Jay Bell Books

When Ben Loved Tim © 2024 Jay Bell

ISBN: ISBN: 979-8-3305-5722-6

WHEN BEN LOVED TIM

JAY BELL

PROLOGUE

Ben's fingers hesitated above the keyboard as he remembered, decades ago, how he had tried to take the maelstrom of feelings in his heart and somehow put them into words. He'd been so incredibly young. And yet, he hadn't felt that way at the time. Not when meeting him. And certainly not when living through everything that followed: The endless allure of love. The inevitable heartbreak of loss. The dreams that had come true and everything that he had never believed possible… Ben liked the idea of going back to relive it all. No matter how bad some of it would hurt. And so, haunted by the memory of a summer long since passed, he began to type.

CHAPTER ONE

My heart is lonely. I realize how ridiculously dramatic that must sound, especially for someone on the verge of turning eighteen. But it's true. I've gotten into the habit of venturing out into the night all by myself, so I can wallow in the sensation, because yearning for love is the only way I get to experience it. Aside from the platonic variety. As I leave the confines of my bedroom, I hear my sister gossiping on the phone through the wall we share. She'll be starting college soon, while living at home, which to me sounds like a fate worse than death. I can't wait to get out of this town. Not because I have anything against it exactly. I just haven't found what I'm looking for. What I *need*.

I pause after descending the stairs. A television is on in the master bedroom, a laugh track urging my parents to find humor in yet another banal sitcom, when really, they should be focusing on each other. I would. If I ever was lucky enough to meet another guy like me, I'd never stop looking at him, touching him, talking to him… I can't imagine a TV show competing with that. And yet, as I stumble out into a humid summer night, I see more blue flickers in the windows. All down the street in fact, the hypnotic glow from electronic screens trapping the residents in a living slumber. Which is difficult for me to relate to, because I feel like I've only recently woken up. And not in the groggy kind of way that I'll feel each morning once school starts again. No, my awakening happened when my best friend moved away.

I'm not sure if I loved him. But I think I could have. We always had fun together, and he was handsome enough. I caught myself staring at him more as our bodies began to change. When he moved to another state with his family, that only made it worse, since I could pretend he missed me just as much. Without him there in the flesh, turning his head each time a pretty girl walked by, I could rewrite the past so that he had started to notice me instead. I convinced myself that's exactly what had happened just before we'd been torn apart. And so I snuck on a bus that was headed to his new home, trying to pass myself off as the kid of another passenger. I didn't even make it out of the station. My mom had to come pick me up. That's when I told her. I didn't put a title on it. Not at the time. But as we sat in the parking lot, I felt I at least owed her an explanation.

"He can come stay with us for a visit, honey," my mom had said. "Or your father and I could drive you up to see him. Why would you try sneaking off like that?"

"Because I wanted him to know how I feel," I'd replied from around a tight throat.

I suppose it was the grand gesture that appealed to me. The romantic notion of showing up at his door unexpectedly and having it stir in him what I had found increasingly difficult to ignore. Although these days I suspect that I was merely in love with the idea of love. If that makes sense. My mom had understood. I'm very lucky in that regard. Destined to die alone without ever knowing the touch of another man's lips, sure, but at least my mom and dad are okay with me being gay. They don't always get it. Neither do I. But they make me feel loved.

And yet, here I am, walking the streets like a junkie on the prowl for a different sort of fix, because the high I crave can't be provided by my family. Or even my current best friend, as awesome as she is. I need *him*. My nameless lover who I have never seen. The man of potential who remains a shadowy figure in my dreams. Not the endless guys who fill my fantasies. I can picture them just fine and imagine them gleefully while jacking off. That always feels good, but it also isn't enough. I want the impossible boy who lets me love him and—even more unlikely—actually loves me back.

And so here I am, walking down a suburban street in the middle of the night to be closer to someone who doesn't exist. But the dream feels more possible here, away from all the distractions of modern life. No ringing phones, no television chatter, no seductive computer screens. Just the hum of cicadas in the trees and the gentle glow of lightning bugs drifting above the grass. I guess, like me, they're out here seeking a mate. As I turn down a paved path that leads through a park, I can't help but wonder what sort of insect I would be. What sound would I need to produce, what exotic dance would I need to perform, to attract another like myself? Do I need to figure out how to make my butt glow green? I laugh at the idea before I begin to sing. Like the feelings in my heart, the need often comes unbidden and is just as instinctual. I can't remember learning how. For me it's a natural extension of my voice. In the same way people graduate from crawling to walking to running. I had gone from gurgling to talking to singing, and according to my dad, I rarely ever stopped. Even when he wanted me to, which he only says with teasing affection. People tend to like the sound of my voice. When I'm singing anyway.

The cicadas provide the backing vocals as I really start to belt out a song. That's another perk of going on these night walks. The world feels like it belongs to me alone. And the occasional dog walker. But for the most part, I can do silly things, like grabbing the chain of a playground swing to twirl in a circle, as if I'm in some sort of hokey musical. I'm still singing when I return to the paved path, getting so into it that I clench my eyes shut. That's when the sound of a drum joins my song, a steady *thump thump thump* of percussion that grows louder until I open my eyes in confusion. My voice strangles to a halt, but the drum keeps pounding, matching the beat of my heart because I'm not alone. And he's handsome!

The guy running toward me is my age. His black hair is short and spiky, his brown skin wet from exertion. Muscled arms continue to pump as wind-blown clothes cling possessively to the contours of his body, revealing tight pecs and a flat stomach with subtle ridges that my fevered imagination interprets as abs. The package in his athletic shorts bounces left and right, like a dog wagging its tail in greeting, but I don't allow my gaze to linger there, even though it would like to set up camp… by pitching a tent next to his. I notice the dark hair on his legs before electric blue shoes capture my attention, but they're unable to hold it, because I need to see that handsome face again. Which is a whole lot closer now.

I notice the way his strong brow furrows, thick eyebrows crinkling in the middle above silver eyes that make the breath catch in my throat when they meet mine. I can't say anything, my voice rendered powerless as he jogs past me with puzzled concern. I finally manage to breathe in and can taste his sweat on the gust of air left in his wake. I stare openly while watching him go, desperately trying to memorize each detail as the shadows reclaim him. He passes by a lamp post, his shoes reflecting the light in fleeting flashes, distant blue dots that blink on and off like a new sort of lightning bug. If only I knew how to answer his call.

My chest is heaving, first with excitement, then with laughter. I'm such an idiot! I literally stopped in my tracks when noticing him and then stood there the whole time, gawping like a tourist.

That's just it though. I've never seen anyone like him before. I have an encyclopedic knowledge of the hot guys in our school. I can summon them up with almost perfect recall. If I had ever seen him before, the boy in the blue shoes, I never would have forgotten. Ever. And I won't! I'll be thinking of him on the way home, on the way up the stairs, on the way into my room, and especially when I'm behind a locked door. Because I might not have anyone to love, but at least now the shadowy figure in my dreams has a face. And an incredible body!

"What do you think?"

Allison holds up another shirt to my chest, but it barely registers. The door to the second-hand clothing shop has just opened, and in the full-length mirror, I see a dark-haired guy walk in. I perk up, certain this is the moment we'll formally meet, but I deflate again when noticing how pale the newcomer is. My guy has a perfect tan or naturally brown skin, I'm not sure which, but I keep wondering because—

"Ben!" my best friend says in frustration. "I'm not doing this for fun, you know."

My attention flicks to her reflection in the mirror, where her dark expressive eyes are slowly losing patience. "Sorry, Mom," I tease. "I was thinking about all the school supplies we still need to buy."

"I know exactly what you were thinking of," Allison says, glancing over her shoulder as the guy walks behind us. She jiggles the shirt. "What do you think? Will your new boyfriend like this one? It matches your eyes."

I consider myself in the mirror, not entirely disappointed with what I see. I always feel more attractive during the summer, when the sun highlights my brown hair, making it appear blond. My skin actually has some color at the moment, which is saying a lot, because otherwise I'm hopelessly white. Allison never fails to remind me of that, usually with a playful smirk. We're quite the contrast in that regard, her ebony skin glowing with a natural sheen that I envy. Both of us are skinny, which works in her favor more than it does mine. I can only assume that, if I ever meet another guy like me, he'll wish I had the same sort of muscles I long to squeeze. I never seem to put on weight, even when I try, and the only thing that push-ups inflate is my insecurity.

"Umm…." I say helpfully before shrugging.

Allison wraps her arms around me from behind. "You're the doll I always wanted when I was a little girl. Let me find a few casual options and you can try them on for me. I mean, for him."

I laugh, not worried about her having unrequited feelings. Allison loves me. I love her back. But thankfully there has never been anything more between us. Not that I would mind. If there was ever an exception to the rule, I'd want it to be her. Allison is wonderfully patient when helping me choose outfits. I still get the final say, but only after she has whittled down the options with her superior sense of style. I need all the help I can get, if I don't want to end high school without having gone on a single date. I'm not ugly. I wouldn't describe myself as hot. I'm just some guy in search of the same.

Which of course is on my mind as we begin the drive home in Allison's ratty old car. The windows have been perpetually rolled down ever since the AC stopped working at the start of summer. Radio is the only option, the slightly bent antenna attached with duct tape by yours truly, so we at least have music to sing along to. That's one of our greatest bonds. Allison has one hell of a voice. I like it better than my own. But together…

She grips the steering wheel tighter and looks over at me, her expression pure joy as we sing the chorus of an overplayed hit, our voices in perfect harmony. My duets with her are some of the only moments that I feel complete, the restlessness in me temporarily soothed. What more could I possibly need than another carefree afternoon with my very best friend? She's pretty much my *only* friend, but that's okay. Quality over quantity.

The song comes to an end just as we reach our neighborhood. Allison eases off the accelerator and turns down the radio. "Which street do you want to try today?" she asks.

We've been making little detours recently in the hope of finding Mr. Blue Shoes, as I've come to think of him. I've seen him a few times now. I go out every single night, instead of waiting until the mood strikes me, and on occasion it pays off. Whenever he jogs past me, it's always in a different part of the neighborhood, making me wonder where he lives. For all I know, he could be the boy next door, or across the street, or around the block from me where Allison lives. I'm not sure. It's hard to follow a guy home while he's running. When people talk about the thrill of the chase, I don't think they mean it so literally. But I still want to know. Not so I can peep in his windows like a perv, although a casual glance when walking by wouldn't hurt. I'm simply desperate to learn more about him. Anything at all really.

"Let's try the new subdivision," I suggest, feeling guilty since it's a bit more out of the way.

Allison is game as always. "So has Blue Shoes seen you on your skates yet?"

"First of all," I say in mock sternness, "it's *Mister* Blue Shoes. We're not on a first name basis yet. And yes, my little scheme paid off just the other night." I figured I'd have a better chance of keeping up with him that way. Suddenly taking an interest in jogging felt too obvious, so I dusted off a pair of skates my parents had given me for my sixteenth birthday. I'd told them I wanted wheels, but not a car, since I'm a terrible driver. Skates sounded fun. Unfortunately, they bought the inline variety, and I never really got the hang of them. Now I'm highly motivated to try again.

"Paid off how?" Allison asked after hitting the turn signal.

"It was incredibly hot," I assure her. "I was skating down the sidewalk, and Mr. Blue Shoes was running toward me. When we got close enough to pass each other, I tried to swerve out of his way, but uh.. You know how I am. He ended up jogging through the grass to avoid me while I kept going, pinwheeling my arms like an idiot while trying to regain my balance. So what is that? First base? Second?"

Allison laughs. "Did you manage to turn around and follow him?"

"I can barely stop on those things. Turning around is beyond my abilities. But he was running in this direction so…"

We both look out the windows, as if expecting to see him. The neighborhood we're driving through is full of newly constructed homes with three-car garages. I'm not impressed. The trees in each yard are thin and spindly, as if they'd been injected there, like a landscaper's version of a hair transplant. Each house is a template, one of a handful of cookie-cutter shapes that are only distinguished by beige or gray paint. I suppose our own neighborhood isn't so different, but decades of families living there while adding personal touches has given it charm and character.

"Do you remember when this was all a field?" Allison asks longingly. "We used to play here!"

"Yeah," I reply, even though it's a revised version of history that we both willingly adhere to. The truth is that Allison used to be friends with my sister, Karen. So yes, we were around each other as kids, and by default, we sometimes interacted or even played together. But it wasn't until Karen started high school and decided that she couldn't be seen with Allison—who was a year younger and still in junior high—that things really changed. Especially after my own best friend moved away. Ever since then it's been me and her, and it feels so much better that it's easy to forget our actual—

"Ben!" Allison says suddenly, grabbing my arm in excitement. "Is that him? It has to be! He's got the shoes and everything!"

I see a guy mowing the lawn and instantly know that she's right. I could have identified him by silhouette alone. My pulse picks up in excitement.

"Should I pull over?" Allison asks as the car begins to swerve toward the curb.

"No!" I slide down in my seat, as low as I can manage. "Keep driving!"

"What?" Allison asks in confusion. The car continues to slow. "How come?"

"Just do it!" I hiss. "Please!"

The car moves back to the center of the lane, but as we pass Mr. Blue Shoes, Allison is staring openly. "Mm-mm-mm!" she says as if offered a slice of delicious pie. "I can see why you're so obsessed. If he's straight…"

"It'll break my heart," I tell her, pushing myself up to a normal height again.

"So what's the game plan here?" Allison asks. "You're going to talk to him, right?"

"Now?" I ask incredulously. "No way!"

She narrows her eyes at me. "So what are you gonna do? Wait until night and hide across the street from his house, so you can keep admiring him from afar?"

"We've gotten close before," I say in my defense.

"Fine, so you've admired him from not-so far, which isn't much better. Make your move!"

"How?"

The car pulls over to the side of the street. "I don't know, but you're about to figure it out."

"What do you mean?" I ask, my panic already rising.

"I'm pushing you out of the nest," Allison says, nodding at the door on my side. "Go on now."

"But—" I try.

"I've been listening to you talk about this guy nonstop for weeks. And driving around so you can find him. I did *not* do all of that for nothing."

"Okay," I say, reaching for the door handle with a sweaty palm.

Allison puts her hand on my shoulder. "You've got this, Ben. You're cute, you're smart, and if I could turn myself into a gay man, you'd never be single again. I'm not the only one who will feel that way. I promise. You've just got to put yourself out there."

"Thanks," I say, feeling a surge of affection for her. "I love you too."

"Call me when you're home," Allison says, "and tell me everything. No matter how late it is." She waggles her eyebrows.

"I wish," I say with a mad chuckle. Then, before I can second-guess myself, I open the car door and climb out. My legs are stiff as I hobble to the sidewalk. Allison drives away, reminding me of how vulnerable I felt during the first day of kindergarten, after my mom left me there. That had been scary, but I'm not a little kid anymore, so this should be easy. Right?

I straighten up and begin walking toward his house. I can see Mr. Blue Shoes mowing the yard, one row at a time. There's not much left. In fact, he's getting nearer to the sidewalk. I pick up the pace, figuring that might present the ideal opportunity. Like he'll have to shut off the lawnmower to prevent grass from blowing all over me, since he isn't using a bag, and then I'll say… What, exactly?

I consider myself a creative person. I sometimes come up with my own song lyrics and have even tried to write stories. Without much luck. I'm starting to see why, because I'm drawing a blank. I could ask where he got his shoes. I've searched for them in stores without success. He probably bought them in a foreign country. I'm convinced that his family moved here from overseas. Italy or Spain, judging from the dark hair, or maybe he's Middle Eastern, since his skin is so delectably brown. I can't wait to see everything up close and in the daylight. My head is bowed to look at the sidewalk, when really, my eyes are tracking him. Mr. Blue Shoes turns at the end of the yard nearest me and begins walking in the same direction that I'm traveling. After a short sprint, I'm just a few paces behind him. He's wearing a sleeveless gray shirt, and I'm absolutely captivated by his round meaty shoulders. They glisten with tiny beads of sweat, making me want to lick them clean. I don't care how that sounds. If he turned around and asked me to, I'd shrug and start tonguing away. Why is he wearing a shirt at all? In this heat? And with that body? I'd be strutting around next to naked, if I was him. Oh god! He's nearing the driveway, and when reaching it, he'll turn around and we'll be face to face.

The lawn mower sputters and stops. I'm just about to pass him and still don't know what I'm going to say. I suppose "Hello" would be a good start. Yeah! I'll be all like "Hey, are you new to the neighborhood? Let me show you around. Oh, is that an Italian accent I hear? I happen to love pizza. We have so much in common! Now about that sweaty body of yours, I have an unorthodox solution." I watch as he swipes an arm across his forehead. So maybe it'll be a team effort.

"Tim?"

My head whips around to find the source of that voice. A woman is standing on the front stoop of the house. Her hair is raven black, her skin an earthy hue like her son. She's definitely his mother. The woman is too beautiful not to be. Her attention flicks to me and back to her son. "Come help me move the couch." She does indeed have an accent, but before I can place it, my skin tingles with his response.

"Yeah, okay."

Just two words, but the voice is deep and kind of husky. I'm already enamored with it. I tense as he turns, just as I'm passing him, but his back remains to me. I keep walking, only daring to glance over my shoulder when I've made it to the next driveway, and see him disappear into the house.

Allison is going to be disappointed. I know she will, but I'm *beyond* thrilled, because I know where he lives now. I'll know the sound of his voice when imagining him whispering seductive words into my ear. Best of all, I know his name. And it's one of my favorites, more so now than ever before. I wait until I'm at the end of the block before I stop biting my bottom lip long enough to try it on for size.

"Tim."

CHAPTER TWO

"We finally made it," Allison says after parking her car. She glances over at me and smiles. "We're top of the food chain. Remember how terrified we were our first day as freshmen?"

"I've blocked it out," I say, already scanning the school parking lot.

"This is a moment to remember," Allison replies dramatically. "We're seniors now. Every single day will bring us closer to college. We're practically grownups!"

"I'm not in a rush," I tell her when getting out of the car, because there are goals I would like to meet first. Like kissing another human being who isn't a relative. Or my best friend. But that was only practicing and definitely didn't count!

"I can't wait," Allison says. "I'm ready to be out on my own."

My own problems recede long enough for me to shoot her a sympathetic wince. Allison's home life is far from ideal. I worry about that. A lot. Especially the way she tends to shrug it off, like now. She sees my concerned expression and chooses to misinterpret it. "I mean until *we're* out on our own. And living together." As if there was any doubt. We've practically had it all planned since that first day of freshman year. Which is how I know she's intentionally deflecting. Especially when she adds, "Maybe by then it'll be three of us living together."

"Planning on getting knocked up?" I tease, even though I know exactly what she means. The ploy to distract me works. As we go inside and navigate the school hallways, my eyes dart from face to face, trying to find one with stunning silver eyes, but Tim continues to elude me. Allison and I set out to find our new lockers and discover that they are across the hall from one another this year. Which is perfect, since it means we'll see each other between classes. The only one we have together is choir, and that's not enough for either of us.

"I'm off to U.S. Government and Politics," Allison says with a weary sigh. "Although I suppose it's necessary if I'm to become president someday."

"I'll be in gym class," I say, "which is bound to be useful in my career as a professional basketball player." That's pure sarcasm, of course, because I only reach five foot eight on a tape measure by standing up really *really* straight. And I've always sucked at sports. Maybe if our school offered horse racing as an elective, I would have made a good jockey. Assuming I didn't fall off constantly. I'm not the most coordinated guy.

"I hope you get lucky," Allison says with a broad smile.

I gasp as if scandalized. "Not on the first date!"

"You know what I mean," she says. "See you at lunch!"

I do know. The potential has me buzzing. Tim might be in my gym class. Which will be absolute torture if he's within range when I'm changing into the horrible school-issued athletic uniforms. I can hardly wait! For the first time in my life, I rush to the school gymnasium and am swiftly disappointed. I recognize a few faces—other freaks and losers that I'll cluster close to for safety—but none of them are my dream guy.

On the way to my second period literature class, I search the halls with an earnestness only matched by a parent seeking a missing child. My gaze lingers on some of the more handsome boys, because I'm only human. And not married to anyone yet. Although I'm not against the idea if Tim insists. I soon regret not being more discreet when I notice Bryce, the biggest jerk in our school in both size and attitude. Irritatingly enough, he's also extremely attractive. Bryce is one of the popular kids. He's on the football team and has always looked older than he really is, like he's already in college. I didn't run into him over the summer, thankfully, but that lowered my immunity to his beefy muscles that have all too often drawn my attention. Like now.

"Look who it is!" Bryce says, having caught my stare. "It's Ben Dover." That is *definitely* not my last name. It's a dumb joke. Bryce jostles one of his friends. "Hey guys, don't drop the soap!"

I close my eyes and release a long drawn-out sigh before stopping to address him. "Those insults aren't compatible," I say. "You accuse me of bending over while also taking advantage of anyone who does the same. How would that work exactly? Do you think gay people bump their butts together when having sex?"

Bryce's strong brow furrows up. "Huh?" He's always been dumb as a rock. And just as brutal. "Are you making fun of me?" he says, taking a step forward while clenching a fist.

"I was trying to help you make fun of me more effectively," I say, already walking away, because I might be recklessly brave at times, but I'm not suicidal.

"Hey, fuck you!" Bryce shouts after me. I don't respond, which is probably why he feels the need to add, "Fag!"

That's the shitty thing about my situation. Not that assholes exist. My dad assures me that they're something to contend with at any age. He's been great about coaching me on how to deal with them. My dad says it's best to not let them see you react, no matter how they make you feel on the inside. But it bothers me that everyone knows the truth. I already came out of the closet. Or was outed, depending on how you look at it. Which I don't regret exactly, but I got all the drawbacks with none of the benefits. Case in point…

When you're younger, your social circles aren't as defined. Learning that someone in your class has an exciting new video game or whatever can be enough motivation to fish for a sleepover invitation. It was on one such occasion that I first messed around with a guy. We played video games for most of the evening. After his parents went to sleep, he took out a nudie magazine hidden between his mattress and box spring. My initial excitement was replaced by disappointment when it offered only naked women.

"Where are all the men?" I had asked rather cluelessly.

I still remember how the guy looked at me as if I was crazy.

"It's not like a porno," he'd replied. "Check her out! Have you ever seen boobs that big?"

I'm always surprised that guys care about such things. To me it would be like going around and sizing up everyone's ears to find the largest pair. Now when it comes to pecs, yeah, that makes sense! And of course, as I would learn that night, size could be exciting in other ways.

"Pretty hot, huh?" the guy had said, nodding at the open magazine. "The only problem is that it's hard to jack off when your hands are full."

I wasn't completely naïve, even back then. I knew perfectly well that it's easy to hold a magazine one-handed. Just fold the cover back. But luckily, I held my tongue long enough for him to suggest a solution.

"But I guess if we helped each other… And took turns. That would work. Right?"

"Let's find out!"

And we did. Sort of. He wanted to go first, meaning I had to do all the work. Which was fine with me, even when he finished and became theatrically sleepy. "Maybe in the morning," he'd promised. "I'm really tired."

"Yeah, me too," I'd replied, lying awake half the night before sneaking off to lock myself in the bathroom. That wasn't the last time. Not with him. Or a few others, because word began to spread, and I was willing to do more than just use my hands. For a horny teenager, I was in absolute heaven. Even though the encounters were always one-sided, they helped me come to terms with myself, the emotional and physical impulses melding together into one simple concept: I'm gay. Rather foolishly, I thought those other guys would appreciate me clueing them in, like a course map sent from the finish line. I told each of them in turn, expecting to see their faces light up with the same realization.

Instead the opposite happened. No more sleepover invitations. My calls went unanswered. I was a ghost in the halls when they saw me at school. Then the rumors began to spread, and I sure as hell wasn't going to pretend that I'm not gay. The cat was already out of the bag. I figured if there was a chance of finding someone like me, that it paid to advertise. So I came out. Whenever people made the accusation, I proudly confirmed it. *"Yes, that's right, I'm gay. So what?"* Which is how I became Ben Dover. Bengay. Butt-fuck Ben. I've heard them all. And for the most part, I try not to care. But it sucks anyway, because there should have been a silver lining. Some shy guy who approached me when no one else was looking to say, "Are you really? Because I am too."

My throat feels raw as I enter my Spanish class. I just want someone to love. So how come I get so much hate? I think of Tim again, a flame rekindling in my heart as I take a seat. I watch the door, hoping to see him enter. I've been thinking about his mom's accent, which sounded Hispanic. And assuming that Tim can already speak the language, what teenager wouldn't want the easy A? But alas, my rainbow dreams are too big for such a small gray classroom. The teacher shows up, shutting the door behind her, and with it, one more chance to find the companionship I so desperately crave.

Allison has good news for me when we meet in the school cafeteria for lunch.

"I saw him!"

I grab her shoulders and attempt to throttle the information out of her.

"What? When? Where?"

She laughs and twists sideways to escape my grip. "In the same hallway as our old biology class. That has to be a sign."

"I'd like it even better if it was chemistry," I say with a grin. "What was he doing? And wearing? Did he seem like he was looking for anyone? As in me?"

She averts her gaze before glancing around for a table. "Where are we going to sit this year?"

"Same place as always," I say dismissively. "What aren't you telling me?"

Allison sighs. "Tim wasn't alone. He was walking with Stacy and Darryl."

I groan, because they're two of the popular kids. As in, the *most* popular. Darryl looks like a toad, and if his family wasn't filthy rich, would probably be at the bottom of the social pecking order like we are. Stacy is a drop-dead gorgeous brunette who is dating Bryce, but unlike her big dumb ox of a boyfriend, she's viciously smart. And an overachiever. She used to give Allison hell, back before we both learned to avoid their clique.

"Maybe they were picking on him," I suggest, already knowing it can't be true.

"Sorry," Allison says in sympathy as we begin walking toward our usual table. "Maybe he'll figure out that they're terrible people. You could be the one to tell him."

"Yeah, you're right!" I say, perking up again. I have a million horror stories I could share with Tim. Nobody in their right mind would still be friends with those jerks after learning the truth. Unless he's cut from the same cloth.

"Of course, that means you'll actually have to *talk* to him," Allison presses.

"What should I do, go to his house after school as a concerned citizen?"

"If that's what it takes," she says. "Or maybe you'll have a class together. You've got three more chances." She's fighting down a smile as we sit across from each other. "I umm… might have gotten lucky. Guess who chose to sit next to me in calculus?"

"Was it Tim?" I ask with a straight face.

"No! You have a one-track mind. It was Ronnie."

I play dumb. "Who?"

Allison arches one of her eyebrows. "You *know* who he is. You had a crush on him too."

Which still stings a little, because Allison had ended up dating him sophomore year. Not that I had a chance in hell. Ronnie is straight. He wasn't one of the guys I messed around with. But that's when it started to feel weird, because Allison had finally landed her first boyfriend, which convinced me that I would too. And yet, here I am, hopelessly single while she's gone on to date other guys, my envy increasing with each.

"I thought Ronnie was too immature for you," I say.

"He was. And maybe he still is." Allison smirks and shakes her head. "But you should see the boy, because he has gotten fine as hell!"

"He was always hot," I say with a sigh. Then I force a smile, wanting to support my best friend. "So what do you think? Are you going to make a move? Or give him another chance?"

We discuss the possibility before moving on to other subjects until the end of lunch. Tim isn't in the following period, and I don't really expect to see him in choir—although I'm sure he'd be a baritone—so anticipation is high when I reach my final class of the day, physics. Instead of individual desks, wide tables seat two. I watch the door, the chair next to mine remaining empty. It soon becomes one of the only available seats. Which I don't take personally, because this is perfect. I can already imagine meeting Allison after school and getting to say, "I got lucky too!"

I'm still watching the door when someone I recognize finally shows up. My stomach sinks as a gangly guy with red hair stumbles on his way inside, his eyes filled with anxiety as he surveys the classroom. Danny seems relieved when noticing the empty seat next to me.

"Hi, Ben," he says, clutching a backpack with two loose straps to his chest. "Can I sit here?"

"Yeah, of course," I assure him, trying to hide my disappointment.

Danny drops his backpack on the table, the chair scraping loudly across the floor as he sits. I don't have anything against him. He's a fellow outcast, like me, although for different reasons. Danny is socially awkward. And he's weird. I stare as he takes out a ridiculous number of pens and pencils and begins arranging them into rows. He notices me watching him.

"Did you have a good summer?" he asks.

"No," I say, even though it was fine.

"Me neither," Danny says with a sigh.

"What happened to your backpack?" I ask, pushing it and the loose straps pointedly toward his side of the table.

"Bryce grabbed it in the hall and swung me around." Danny is rubbing his nose. "I hit the wall and it really hurt. So I'm just going to carry it from now on."

"That guy is an asshole," I mutter.

Danny's head whips left and right, like he's worried about getting in trouble for the foul language. Then he cackles. "Yeah, he really is! Bryce is a total idiot. I bet he's got a super low GPA. The lowest in the whole school." Which of course is a segue to Danny's favorite subject. He's always been grade-obsessed, competitively slamming his pencil down at the end of each test and quiz before looking around with gleeful pride. Which is annoying, sure, but I don't get why people like him sink to the bottom while Bryce, Darryl, and the other jerks rise to the top. I try to imagine an alternate reality where people care more about the valedictorian than the prom queen and pep rallies are held before the chess club's big game. As fond as I am of muscles, I'd willingly go without to be a part of that world.

So maybe Tim isn't the guy for me. I glance at Danny. I don't find him attractive. Nor do we have much in common. I've never been tempted to hang out with him after school. Am I just as bad as the rest of them? Prioritizing a handsome face instead of caring about the substance beneath? I'd be willing to find out what kind of person Tim is, if given the opportunity. I promise myself, the next time I see him, to finally make it happen. I picture myself waving him down while he's mowing the lawn, just so I can introduce myself. If he's the kind of guy I need him to be, Tim won't mind. He'll love me for it.

At the end of class, I meet Allison by her locker before we head outside. I'm searching the dispersing crowds when I finally see him. Allison does too. She nudges me before noticing that I'm already looking across the parking lot to where a group of popular kids are gathered around a sleek black sports car. Bryce, Stacy, Darryl, and yeah, Tim. He's got this victorious grin on his face, like he's just won the lottery, and I suppose he has. I'm certain he didn't go to our school before—I'd bet my life on it—and yet on his first day he already ranks among the elite. I don't question why. You've gotta be hot or rich to be popular, and I'm pretty sure he's both. I watch Tim unlock the door to a sports car that sure looks new before he steps aside so the others can check out the interior. Even now, at a distance and surrounded by people I despise, I still find him incredibly attractive. When a thin blond girl named Krista bounds across the parking lot and grabs his arm, I'm not the least bit surprised.

"Oh well," I say with a sigh. "It was a nice fantasy. I'll add him to the list of all my other imaginary ex-boyfriends."

"Give it time," Allison says. "Once he figures out that his new friends are bastards, he'll need a shoulder to cry on. And it'll be yours."

I appreciate her attempt to lift my spirits, but it's way too late for that. "He's one of them," I say, turning toward her car. "Even if he was gay—which obviously isn't true—he'd never notice someone like me."

"He'd be crazy not to!" Allison says in shock. "I still think you should talk to him."

"You don't get it!" I growl. "You can flirt with any guy in this school without having to worry about getting punched in the face. It's really freaking hard, okay?"

She looks wounded, but only momentarily. "And *you* don't get what it's like to be me," she says, placing a hand over her heart. "Not entirely. There are plenty of guys who refuse to date a black girl. Which sucks. Especially when it's someone I actually like. But I'd rather know upfront who they are than experiencing that gut-punch of disappointment later. Wouldn't you?"

I look back to where I last saw Tim. He's holding open the passenger-side door of his car. Krista clutches her hands together as if charmed before climbing inside. All I can do is swallow against the lump in my throat.

"Sorry," I say, turning to Allison. "I didn't mean to snap at you. Of course you understand."

"Maybe I don't," she says, her tone sympathetic as she draws me in for a hug. "I get frustrated too. On your behalf, as corny as that sounds."

"Same here," I say, squeezing her before we let go. "Does this mean you'll remain celibate until college so I don't have to feel sorry for myself anymore?"

"I don't love you *that* much," she teases. "C'mon. Let's go hang out at my place until my dad gets home."

"All right." I decide to leave my self-pity behind. So some hot guy who is out of my league turned out to be straight. Big deal! Life goes on.

And yet, before getting into the car, I can't help but sneak one final peek. My heart skips a beat when I do, because I swear he's looking in my direction. I'm absolutely certain he is when Bryce nudges him, points at me, and says something I can't hear. But I can guess. Tim stares a second longer before his new friends distract him again. I watch him get into his car as the others disperse, and despite all evidence to the contrary—even though it's Krista sitting in the passenger seat instead of me—I still want him to be the guy that I've been waiting for.

CHAPTER THREE

I'm pretty sure the universe hates me. The first week of school wasn't great. Instead of having to search for Tim, it's like he's being dangled in front of me. I keep seeing him in the halls, Krista perpetually wrapped around one of his arms. Which I can't even hate her for, since I would happily do the same. I decided not to go walking at night over the weekend, certain I would see them jogging together or something equally insufferable. I hung out with Allison instead, which was nice, even though she keeps talking about Ronnie. Who admittedly, has indeed gotten much hotter. She made us go to the fast food restaurant where he works so I could see for myself. And he did look very presentable in his work uniform. I was crazy about his mischievous smile and milk chocolate skin back in freshman year, not that I stood a chance then or now. Ronnie clearly has a thing for Allison, so it's only a matter of time. I'm happy for her. Even though I'll soon be the third wheel on their bicycle of love.

My nerves were strained further when she called on Monday morning to tell me her car had broken down. Again. She's been getting a ride with her dad ever since. I refuse to take the bus, or have my mom drop me off, so I'm back on my skates. I'm really getting the hang of them too. I still have to slam into a wall or some other solid object when needing to stop, but I hardly fall down at all anymore. Showing up to school windblown and kind of sweaty isn't ideal. I miss singing with my best friend each morning. But hey, I've nearly convinced myself that life is good, even with a lonely heart. Although I do wish the universe would stop testing me.

I'm sitting in Spanish class when a complete stranger walks through the door.

"Hello class," the man says, peering at us through the glasses on his nose. "I'm afraid your usual teacher, Señora umm…" He flips through papers on her desk before looking to us for help. Nobody says a thing, of course. "Anyway, she's had a bit of a medical emergency, so I'll be stepping in for the time being. My name is Señor Langdon." He looks young, reminding me more of the student teachers who sit in on classes to learn the trade, rather than an experienced substitute. Either way, like sharks smelling blood in the water, the class begins to turn on him.

"Is she dead?" a girl asks. "Or dying?"

"Not at all," Señor Langdon assures her. "I'm sure she'll be back before you know it."

"Unless she has prostate cancer," a guy supplies helpfully.

Señor Langdon raises an eyebrow at this. "That would be an excellent starting point for a lecture on human anatomy, which is sorely needed, it would seem. Unfortunately for you, this is Spanish class. Now then, Señora uh…"

"Vega," I say, deciding that I already like him.

"Thank you!" Señor Langdon says, perking up. "Señora Vega is quite organized in her lesson planning, so you should still be on track by the time she returns. So if you'll please take out your books and turn to page thirty-eight, we'll get started. Interpersonal relationships are the theme. Each of you will choose a partner and write a short dialog, four lines each."

The class doesn't go as it normally would. A substitute always increases the temptation to misbehave, so when pairs of students are called to the front of the class to perform, the conversations are much sillier than usual. Señor Langdon rolls with this rather than scolding anyone, and it's actually kind of fun. When a snickering girl says that she's going to marry a circus clown, Señor Langdon steps in to ask what skills her fiancé has and introduces new vocabulary, like the Spanish term for balloon animal. Which has us all laughing. The grin slides off my face when Darryl and another guy are called to the front of the class.

"I heard you are getting married soon," his partner says in Spanish.

"Yes," Darryl replies with an exaggerated lisp. *"To a man. I am a—"* Darryl shakes his head and reverts to English. And his normal voice. "Sorry, sir. What's the Spanish term for homosexual?"

"Homosexual," Señor Langdon says, pronouncing the word differently than I'm used to hearing it.

"Thank you," Darryl replies cordially. Then, reverting to Spanish—and the lispy voice—he says, *"I am a homosexual."*

People laugh around me. And look in my direction.

"Settle down," Señor Langdon says warningly. He nods at Darryl and his partner. "Let's hear the rest."

"Will your parents be at the wedding?" his partner asks.

"No!" Darryl places the tips of his fingers to his mouth in a

way that's a caricature of femininity. *"They don't get along with my boyfriend."*

"Why is that?" his partner asks in Spanish.

"Because my father called him a—" Darryl scrunches up his face, as if deep in thought, before addressing the teacher again. "Excuse me, sir." His eyes dart to mine and away again. "What's the best translation for the word faggot?"

"I'll give you a hint," Señor Langdon replies dryly. "It sounds an awful lot like detention."

Darryl manages to appear convincingly surprised. "I only wanted to explain that my father was cruel to my boyfriend. Señora Vega always talks about the importance of learning colloquial Spanish."

I sigh inwardly. Unlike his buddy Bryce, Darryl isn't stupid. Which makes him dangerous in a completely different way.

"It still doesn't seem appropriate to me," Señor Langdon says, "but I suppose, for the sake of this exercise, you can use the term *mariposa*."

"As in my father called him a *mariposa*? Am I pronouncing that right?" Darryl's eyes meet mine. He doesn't look away again. *"Mariposa,"* he repeats.

"Your pronunciation could use some work," Señor Langdon says coldly. "Sit down. Both of you. Who's next?"

My hand shoots up. My partner is taken aback, but I don't care. Blood is pounding in my ears as we walk to the front of the class.

"I met a nice girl at the church who I think you would like," my partner says in Spanish.

"No thanks," I reply, having to improvise, which takes a lot, because this isn't my best subject. *"I am a homosexual."*

"All right," Senior Langdon says with a sigh. "Very funny."

"It's not a joke!" I snap.

Señor Langdon considers me a moment. Then he nods. "Continue."

"Umm…" my partner says, since I've gone off script.

"My parents love me," I say in Spanish, my voice cracking. *"And so does my boyfriend."*

The class is completely silent until my partner runs with one of the lines we had planned. *"Then I'll have you both over for dinner."*

"Please let me know when," I finish lamely.

"A much better use of the subject matter," Señor Langdon says with a nod of approval.

My face is burning with indignation as I return to my seat. I glare openly at Darryl, who is wearing a serene smile. "*Mariposa*," he mouths almost inaudibly as I pass.

I continue to hear the slur after class. I already know that it'll accompany me the rest of the year. They can add it to the pile. I don't care. Or at least, I don't want to.

My heart is heavy at the end of the school day. I feel beaten down, despite my defiance, like a dog snarling and barking at the end of its chain. I start to question if it's worth fighting anymore. Maybe I should switch schools. Stay in the closet. Allison could come with me and be my fake girlfriend. I'm seriously tempted. I could finish my senior year anonymously instead of being a constant target. But I can't. It's just not in me. And it wouldn't be fair to my best friend, who has to deal with racist shit without being able to hide who she is, even if she wanted to. So I won't either. Fuck the haters!

I keep Allison company until her dad comes to pick her up, ignoring the way he glares at me. Then I walk with my skates to the edge of the parking lot and continue down a sidewalk, making sure I'm clear of the school before I sit to pull them on. I might be proud of who I am, but I don't need to give my detractors fresh material to work with, and there's a fifty-fifty chance I'll fall when getting to my feet. I don't today. But I do decide to be someone different, just for a little while, to get it out of my system. I head in the opposite direction of my house, wandering into an unfamiliar neighborhood. I skate around while choosing the house I want to live in, pretending that I've already graduated from college. I've begun my career as a marine biologist—an occupation that has never appealed to me, but that's the point. And while I'm out there saving the whales or whatever, maybe I'll see someone lost at sea, a handsome and sweet guy clinging to the last vestiges of his sunken ship. I'll rescue him of course, and he'll insist on taking me out to dinner in gratitude.

I let myself slow and gently collide with a tree to stop, all while shaking my head. I'm hopeless. I know who I am and what I want. People can hate me for that. It won't make a difference. They can lock me up somewhere, or beat me to a pulp, but it won't change how I feel inside. I'm going to love someone or die trying. That's a real possibility because I have a brave heart that refuses to be silenced. Anyone who makes the attempt is in for one hell of a fight.

I notice that the sun is beginning to sink and decide to go home. I'm feeling a lot better by the time I near my own neighborhood. High school might be a bust, but college is where people experiment and figure out who they really are. I'll be there to assist any confused straight guys, and after I've *blown* through enough of them (ha!), chances are that I'll find a pearl among the oysters—another frustrated gay guy like me who is ready for love. My soaring spirits take a tumble when I notice someone jogging on the paved path ahead of me. It's him. Of course it is. Tim's alluring arms are on full display, thanks to the sleeveless shirt, and his butt looks ridiculously pert tucked into the tight nylon shorts he wears. These details annoy me more than they tempt me. It doesn't help that we're in the same park where I first saw him. The very place where this stupid obsession began.

My instinct is to stop somehow and turn around, so I can take a longer route home to avoid him. Then again, why should I? I'm tired of making concessions for people who have already inherited the earth. Movies and TV shows are full of heterosexual couples. Their love is celebrated in song and immortalized in art. They can hold hands in public, kiss each other without being attacked, and don't have to fear being fired from their jobs or rejected by their families for responding to their natural urges. So why do they unleash so much grief on people like me when they already have it all? How petty can you get? Like a king who resents the patch of strawberries growing behind a peasant's hut, when he gorges himself on a feast three times a day. Or exactly like the stupid popular kids—high school royalty—who give the rest of us shit when they should be the most benevolent of all, since they've got it easy. But no, the ones on top always kick at those beneath them, not wanting to share the sunlight, even though there's plenty to go around.

I'm done. I don't care how hot Tim is, or how bad I still want him. He makes me hate that side of myself. I wish I could switch it off, so I don't have to feel it for the wrong person, but I can't. And it pisses me off. I tuck my arms close to my body before lowering myself to pick up speed. The world refuses to make room for me? Fine. I'll cut my own path.

"Get out of my way!" I growl.

Tim looks over his shoulder. Then he turns to face me, his silver eyes widening with panic. He's blocking the path and getting closer by the second. I want him to scurry out of my way in fear, but he seems frozen in place.

"Uh oh!" I say, my arms beginning to pinwheel. "Watch out!"

Tim tries to dive into the grass, but it's too late. I slam into his side just as he leaps, sending him twirling through the air before I lose track. I've bounced off him and am rolling backwards. My skates finally leave the pavement, where I fall onto my rump.

"FUCK!"

I wince, expecting to hear a barrage of insults. Instead the swearing continues, seemingly without direction.

"Shit, shit, shit! Aw man… Damn it!"

I scramble onto my hands and knees, so I can see what became of him. A slope on one side of the paved path leads down to a narrow drainage ditch. Tim is near the bottom, rocking back and forth on his butt while holding one of his legs aloft.

"Sorry!" I cry. "Wait right there. I'll help you!"

I manage to stand but my skates slip on the grass and I lose my balance. I slide down the slope until I end up on my back next to him.

"My hero," Tim grumbles, his eyes widening as I take off the bike helmet that makes me look like a mushroom, but I figure it's better than turning myself into Bryce by accident. "Holy shit!" he says in shock. "You're the gay stalker!"

My mouth falls open. "The what?"

"Nothing," Tim says with a shake of his head. "I mean the night stalker."

That's not much better, but I don't get the chance to tell him, because he winces in pain and groans. I notice the blood dripping down the leg he's still gripping. How did he get so hurt? We both fell on soft grass. Unless a bone snapped on his way down and pushed through his skin.

"Did you break something?" I ask.

"Huh-uh," Tim says. "Feels more like a sprain."

"With that much blood?"

He seems to notice something. I follow his gaze to a jagged rock sticking out of the grass.

"Oh," I say with a guilty swallow.

"It's just a scrape. I'll be fine."

I watch him lower the leg experimentally, but as soon as his heel touches the ground, he lifts it back up again with a grimace. I'm making the same face in sympathy.

"Hold on," I say, pulling at the straps of my Rollerblades. "I'll help you up."

"You're the one who did this to me!" he shoots back.

"Yeah," I say sheepishly as I unshoulder my backpack to get at my shoes, "but that was an accident."

Tim's brow furrows. "It sure didn't look that way to me!"

And he sure looks handsome, even when wearing an incredulous expression. "Umm…." I say in my own defense. Smooth as always!

Tim has gone back to testing his leg anyway. I get my shoes on and hang my skates off my backpack, serenaded the entire time by whimpers of pain. "Maybe we should call an ambulance," I suggest.

"No!' Tim says with intense reluctance. "I'm fine! Just…" He hooks one of his arms, like he has it around an invisible man. That's where I'm supposed to go. I'm staring at the empty space when he holds out his hand. "Help me up."

I swallow, my own hand trembling slightly as I reach for his. His palm is soft when it slides across mine, but his grip is strong as he begins shifting his weight. I lean back, using leverage to pull him to his feet and imagine what would happen if I yanked so hard that he tumbled into my arms. I'm brought back to reality when Tim shakes off my hand and slings an arm around my shoulders.

"Just get me back to the path," he says. "I'll be all right."

Except it isn't that easy because he can only use one leg and has to hop up the slope, even with me supporting him. The first time he starts to slip, I wrap my arm around his torso, my hand ending up on his stomach, but thankfully I don't lose myself in another fantasy. After a struggle, and more swearing from Tim, we make it back to level ground.

"You can let go of me now," he says pointedly.

"I don't think I can," I tell him, and I mean it. I'm not trying to be a creep. "Your house isn't far away if we cut across the park, but you can't hop there on your own."

Tim is looking at me funny. Oh. Right. I don't have a good excuse for knowing where he lives. All I can do is offer an encouraging smile. "Ready to go?"

"Yeah," Tim murmurs. "Straight to the cops."

My face is burning as we begin lurching toward our destination. Now that we're on even ground, I'm painfully aware of everywhere our bodies connect. The bare skin of his bicep is pressed against the back of my neck. Tim's shirt has pulled away from his waist, my pinky and ring finger touching warm naked flesh. I like the way he smells, and how his sweat is soaking into my clothes to join mine. I'm going to lock myself away after this and never show my face in public again, because I'm more of a monster than I realized, but for now, I can't help but revel in being this close to him. Although when I glance over and see the grimace etched onto his face, it's enough of a cold shower for me to say, "I'm really sorry. I suck at skating. I haven't got the whole stopping thing down yet."

His silver eyes dart over to mine and away again. "I've noticed," he says. "You're a lethal weapon on those things."

Right. This isn't the first time I've run him off the path. And that means he remembers me from at least one of those night-time jogs. For better or worse.

"It really was an accident," I say, wanting to assure him that I'm not completely insane. "I'll wear sleigh bells while skating from now on, so people can hear me coming."

Tim snorts in amusement, which delights me more than it should. "This way?" he asks when we reach a shallow row of trees.

"Yeah," I say with a squirm. "Your street is the next one over."

"Uh-huh," he replies, tightening his grip on me as he hops across last year's fallen leaves. "What else do you know about me?"

"Your name," I admit. "Do you know mine?"

He's quiet for a moment. "A version of it."

That's my confirmation. He's definitely heard all about me from his new friends. I might as well run with it. "Most people call me 'that gay guy' or 'what are you lookin' at homo' or on a good day, 'hey, there goes the fag.' Take your pick."

He scowls as we maneuver around a tree. The expression remains. I bet he can't wait to get away from me. "I thought your name was Benjamin," he says at last.

"Almost," I reply, ignoring the pitter-patter of my heart. "Well, I mean, yeah, technically it is but—"

"Hey!" Tim interrupts. "You weren't kidding!"

I glance up. The trees have thinned out enough to see the backyard of someone's house.

"That's our fence over there," Tim says, hopping toward it so fast that I struggle to keep up. I regret suggesting the shortcut. A little more time with him would have been nice. Especially considering the steep price it'll cost me. When his friends learn about this, I'll never hear the end of it.

"Have you lived here long?" I ask, wanting to at least confirm my theories.

"You mean you don't already know?" he teases.

I laugh. "I've never seen you around before so…"

"We moved here during the summer," Tim says.

"From where?" I ask.

He glances at the horizon, orienting on the setting sun before he jerks his head to the right. "About a twelve-hour drive that way."

"Oh. That's far!"

"Yeah. But I could still make it there on my own."

"Do you want to go back?"

"Sometimes," he says. "But not really."

Once in his driveway, we avoid the stairs leading up to the front door by circling around them through the yard.

"Your parents are going to adore me," I say sarcastically.

"Don't worry about it," he says. "They're out of town."

"Really?" My guilt intensifies, because this type of situation is when I want my parents the most. My dad for the practical stuff, like bandaging up a booboo, and my mom for the love and comfort she always provides. They can play either role, and have, but that's been my preference ever since I was little. "Both of them are gone?"

"Yup," Tim says, pulling at a beaded chain around his neck. The really basic kind made up of linked balls, like what Army nametags usually hang from, except his has a key at the end. He attempts to brace himself against the front of the house before giving up and handing it to me. I unlock the door and push it open.

"Nice meeting you, Benjamin," Tim says, grabbing the door frame and hopping out of my grasp. "Make sure you get those sleigh bells, and if you're really good, maybe Santa will make you one of his reindeer."

"Wait!" I say, "I can't leave you on your own!"

"Sure you can," Tim says. "I'll be fine. See ya."

"Okay." The door swings shut and I'm on my own again. "But for the record, it's just Ben," I murmur.

I'm about to leave when I hear a crashing sound. And then more swearing. How am I supposed to walk away from that? Especially when he's all by himself.

"This is ridiculous," I say after opening the front door. "You need my help!"

I glance around and then down at the floor, where Tim is lying on his side. A small decorative table is next to him along with the ceramic shrapnel of a former vase.

"Yeah, all right," he says with a sigh. "Just get me to the couch."

"I hope that wasn't expensive," I say, because even a quick glance around has convinced me that his family is wealthy. The entryway is grand, the height spanning both floors. Stairs lead up to a landing that merges with a hallway. I can see a spacious living room in the direction Tim was attempting to go, and the pristine white couch that was probably his goal.

"Back on your feet," I say, pulling on both his hands this time. Tim catches himself on the wall once up and resumes his struggle. I follow him into a living room that reminds me of the decorating magazines my mom reads. She's the type of interior designer who likes to incorporate the personality of her clients into her work, so they are represented in their surroundings. Everything here feels too prim and proper and in its place. Like there isn't much actual living that goes on. To be fair, Tim's family hasn't been here long. And they have good taste. Although I'm already eyeing the couch with unease.

"I don't think blood is a good accent color for this room," I say.

"Huh?" Tim replies. "Oh. Good call. Grab a blanket or something, will ya?"

I prop him against the wall and follow his instructions to a basket of neatly folded blankets. I spread one over the couch before helping him reach it. Tim sinks into the cushions with a sigh of relief.

"What else?" I ask.

Tim inhales and exhales a few times, as if catching his breath.

Then he gingerly rotates his ankle while wincing. "This happened to me last year," he says, "when I was sliding into home base. I still have the brace upstairs. Oh, and some painkillers. They're both under the sink, in a cardboard box."

"I'll go get them," I say, happy to be of use, since it's the only way I can make up for my transgressions. I race up the stairs to the bathroom. In the cabinet, I find a moving box that has clearly been rifled through numerous times. Some items give me pause, like an old bottle of cologne that I'm tempted to sniff, but for all I know it belongs to his dad. I'd rather go straight to the source. And then I'll check myself into the looney bin. For now, I pocket some adhesive bandages that I find in the box. On my way out of the bathroom, I grab a towel and washcloth. I take all of it downstairs and set it on the couch next to him. "The kitchen is this way?" I ask before heading toward it.

"Yeah, make yourself at home!" I hear Tim call after me.

"Thanks!" I reply, even though I know he's being sarcastic. The kitchen gleams with brand new appliances, but I'm all business as I open cupboards to find a big enough bowl. I fill it with water and carefully carry it back to the living room.

"Dinner is served!" I joke.

Tim laughs when able to see into the bowl. I set it on the floor next to his feet. "What are you doing?" he asks.

"Checking how bad the damage is," I say, dipping the washcloth into the water. I bring it close to his bloody shin and look up, seeking his permission. Tim is already bracing for pain, but he nods. I begin dabbing at the dried blood to reveal the actual wound. Once I see the spot to avoid, I gently wrap my hand around his leg to take hold of his calf. I'm wiping his shin clean when I notice goosebumps race across his skin. Probably because the air conditioner is running. Or maybe it's my touch. The hairs are standing up on his legs where they are dry enough to do so. I hope I don't creep him out. My eyes meet his, but what I see there isn't fear. I'm not sure what's behind them, but my skin has reacted too, tingles racing up my arm.

"Does that feel okay?" I ask.

"Yeah," Tim says, his voice husky. "It's fine."

I keep working, dipping the washcloth into the bowl when needed, the water getting steadily darker, and wonder why we associate red with love. Because of the liquid pumping through our hearts? Or did some ancient Egyptian knock a cute guy off the top of a pyramid when having a bad day? I pat his leg dry, resisting the urge to smile as I apply an adhesive bandage over the cut.

"Doesn't look so bad," Tim says, leaning forward to watch.

"The bleeding has already stopped," I say, nodding in agreement. "What about your ankle?"

"I dunno. Let's check it out." Tim leans forward in an attempt to untie his shoes.

I put my hand on his bare shoulder and gently push. "I've got this," I say.

He leans back, wearing a curious expression as I untie the laces of his blue shoes. I start with the good leg, pulling that shoe off first. I'm braced for stinky socks, which even my twisted libido can't turn into something sexual. Not on such short notice at least. But his socks smell fine. He tenses as I gently wiggle off the other shoe, and so do I, because I can already see how pink and swollen the ankle has become. One of the socks is stained with blood, so I peel those off next, revealing big brown feet with hairy toes. Which I am way more into than I care to acknowledge. Fortunately, the injured ankle continues to distract me.

"You need to see a doctor," I say, looking up in concern.

"Nah, it's fine." Tim grabs the brace next to him. "Just put this on it. Tight, but not too tight, you know?"

I do as he says, feeling horrible with each stifled whimper I hear.

"If it hurts that bad—" I begin.

"That's what these are for," Tim says, jiggling the bottle of painkillers. "Get me something to drink before you go."

I wasn't planning on leaving, but it's his choice, not mine. I go to the kitchen and grab a can of soda from the fridge. After I hand it to him, I can't get myself to turn away.

"When do your parents get back?" I ask.

"Next week," he says.

"But they'll come home early, right? When they hear what happened?"

Tim snorts. "I'm sure they'll paddle across the ocean just as fast as they can."

"My mom would swim if she had to. Wait, what do you mean the ocean? Are they out of the county?"

"I'm fine," Tim says, tossing a pair of pills into his mouth before washing them down. "And soon I'll be even better."

"Maybe I should stick around," I suggest. "What if you need something?"

"I'll crawl. It really isn't that hard."

I gnaw on my bottom lip, but he's looking less patient by the second, so I finally turn away. I grab my backpack and dig through it to find a piece of paper and a pen. I write down my phone number. "Just in case," I say, holding it out to him.

He stares instead of taking the paper from me. I feel vulnerable.

"Okay?" I prompt, stretching my arm out farther. "Whatever you need. I'll come running."

Tim finally grabs the piece of paper. "I'm good. But okay."

"So I guess umm… See you around."

He merely smirks in response.

I see myself out, deciding that I will indeed move to a different town to begin a new life, because this has been one of the most humiliating experiences of my life. And simultaneously one of the most exciting.

CHAPTER FOUR

Tim is all I can think about while I'm eating dinner with my family. As soon as we finish and I've cleared the table, I leave Karen to fill the dishwasher so I can do medical research. I feel like I'm fighting against the clock to find a desperately needed cure, although all I come up with is bad news. Tim isn't okay.

"I'm gonna go hang out with Allison!" I tell my parents as I race past the living room.

"Don't forget that it's a school night!" my mom shouts after me.

Jogging isn't an interest of mine, and by the time I show up on Tim's doorstep sweaty and panting, I decide that it never will be. I ring the bell and knock before worrying that he'll fall in the entryway again, so I try the door, which is still unlocked.

"Hello?" I call, sticking my head in. "It's me!"

I hear laughter before he responds. "Get in here, you weirdo!"

I find Tim exactly where I left him, except now the television is on, and he's pulled the blankets close to cover himself. His face is pale.

"How do you feel?" I ask.

Tim raises the remote to mute the TV. "Great! Kind of cold though." He shoves off the blanket. "Although now I'm kinda hot. And hungry."

"How's the ankle?" I ask, taking a step closer to see.

"Oh you know…" Tim says, leaning forward to check. Then he leans back slowly with a haunted expression. "It'll be fine. I can barely feel it."

"How could you not?" I ask, turning on a lamp. The added light reveals swelling above the brace, like the top of a muffin. "Tim! That doesn't look good!"

"It's getting better, I swear!" He reaches for the bottle of painkillers. "Could you grab me another Coke?"

"Just a minute," I say, getting on my knees in front of him, but even I don't find this moment sexy. I start to unfasten the brace.

"What are you doing?" he asks, jerking his leg away before hissing in pain.

"I looked it up," I tell him, gently taking hold of his foot and moving it close again. "I think you have a grade two sprain."

"Meaning what?" he asks.

"That you tore something." I suck in air as the brace falls away, revealing bloated flesh that is already starting to bruise. "We've gotta get you to the hospital!"

"Or what?" he asks, as if wanting to weigh his options.

"Or it won't heal right and you'll always be in pain. *And* you won't be able to play sports anymore." I'm expecting that last bit to upset him the most.

Instead he twirls his index finger in the air and says, "Whoop-de-doo!"

I sit back, confused by his apathy. "If you let it heal on its own, you might not be able to walk the same afterwards. And you sure as hell won't be able to run on it anymore."

This seems to sober him up. "For real?"

"Yes! We need to go to the emergency room."

Tim crosses his arms over his chest. "Maybe tomorrow. If it's still bugging me."

"Tonight," I say, getting to my feet with determination. "I'll call an ambulance. Or my parents. They can drive us."

"Wait!" Tim says, sounding panicked "We don't have to get anyone involved. Do we?"

I shrug, not seeing why it would matter. "You can't drive yourself," I say, nodding to the injury, which is on his right leg. "I can't imagine you pushing down on the gas pedal with that thing."

"Yeah, but maybe..." I watch him clench his jaw as he struggles within himself. Then he perks up. "You can drive, right?"

I freeze. "I mean, technically."

His brow furrows at this. "You don't have a license?"

"I do." It took me three attempts to pass the test, but I keep that to myself.

"All right," Tim says as he tries to push himself up. "You can drive us there."

"In your car?" I ask, already loving the idea.

Tim laughs. "In my mom's minivan."

"No way!" I shoot back. "I've seen what you drive—"

"Of course you have," Tim interjects.

"—and it's *way* cooler," I finish.

This seems to please him. "You're into cars?"

"Super into them," I lie.

He eyes me a second before offering his hand so I can help him up. "What's your favorite kind?" he asks.

"I love Mustangs and um… Broncos and also uh…. Ponies. Because of the horse power," I finish lamely, figuring that I've already revealed myself as a fraud.

"You're into pony cars?" he asks with a grin. "Those are my favorite too!"

He starts naming different makes and models. I don't have a clue what he's talking about, but all I have to do is nod and say "Yeah, exactly!" as we hop through the kitchen to the garage door.

I get him situated in the passenger seat of the whatever-it-is he owns. I just know that, like the owner, the car has an impressive build. I return inside for the key and a pair of sandals I saw by the front door. Before long, we're pulling out of the garage. Slowly.

"Watch the side mirrors!" Tim cries in alarm.

"Huh?"

"Stop!"

I hit the brakes and glance over. The passenger-side mirror is a fraction of an inch from hitting the wooden frame around the garage door.

"Oops!" I say, driving forward before I try to pull out again.

Tim's head is whipping around in concern at this point. Especially when the second attempt doesn't go any better. "Why do you keep reversing at an angle?" he demands.

"Because I can't even drive straight," I deadpan.

I finally get it right on the third try.

"So it's true?" he asks as we cruise down his street.

"What?"

"The gay thing."

"You think I made it up for fun?" I ask with a playful smile.

Tim shrugs. "Just because someone says something bad about you, doesn't mean that it's true."

The grin slides off my face. "Is that how you see it? As a bad thing?"

Tim seems distracted. "That was a four-way stop back there."

"I didn't see anyone else," I say with a shrug. "So do you?"

"What?"

"Have a problem with me being gay." I look over at him, a

lump already forming in my throat. I'm braced for the worst, but like Allison said, it's better to know early on. "I'll still drive you to the hospital. No matter what you think."

Tim searches my eyes. "I don't know," he says. "It's just… different."

"Different," I repeat before returning my attention to the road. "Okay, but in a good way or a bad way? Because it was different when the school cafeteria started microwaving their pizzas, but nobody actually likes it."

"I don't have a problem with you," Tim says, reaching over to grab the wheel. He guides us toward the center of the lane again. "But if you wreck my car, it'll get real personal real quick."

"Is that a promise?" I ask, placing my hand over his, but only to move it off the steering wheel. And yeah, for the fleeting physical contact as well.

"You're crazy," Tim says with a chuckle. "So what do you think?"

He nods in front of him. I examine the world outside the windshield and am none the wiser. "About what?"

"My car!" he says incredulously. "Do you realize how many cylinders this baby has?"

I hazard a guess. "One for each wheel?"

"Huh?"

"Isn't that how it works? The wheels go on the cylinders, right?"

"You're thinking of axles," Tim says, "but even then, this car wouldn't have four. Are you messing with me?"

"Ha ha! Yeah… Totally. It's a beautiful car." Whatever it is.

"Thanks. My parents gave it to me for my eighteenth birthday."

"An older man!" I breathe. "Just how I like them! And rich too. Make sure to leave me something in your will, gramps."

Tim laughs. "How old are you?"

"Seventeen. But only for another month. If you need a roommate in the retirement home, give me a call."

Tim's attention is fixed on the street. "The light is about to change," he says.

"That's convenient," I reply.

"About to turn *red*," he emphasizes. "Slow down!"

"I can make it."

"No you can't!"

I don't see what all the fuss is about. We blow through the intersection unscathed. The other drivers are so impressed by my skill that they honk in tribute.

"Is it too late to call an ambulance?" Tim moans. "You know what? Take me home. I don't care if I ever walk again."

"We're almost there," I assure him.

When we reach the hospital, I drop him off at the emergency room doors, where he leans against a pillar supporting the covered entrance and watches me park. Once we've reunited, I make him get into one of the wheelchairs we find near the doors, which feels like putting a cute guy in my shopping cart. I'd push him through the express lane checkout if that was an option. No need for a return receipt. Instead we venture inside to the front desk and explain the situation to the woman stationed there.

"Do you have insurance?" she asks.

Tim shrugs. "Probably."

"Where are your parents?"

"Out of town."

"But they're rich," I explain, "so if they don't have insurance, they'll pay in cash. Or do you accept gold bullion?"

The receptionist eyes us wearily before sliding a clipboard over the counter. "Fill out what you know and someone will see you soon."

I snatch the clipboard, and after rolling Tim over to the waiting area, delight in asking him all manner of personal questions.

"August twenty-fourth," he says when we get to his date of birth.

"Wow, that was just a few weeks ago!" I say in surprise.

Tim sounds muted in his response. "Yeah."

"Must have been a good one. You got an amazing car."

Tim shrugs. "It sucked not knowing anyone here. I didn't have any friends to hang out with."

"Well you do now," I say, flashing him a hokey smile. Which makes him laugh. "Do want me to be your emergency contact?" I ask after consulting the form again. "I mean, it would obviously be your parents if they were in town. But until then?"

Tim sighs. "They're going to kill me."

"Hey, none of this is your fault."

He shakes his head. "Doesn't matter. If their trip gets cut short, they'll be pissed."

"But only in the concerned and overbearing kind of way, right?"

Tim eyes me like I'm not making sense. Then he studies his sandaled feet, wiggling his toes. "I got a really bad flu when I was fourteen. Like the high fever kind that makes you feel crazy. I cried so much that my parents had to fly home early. I wish they hadn't bothered, because I was feeling better by the time they got back. They probably thought I was faking it. My dad was in a shitty mood because of some business deal I messed up. I don't know exactly, but it's the same situation. Right now they're traveling with another couple who have connections my dad needs. It's a wining and dining type thing." Tim scowls. "I'd rather be a gimp for the next two weeks than to have him hate me more than he already does." He clenches his jaw as he turns his head away.

"I'm sure he doesn't hate you," I try.

Tim doesn't respond.

"What about your mom?" I ask.

He looks at me again, his features softening. "She'll be mad that I didn't tell her sooner. So I guess I'm in trouble either way."

"What if they never find out?"

"What do you mean?"

I don't get a chance to explain. A nurse calls Tim's name. I follow him down a hall, where he's weighed and measured (six feet tall and a hundred and seventy pounds) before we're shown to an exam room. I try to keep his spirits high while we wait. When the doctor shows up to examine him, the sprain is severe enough that we're told he'll be there through the night.

"I can pick you up in the morning," I say during a brief moment when we're alone.

"Yeah, all right," Tim says, gnawing on a thumbnail.

"I'm really sorry," I tell him. "I didn't mean for any of this to happen. I'll make it up to you."

He perks up. "Will you walk home instead of taking my car?"

"Nope! But I do have a plan. So you don't get in trouble."

Which might land me in hot water, but I figure it's the least I can do. Before I can explain, a nurse arrives with a wheelchair to take him to his room for the night. I walk with them to the elevators, but he's going up while I'm going down. (If only.)

"Everything will be fine," I tell him as he's rolled into the elevator. "Don't worry. Okay?"

The last thing I see before the doors close are concerned silver eyes. It'll be all right. I'm going to take good care of him. Like a bird with a broken wing, I'll nurse him back to health before releasing him into the wild. Or in this case, back into the clutches of the popular kids. I'll need help though. Lucky for me, I've got the greatest friend a guy could ever wish for.

I call Allison in the morning, a minute after her alarm is set to go off. Yes, we know each other that well.

"I'm giving you a ride to school," I tell her.

"Really?" she asks. "Is your mom driving us?"

"Nope! I'll be there as soon as your dad leaves. I need your help."

"Of course you do," she says around a yawn.

Allison is much more alert when I pull up in a brand-new sports car and climb out.

"I can't believe it!" she says when leaping down the steps to the driveway. "Is this an early birthday present? Wait... It's the same car that Tim has! Is that why you chose it?"

"It's way better than that. This *is* his car. I put him in the hospital!" I blanch at my own confession. "Wait... That sounds bad."

Allison raises an eyebrow. "Then you better start talking."

I tell her everything as we go inside her house. She's already shaking her head halfway through my story. She's never shied away from telling me hard truths—especially when I make mistakes—but she's also my best friend and has always supported me. So at the end of my recap, she says, "The boy only has himself to blame for being so damn fine."

"Exactly!" I say with a maddened cackle.

Her dark eyes are probing, her tone gentle when she asks, "Does he like you back?"

"I don't know," I admit. "Right now, I just want to focus on helping him. I figure he'll be back on his feet by the time his parents get home. More or less. If I take care of him until then, they won't need to come home early, and I'll..." I swallow before continuing. "I'll get to spend time with him."

"Ben," Allison says, in a way that makes it sound like her heart is breaking for me.

"I need your help," I say while I still have her sympathy. "Tim won't be in school today. His mom has to call the front office to let them know."

"But you just said—" she begins before her eyes widen. "No!"

"Please!" I literally beg. My hands are clutched in front of my chest and everything. "One quick call. That's it. Oh… And I need you to do a Mexican accent."

"Oh my god," Allison rolls her eyes. "Remind me why I love you."

"So you'll do it?" I ask.

She sighs. "Of course. Help me practice first. You be the front office."

I hold up a pinky and thumb to the side of my face. "Hello! This is the most boring high school in the world. How can I help you?"

The accent Allison does is terrible, so I'm glad she suggested a trial run. We get it ironed out, upgrading Tim's injury to a broken ankle, so they won't expect him back for the rest of the week. We even inform the office that his close personal friend—yours truly—will be bringing his assignments home to him.

"Thank you," I tell Allison after she hangs up. "That takes care of him. Now I just need to get away with the rest."

"Which is what exactly?" she asks as we gather our things to leave.

I grimace, knowing that she won't like my plan. "I'm going to cut class today."

"Ben! Why?"

"I need to pick him up from the hospital." I hold up a hand to ward off a lecture. "I won't get caught. You know how they take attendance in second period? As long as I'm there when that happens, I should be good. Nobody will expect me to leave again."

Allison is already shaking her head. "Unless a teacher notices you missing. Mrs. Hammond will. You know we're her star pupils."

Our choir teacher. She's right. "You can cover for me. Tell her that I got food poisoning. It'll only be for one day."

Allison exhales. "Fine. But you shouldn't leave until lunch."

"How come?"

"So your best friend won't have to eat all by herself. That's also when some seniors leave for the work release program. So you're less likely to be noticed when driving away in this showy thing."

"You're a genius!" I say, holding open the passenger-side door of Tim's car for her.

Once we're both inside, I turn on the ignition and rev the engine, expecting her to be impressed. Instead she still looks concerned.

"You know," Allison says softly, "there is another way. You could tell your mom. She would pick Tim up from the hospital. And make sure he's taken care of. Like she did for me, after my mom died."

I can still remember being sent to school with two sack lunches, so Allison's father wouldn't have to pack one. Which had bothered me at the time, because Allison was Karen's friend, not mine, but we were in the same grade and shared the same lunch break. The first time I gave Allison one of the home-packed meals, she cried. Not knowing what to do, I sat next to her. We ate together, mostly in silence, while she continued to sniffle.

"I really liked her," I had said toward the end of the meal. On occasion, my parents would send me with Karen on her playdates with Allison, most likely wanting privacy for reasons I'd rather not imagine. I would inevitably get bored when my sister and Allison started playing with dolls and would wander through the house. Allison's mom would usually offer me a cookie and let me hang out with her instead. Which was great, because she was always willing to watch cartoons with me or whatever else I wanted. So while I didn't truly understand death back then, I felt a loss, and it had seemed important to say so.

"I want her back," Allison had responded before starting to cry again.

I remember glaring at a pair of boys who had laughed at her tears and telling them to shut up. I can't count how many times Allison has defended me in the years since. And she's right. My mom would be more than willing to help take care of Tim. All I need to do is ask. And yet…

"I need this," I admit turning to my best friend, who is no longer a little girl. "I'm not going to find someone to love. Not while I'm in high school. So as crazy as it sounds, I like the idea of getting to be a part of his life. Even for a week or two. I'll be able to pretend that we're something more than we really are. Years from now, when you and me are looking back and talking about old boyfriends, Tim will be my high school sweetheart. Even though he'll never have known."

"What if you *do* fall in love with him?" Allison presses. "And it's not just pretend?"

"I want that too," I say with a tight throat. "It would be better than nothing."

"Oh honey…" Allison places her hand over mine and squeezes. "I do worry. Not because you crippled a hot boy and are basically planning on holding him captive. You're my kind of crazy. But I don't want you to get hurt."

I put on a reassuring smile. "At least I'd be feeling something." Not that I'm numb inside. I simply haven't gotten to experience any aspect of that kind of love. Unless a fleeting crush counts. I've had plenty of those. Maybe that's all Tim will turn out to be. But I don't think so. "And if worse comes to worst…" I say as the car goes over the curb during a tight turn. I look over at Allison affectionately.

"We'll always be there for each other," she confirms.

CHAPTER FIVE

I take my friend's advice and don't leave school until after lunch. The wait is torturous. I'm tempted to break the speed limit on the way to the hospital, but I play by the rules, not wanting my prize to slip from my grasp. I feel a little funny about that. I know Allison was joking when she said I plan on holding him captive, but it is kind of messed up to prevent someone's parents from finding out their child has been in a serious accident. Especially when you're the guy who put him in the hospital. I promise myself to spell it all out to Tim, so he can make his own decision. I really *really* hope he likes my plan.

I feel less certain when I get to his hospital room and he's flirting with a nurse. I wait patiently as she finishes her duties. He's got a shit-eating grin on his face as she leaves, although I'm happy it doesn't disappear just because she does.

"Benjamin!" Tim says, sounding upbeat. "How's my car?"

"I'm doing fine, thanks," I reply sarcastically. "And so is your car," I add when he starts to look worried. "What about you?"

"They've got me all patched up," he says, rocking his bad leg back and forth, which is covered up to the shin by a massive boot. A series of thick horizontal straps lead down to his foot, where socked toes stick out of the tip.

"What is that?" I ask, moving closer to see.

"The doctor called it a walking boot. I'll still need crutches for a little while, but pretty soon, I'll be as good as new."

I can already see my plans unraveling. "So you can go back to school tomorrow?"

Tim blanches at the idea. "I dunno. The doctor said I'm supposed to take it easy." His reluctant expression matches my own. "Do you think I have to?"

"Probably not. I had my friend call the school this morning. She um… pretended to be your mom." His brow furrows, so I force myself to press on, surprised by how much nuttier this sounds than it did this morning. "My friend messed up and said you'd broken your ankle. So I figure they aren't expecting you back this week. Or maybe even next."

"No shit?" Tim asks.

I can't tell if he's happy or not, and I don't get to ask, because we're interrupted. I take a step back during the discharge procedure, paying extra attention when the nurse goes over everything he'll need to remember, like his medications and how careful he'll have to be. She helps him get into a wheelchair, which I am soon walking behind while pushing him down the hall. I figure now is the best time to tell him the rest. If he hates the idea, I won't be able to see his face, and more importantly, he won't be able to see mine.

"I know you're worried about your parents finding out," I say. "My friend can talk to the school if they have any questions. I'll bring your homework and help you with it. And cook for you. And do anything else you need until your parents come back. By the time they get here, it sounds like you'll already be walking around. By then it really will be a minor sprain, so I can't imagine your mom being too upset."

Tim is quiet as I wheel him into the elevator. He doesn't speak until the doors close, sealing us in. He looks up, silver eyes seeking mine. "You'd really do all that for me?"

"Yeah!" I say eagerly. "I mean, this whole thing is my fault. I owe you that much."

"Sure, but you don't have to," he says. "I'm not pissed at you or anything. Accidents happen."

"I want to," I admit. The elevator dings then, as if emphasizing the point. "Really," I add when he continues to stare.

Then he smiles, and it just about makes me melt.

"Cool," he says. "Get me out of here. I can't wait to see my car!"

I roll my eyes, but I'm smiling too. I've been as honest as I can, without baring my soul entirely, and he truly does seem fine with the plan. I'm tempted to ask if he's high on painkillers, but I figure even if he is, Tim can change his mind later if he wants. But I sure hope he doesn't.

After a ridiculous debate where he insists he can drive with a massive boot on his foot, I get him loaded into the passenger seat. I try to pay more attention to the road while driving him home, not wanting to give him any reason to doubt that I can take good care of him. I really want this to work. More than anything.

"Hey, shouldn't *you* be in school?" Tim asks along the way.

I make sure my smile is enigmatic. "I'm supposed to be."

"You cut class?" Tim cackles when I nod and asks. "For me?"

"Yeah. Why not?"

He laughs again, "You're a wild one, Benjamin."

As soon as we reach his house, he puts me to work, more comfortable with the arrangement than I would have guessed. "I'm already sick of that couch," he says, leaning on a crutch as we survey the living room. "Going up and down the stairs to my bed will be a pain. Let's set up camp in my dad's den."

I try to imagine what his father looks like and picture a wolf. I follow Tim to the back of the house and enter a room that feels more like a hunting lodge. Tim makes his way to a dark leather couch, where he sits and props his boot on the rough-hewn coffee table in front of it. I continue to glance around. Wooden bookshelves built into the walls are filled with thick tomes that have somber spines. Any remaining space is filled with a scattering of trophies, an antique globe, and the occasional framed photo. I move to one and see a man with stark white hair and the same silver eyes as his son. Not too far off from the wolf I was envisioning. His stern face isn't as handsome as Tim's, especially in contrast to the woman at his side, who radiates beauty. I tear my gaze away, noticing framed sports memorabilia, a wet bar, and some poor creature who has been reduced to a stuffed head on the wall.

"Pretty cool, huh?" Tim asks.

I turn and see him gesturing at a massive big-screen TV.

"It certainly makes an impression," I reply diplomatically. I'm guessing his dad isn't a touchy-feely sort of guy. Unlike my own father, who is so sappy that he'll shamelessly weep while telling me and my sister how much we're loved. Don't get me started on how crazy he is about my mom. He'd do anything for her.

"We're gonna have to fill up the mini-fridge with Cokes," Tim says from the couch. "The only thing in there is beer. Which doesn't sound so bad at the moment."

"You're not supposed to drink alcohol with your pills," I murmur.

"Yeah, yeah," Tim says. "I'm buzzing anyway. It's good to be home. I didn't sleep so well last night. Hey, I'll need my favorite pillow down here. And a blanket. Maybe some snacks." He pulls at the muscle shirt he's wearing and sniffs. "Ugh! You know what I really need? A change of clothes. And a shower."

"How about a bath instead? So you don't slip."

"Yeah, okay. Will you run one for me?"

"Sure," I reply, still surprised by how quickly he's taken to the situation. "Were you raised by a nanny or something?"

"No. How come?"

I shrug innocently. "Do you have a stay-at-home mom?"

"Nah. She works as a translator." He scrunches up his face. "Are you saying I'm spoiled?"

"You just seem like you're used to having servants."

Tim shrugs. "Hey, you offered. I can do it all myself." He pushes against the couch, as if he's going to get up, although I'm pretty sure he's bluffing.

"Stay put," I tell him. "I'll get your bath ready."

While watching the tub slowly fill with water, it finally sinks in that this is really happening. I'm going to be Tim's make-believe wife for the next week! Maybe even longer. If only I could figure out some way of staying home from school. How hard would it be to sprain my own ankle? Or maybe a wrist. Although I can already imagine the jokes if I did. I return to the living room and insist on helping Tim up. We haven't touched yet today. His hand slides into mine for the fourth time since we've met. I've been keeping count. And I pray it won't be the last, because I want to memorize how it feels. Years from now—decades even—I want to close my eyes and be whisked back to this moment. I release his hand unwillingly and follow him to the bathroom, where he stops and stares.

"Why are there bubbles?" Tim asks.

I shake my head, not understanding. "Why wouldn't there be?"

"I dunno," he says with a shrug. "It's a little…"

"Girly?" I supply.

Another shrug. "I mean… Sort of. Yeah."

"Oh whatever," I say with an eye roll. "You didn't take bubble baths growing up? Because I sure did. And back then, it came in a pink bottle."

"I loved that stuff!" Tim says.

I gasp theatrically. "You've taken a bubble bath before? And it didn't make your penis fall off?"

Tim laughs. "Stick around and find out."

"Speaking of which," I say, since he broached the subject. "Do you need help getting undressed?"

"You wish."

"Yeah, obviously," I say shamelessly. "I'm gay, remember?"

"You make it hard to forget," he says with a grin. "I'll be okay. But I could use a change of clothes."

"Sure!" I begin lifting my T-shirt. "Let's trade."

"From my bedroom," he says. God I love his smile. I could stare at it all day. And I might!

"Anything in particular?"

He looks me over. "You've got good taste. Surprise me. Just make sure to grab jogging shorts, since they'll be easier to pull over this thing. I don't want to take it off until I have to, so I'll be in good shape when my parents get home."

"Okay. Just be careful on your way in."

I wait in the hall and listen to the sound of sloshing water until I'm certain that he's safely settled. Then I rush up the stairs to locate his bedroom, already excited by the prospect. I shut the door behind me when I find it, wanting to be completely surrounded by him. The room smells like Tim, so I take a deep breath, and another and another, until I'm practically dizzy. I let myself fall onto his bed, clutch his pillow to my chest, and then roll over on my back while imagining him above me. I bite my lower lip and get up to see what else I can find. The posters on his wall are predictable, featuring baseball players, cars, and swimsuit models. With one notable exception. An abstract painting hangs on the wall. In it, swirls of colors collide with a dark gray barrier, like a rolling tide trying to break through a dam. I spin around in an attempt to spot anything similar. A baseball bat leans in one corner, a boom box with fat speakers sits on his dresser, and a bikini-clad woman winks from a poster near his bed. Everything I'd expect to see in a jock's room. And then there's the painting. Did he hang it there? Does it resonate with him somehow? I stare, trying to interpret the meaning behind the art, before I remember what I'm here for.

I move to his dresser and begin opening drawers. I find a black T-shirt that will go great with his hair and a pair of maroon jogging shorts that will look nice against his brown skin. Then I open his underwear drawer and stare before grabbing a pair of gray boxer briefs. I hold them up, trying to determine if the fabric in front seems abnormally stretched, as if it struggled previously to contain his massive package. I'm none the wiser for my efforts, but I do notice a black book tucked into one corner of the drawer.

No words decorate the cover. Is it a diary? I'm not sure, but I decide to leave the book untouched. I want him to offer his secrets to me freely instead of stealing them. I gather up his clothes and glance at the painting on my way out.

I linger upstairs, peeking into his parents' bedroom, which has a definite theme. A large decorative crucifix hangs above the bed. A framed painting of Jesus is propped up on the nightstand, a copy of the Bible resting next to it, the cover worn and slightly curled from use. I hiss like a vampire and slowly retreat. Not that I have anything against religion, but it sure seems to have a problem with people like me.

I return downstairs and stop in the hall, just before the bathroom. "I've got your clothes," I call. "Want me to set them by the door?"

"Nah. Come on in!"

I won't make him ask twice. I walk into the bathroom, surprised that the shower curtain isn't pulled shut. I'd be able to see *all* of Tim, if I hadn't been so generous with the damn bubbles. He has his booted foot propped up on the side of the tub, the rest of him lost beneath the suds until his impressive chest rises out of the water like a sculpted cliffside that I want to hump. Those piercing eyes are watching me watch him, and they sure don't seem to mind. His hair is wet and slicked back, which is a good look for him, although I prefer the messy spikes.

"What did you get?" he asks, nodding at the stack of clothes. I show him, and he seems pleased with my choices until I reach the underwear. "Those'll get ruined if I stretch them over my boot," he says. "Feel free to keep them."

"Are you joking?" I ask. "Because I don't want to hear about it later when they've gone missing."

"Yeah, I was joking!" he says, swiping at the bubbles and sending some flying in my direction. "You don't actually want them. Do you?"

"Not until after they've been freshly worn," I say with a grin. "I'll leave it all here for you." I set the stack on the shut toilet lid.

"Hey!" he says when I turn to leave. "Stick around. Keep me company."

"For real?" I make a face. "Is this a popular kid thing? You guys are all attention starved?"

His eyes dart away and his brow furrows, like I've struck a

nerve. I don't like the idea that I've hurt him somehow. The ankle was bad enough.

"I'm just jealous," I say, sliding down to the floor with my back against the sink cabinet. "Tell me what it's like."

"Being popular?" Tim shrugs, the water sloshing around his beefy shoulders. "I used to like it. Everyone knows who you are, even if you don't know them, so you've got all the friends you'd ever need. You get invited to parties and stuff, which is cool, and it feels good when people look up to you. This one guy at my old school started dressing just like me. My friends teased him, but I thought it was flattering, you know?"

"I do know," I retort. "About the teasing part."

"Oh." Tim grimaces. "Some of the popular kids can be assholes, but we're not all bad. I'm always nice to everyone."

"Are you?" I don't say this to challenge him. I really want to know.

"Yeah," he says easily. "I don't think I'm better than anyone. I never signed up to be popular. It's not like I cozied up to someone trying to get there. It just sort of happened."

"Because you're rich and hot," I explain.

Tim looks surprised. "You think so?"

I nod. "That's how it works. You've got to be one or the other. And if you're both…" I move a flattened palm through the air, like an airplane taking off at a steep angle.

"No," Tim says, shaking his head. "Do you really think I'm hot?"

I laugh. "Are you kidding me? Yes!"

He flashes a cocky grin. "Thanks."

"Don't tell me you're insecure."

Tim shrugs. "What's it like being you?"

"Pretty much the same, but in reverse. Nobody knows the real me, but they all know my name. And my reputation. I'm the gay guy who's only good for a secret blowjob. And afterwards, nobody wants to be seen with me. Especially since I came out."

The saddest part is that I'm telling him on purpose. I want Tim to know that the option is on the table. It hasn't been for a long time. I value myself too much these days. But for him, I'll make an exception.

Tim's expression is hard to read. His words aren't much clearer. "That's messed up."

The services I've performed? Or the way I was treated afterwards? I'm not sure, and I don't get a chance to ask, because he adds, "I know what it's like."

That gets my attention. "You've been secretly blowing guys too?"

Tim chuckles. "No. But where I used to live…" The smile slides off his face. "Being popular isn't always a good thing."

"How come?"

He shakes his head, like it's not important.

I remain silent, noticing his reluctance when he starts to speak.

"Some people want to see you fail," he says at last. "Maybe they resent you for being popular. I don't know. But they watch, waiting for you to mess up or say the wrong thing. And if you do, it's headline news. Like if some random guy pukes during lunch, a handful of people might gossip about it for the rest of the day. But if you're popular, *everyone* hears about it. And they don't let you forget."

I study him for a moment. "So how much did you barf?"

"It wasn't that," he grumbles.

"Then what?"

Tim frowns. "Forget about it."

"I can keep a secret," I assure him. "All those guys who used to invite me over? I didn't speak a word of what we did. Not to anyone. I was too worried it would stop the fun. They weren't as discreet. So I know how quickly word gets around. And how bad it can be when it does. I wouldn't do that to you."

Tim's expression is guarded as he weighs my sincerity. I let him stare into my eyes, wanting him to see everything contained there. I would be loyal to him. If given the chance.

"Before we moved," he says at last. "I was dating this girl." He shakes his head, as if needing to start over. "Her name was Carla. The first time I saw her, she was in a bikini at a pool party, and man, it was like something out of a movie. Suddenly the whole world was moving in slow motion."

I'm already jealous of her.

"So we started talking and hit it off," Tim continues. "She was my first serious girlfriend. And I was her first time. Which makes it so messed up that she…" He eyes me again, his expression vulnerable.

"What?" I ask, leaning forward.

Tim takes a deep breath. "She said that I raped her."

The bathroom is silent in the wake of this confession.

Tim sighs. "When people hear that kind of thing, they assume it's true. Guilty until proven innocent. Which is seriously fucked up." He glares. "Go ahead and ask if I actually raped her. I can tell you want to."

"No need," I assure him. If I thought Tim was capable of that, I'd get up and walk the hell out. And I know he's right about the rest, because if Bryce was facing the same allegations, I'd be tempted to tell people that yeah, he probably *did* do it. Mostly because I want to see him fall. But not for something that isn't true. As much as I hate Bryce, there's a big difference between being an insensitive jerk and committing a horrific crime. Although plenty of gray area lies between the two. "What happened exactly? Were you drunk or something?"

Tim scoffs. "We dated for most of junior year. We had sex dozens of times and it was *always* consensual. The bedroom is where we got along best, because otherwise… Carla had a mean streak. She was always making fun of me in front of her friends and treating me like crap. I don't know why. Her home life was kind of messed up, which is something we had in common. But I couldn't take it anymore and broke up with her."

I wait for him to say more. Like they had sex one final time afterwards, and she regretted it, or anything that could even begin to justify such a serious allegation. "So when did you supposedly…" I trail off, not wanting to say it aloud.

"At a party. I was hanging with my best friend during the whole thing. And after. So thank fucking god I had an alibi. But people hear that and say, 'Of course his best friend would have his back. I bet he helped!'" Tim's lips pull back in disgust. "I'd rather die than do that to someone!"

"That's terrible. How did everything play out?"

"I spent the rest of the school year being called a rapist by people I didn't even know. *That's* why being popular sucks. It doesn't take much to go from famous to infamous. My parents got involved. You should have seen my mom's face. It was the worst. Carla didn't take it to the police, but she told anyone who would listen." Tim winces while sinking lower into the tub. "Why am I even talking about this? Leaving it behind was the only good thing about moving here."

"I'll never breathe a word to anyone," I promise him. "Not

even my best friend." Which is saying a lot, because we tell each other everything.

"Thanks," Tim replies, seeming haunted by the memories.

"So if being popular backfired on you," I say, "why are you friends with Bryce and the rest of them?"

"Hey, they found me. All I did was flirt with Krista. She introduced me to the others. I was glad to have friends again. It was my first day of school. I didn't know who anyone was, or their status."

"But now that you do…" I prompt.

Tim shrugs. "They're good to me. And from what you said, people turn on you whether you're popular or not, so it doesn't really matter."

"Not so fast," I say, sitting up straighter. "People hating you for something that isn't true is *not* the same as them hating who you really are."

Tim studies me. "Which do you think is worse?"

I blink in surprise. "I'm honestly not sure. I get to feel proud of who I am, at least. But moving to a different town wouldn't help. Not unless I wanted to live a lie."

"Ever been tempted?"

"Yes." I gnaw my bottom lip for a moment. "But I won't."

"How come?" He seems genuinely curious.

"Because it's my only chance of finding love. It pays to advertise."

"Oh yeah?"

My shoulders slump. "In theory. I've never had a boyfriend before."

"That's crazy," Tim says. "Can't you… I don't know. Find some other way to advertise?"

"For a casual hookup? No problem. That would be easy. But I want love."

I wait for him to scoff or snort. He's looking me over in a way that's hard to define. Not like I've been eyeing him from day one. He isn't lusting after me exactly. Instead he seems to be taking it all in. Including some of my surroundings. I don't know what's going on, but when he snaps out of this state, he appears self-conscious. Especially when glancing at the tub.

"Whoa!" he says, trying to reach the shower curtain. "These bubbles are getting awfully thin."

I regret not sitting somewhere higher, so I'd have a better view. Considering the raging hormones pent up inside of me, it's a testament to the conversation we just had that I wasn't thinking of his body at all. I don't want to cheapen that by sneaking a peek now. So I keep my head down when standing. I grab the towel and set it on the floor next to the tub before pulling the shower curtain shut.

"Be careful when drying off," I say.

I don't jokingly offer to help. I haven't exactly been subtle. He knows I'm attracted to him, and what I am willing to do. I'm surprised to find that sex isn't at the forefront of my thoughts. What I really hope, once he's finished bathing and has dressed, is that Tim will want to spend more time talking together.

CHAPTER SIX

I get my wish. Tim stretches himself out on the couch in his father's den. I angle one of the side chairs to face him. We talk a little more about our pasts, and after a while, his eyelids begin to droop. I don't take it personally. I figure it's either the painkillers or the rough night at the hospital. I let him sleep, using the opportunity to study his face, which I find incredibly handsome, even without those silver eyes lighting up the room. I like his strong nose and his kissable lips. His hair isn't styled and looks soft to the touch. I wish I could run my fingers through it. Or snuggle up with him on the couch, because I wouldn't mind a nap. I check the clock and become instantly alert. School is almost over! I'm supposed to pick up Allison!

I take his car keys, and as quietly as possible, leave the house. I'm not too late when pulling up to the school. I can tell that Allison was getting worried, but when she sees me, she perks up and hops inside.

"Tell me everything!" she cries.

I do. Except for the allegations that I promised to keep secret.

"He's really nice," I finish, frustrated that it's so hard to convey the magnitude of feelings developing inside of me.

"I'm happy for you," Allison says. "So what's the plan? Are we hanging out at your place? Or going shopping somewhere? Oh! There's a new album I *need* you to hear. You're going to love it!"

I wince apologetically. "I have to go back to Tim's place, so I can make him dinner."

"Boo!" Allison says, drawing the word out. "I can't believe he's taking my place already." She grins to show she's not actually upset. "For the record, I have romantic plans of my own."

"You do?"

Allison nods happily. "Ronnie wants to take me out for ice cream tomorrow."

"For ice cream?" I repeat with a snort. "What is he, your grandpa?"

"I think it's sweet," Allison says, shoving me playfully. "Coffee would have been more sophisticated, but this way, I don't have to pretend to like it."

"So is this a date?" I ask.

Allison scrunches up her nose. "More like a pre-date, I guess. Which is good, because I'm not sure about Ronnie."

"But he's so cute!"

"True, but there's a reason we broke up freshman year. We'll see how much he's changed. If he has…" She eyes me knowingly. "Pretty soon we'll both be busy gettin' *biz-eh!*"

I'm so taken by the idea that I have to slam on the brakes to avoid rear-ending a car. Which is ironic, because I was thinking about getting rear-ended myself. Allison doesn't complain about the sudden stop. She's not the best driver either.

"I still have time to hang out," I tell her.

"Good!" Allison reaches for the radio. "Let's listen to some tracks."

"One more thing," I say. "After I have dinner with my family, I'm going to leave so I can hang out with you. Wink wink. So if it comes up later…"

"I'll say we've been practicing for the talent show."

"Oh god," I say with an exaggerated shudder. "I'm glad that isn't until the end of the year, or we'd be hearing about it from Mrs. Hammond every day."

"You'd think," Allison replies, "but guess what?"

"No!"

"Yup! She asked why you weren't in class—which went fine, by the way—and wanted to know if we'd given any thought to which song we want to perform."

"She doesn't expect us to start practicing *now*," I say in disbelief.

Allison shrugs. "Last year we weaseled out of it by saying we didn't have time to prepare."

"I'll come up with a better excuse," I promise her.

Our choir teacher is great. Performing on stage doesn't intimidate me. It's the specific audience that I dread. No matter how much ass we kick, a lot of people will pretend to hate the song because the local homo is singing it.

"But if we *did* enter the talent show," Allison says casually, "which song would we choose?"

She isn't as against the idea as I am, so I humor her and discuss potential candidates all the way home. We have fun hanging out there, like we always do, until my mom knocks on my bedroom door. I inherited a lot from her, such as the short and slight build. Her shoulder-length hair is blond too, and not just in the summer. Which makes me worry that I inherited my hair from my dad, who doesn't have much of it left.

"Are you staying for dinner?" my mom asks Allison.

"No thanks, Mrs. B! My dad promised to bring home takeout."

"Oh, that's nice," my mom says with a friendly smile. Her eyes move to mine. "Come set the table after you've said goodbye."

I walk with Allison to where the sidewalk meets the driveway. She lives just around the block. I parked Tim's car at the halfway point, since it would raise too many questions.

"Don't forget that we're hanging out tonight," I say with an exaggerated wink.

Allison hesitates before nodding. "I'm still cool with that," she replies, "but I think you should tell your mom about Tim."

"What?" I recoil from the suggestion. "Why?"

She holds up her palms. "Not *everything*. Just tell her that you've made a new friend. Because think about it, if things start to sizzle between you guys, and the weekend is coming up…"

I shake my head, still not seeing the big picture.

"You can't pretend that you're staying the night at my house," she clarifies.

Her father would never allow it, even though he knows I'm not interested in women. It finally clicks!

"But I *can* say that I'm staying with my new straight buddy," I breathe, getting it at last. "You're a genius!"

"I do what I can," Allison says before we hug and part ways.

I eagerly execute her plan during dinner. I tell my family about the new guy in town while trying to rein in my enthusiasm.

"That's wonderful, honey!" my mother replies. "I'm glad you've made a new friend." A trace of worry betrays her cheerful demeanor. "Does he know about you?"

"How could he not?" my father asks in confusion. "They're friends."

"Obviously," my mother says patiently. "I mean—"

"Does he know that you're cursed?" my sister supplies helpfully. That's how she always refers to my sexual orientation.

"Karen!" our mom says in chastising tones. "Eat your broccoli."

My sister looks offended by the suggestion. "What am I, five years old?"

"When you talk to your brother that way, it sure sounds like you are," my mother retorts.

"You're still *my* baby," my father says warmly. "And always will be."

Karen is his favorite. Which is fine. Someone has to actually like her.

I turn to my mom. "Tim knows about me. And he's cool with it."

"Good!" my mom says, seeming relieved. "You'll have to invite him over sometime, so we can meet."

Not too soon though. She'll definitely have my number when seeing how hot he is. I can barely wait to refresh my memory. As soon as I'm free, I run to his car and make the short drive over to Tim's house. I let myself in and find him on the couch in the den. He's twisted around so he can see the doorway.

"There you are!" he says. "I was starting to think you wouldn't show."

"Did you miss me?" I ask.

"Yeah!" he says, thrilling me briefly. "I'm starving."

It's good to be wanted, I suppose, no matter the reason. "I'll whip something up. Any requests?"

"Pizza," he says, smiling at me before he turns to face the TV again.

Being in a different room than him and yet so close is torture. I'm relieved to find a pizza in the freezer, since I wouldn't know what to do otherwise. Order one, I guess, which requires money that I don't have. While waiting for the oven to heat up, I spot a kitchen radio and turn it on. After tuning to a station I like, I begin singing along with one love song and then another, appreciating the lyrics like never before. I dance around the kitchen once the pizza is in the oven, making sure to check on its progress through the glass door. I turn around on one such occasion and notice that I'm not alone. Tim is leaning on a crutch while watching me. And he has a funny look on his face. Probably because I was bent over and shaking my rump just a second ago.

"Hey!" I say with an embarrassed laugh.

"Hey yourself," Tim replies. "Was that you singing?"

"Oh. Ha ha! Yeah."

"You've got one hell of a voice," he says.

I'm not sure if he means the volume or the quality, but one of my favorite songs starts to play. Or more accurately, a new version of an old classic. I grab a wooden spoon and use it as a microphone as I croon along with the lyrics. Tim's eyes go wide, then he grins as I put on a show for him. I perform like I'm on stage in front of a packed stadium. I strut the length of the kitchen while working the adoring fans in the front row. Halfway through the song, I stop singing and let the imaginary mic drop to my side, but he shakes his head.

"Keep going, Benjamin!"

"Really?" I ask in disbelief.

He almost looks pained that I've stopped. "Yeah!"

I set aside the wooden spoon and resume singing, but I'm not hamming it up this time. I go deep inside myself, everything I feel exploding out through my voice a split second later. I stand in place, closing my eyes on occasion when overwhelmed by the intoxication that comes with being a conduit for a universal symphony. I don't know how else to describe it. In moments like this, I'm connected to something more. A nameless god or the fabric of the universe or the unseen connection between everything living. I'm not sure. But as the song ends, I'm only looking at him. And he's staring back, as if he finally sees me for the first time.

When the DJ starts talking, Tim scowls and hobbles over to the radio to shut it off. Then he turns to face me. "That was…" He doesn't find the words. Which is fine, because getting to sing for him was already enough for me.

"Oh shit!" I exclaim suddenly. "The pizza!"

I throw open the oven door, a swirl of smoke coming out, but only the edges of the crust are burnt. Which for me, is as golden-brown as it ever gets.

"Dinner is served!" I say. "Almost. Do you guys have a pizza cutter?"

"Uh… yeah," Tim says. "The drawer next to the sink." He watches me as I work. "That was really nice."

"Thanks," I reply. "It's kind of my thing. I figure everyone has a talent, whether they've discovered it or not. You play baseball, right?"

"Yeah, I guess," Tim says.

"You can't remember?" I tease. "Uh-oh! Did you bump your head when I knocked you down?"

He laughs while opening a cabinet. "Baseball is more my dad's thing. How many plates?"

"Just one. I already ate."

"Thank god!" Tim says, watching as I start stacking slices. "I would have shared, but I really don't want to."

"Fine with me," I reply. "Where do you want to eat?"

"In the den," he says, already heading that way. "We'll put on some music videos. I wanna hear you sing again."

"Seriously?" I ask while following.

I'm not sure if he hears me, because he's moving surprisingly fast for a guy with a bum leg. He must be really hungry! Before long, Tim is sitting on the couch with a slice of pizza in each hand, alternating between each when taking bites (who does that?) while I serenade him during the songs I know well enough. He has pizza sauce in the corner of his mouth when he's done eating. I want to kiss it away. That would sound gross if anyone else described the scenario to me, but I'm just that crazy about him.

"I think you need a napkin," I say when I can't get the fantasy out of my mind.

"Oh!" Tim rubs his mouth on the back of his hand. "Did I get it?"

"No," I say. Even though he did.

I watch him repeat the ritual over and over. "Nope. Still there. A little to the left. Try again."

He finally squints in suspicion. "You're messing with me."

"How could I not? You make it so easy." He's rolling his eyes and I'm laughing as I stand to collect his plate. "Want more to drink?" I offer.

"Yeah! Thanks."

I'm all aflutter when leaving the room, like I've just gone on a dream date, when in reality, I'm the worst paid waiter in town. Cleaning up doesn't take long. I'm eager to rejoin him. On the return trip down the hall, a shrill ringing sound falls silent just before I reach the den.

"Krista!" I hear Tim say. "Hey!"

When I enter the room, he has a phone pressed against his ear.

"No, I'm okay," Tim says into it. "I took a spill and messed up my ankle, that's all. Huh? No, I was out jogging. I must have tripped over a rock. Lame, right?"

My heart is in my throat as I quietly sit, and it plummets right down to my stomach when Tim notices me and mouths an explanation.

"My girlfriend."

I nod in understanding, because it makes perfect sense. Of course he has a girlfriend. Who else would it be if not Krista? Me? I'm not pretty or popular. They're two of a kind. I'm nobody, my role in the story replaced by a rock that Tim purportedly tripped over. When it becomes obvious that he isn't going to call her back some other time, I stand to leave.

Tim tries to communicate something with his face.

I ignore him and collect my things, surprised when a hand wraps around my wrist to stop me. Tim has gotten to his feet, the phone pinned between his ear and shoulder as he balances himself against the back of the chair I'd been sitting in.

"Hold up," he says into the phone. "Be right back."

He lets go of my wrist so he can grab the phone and toss it on the couch. "Where are you going?"

"Home," I say, without offering a reason.

"Will I see you tomorrow? Like in the morning?" His eyebrows are raised in anticipation of my answer, as if it matters to him.

I sigh inwardly before offering a reassuring smile. "Yeah. I'll see you then."

"Cool."

He sits back on the couch. I hightail it out of there, not wanting to hear more of their conversation. Although one last snippet reaches my ears.

"Sorry, a friend stopped by. What were you saying?"

It's not a bad consolation prize. He considers me a friend. Which is a timely reminder of the facts: Tim is straight and taken. I'm gay and lonely. Nothing I didn't know when going in, but the dream was so intoxicating that I nearly lost myself in it. Even now, as I climb into his car and run my hands along the steering wheel, I can't help hoping that it'll still come true somehow. Maybe that's why I feel the need to take part of him with me like this, instead of making the short walk home.

The rest of the school week is the most wonderful rerun. I've been stopping by Tim's house every morning before class. And um… *during* school, because I haven't been going to PE. I don't think the coach can tell me apart from the other underperformers, or else I wouldn't have gotten a solid 'B' in the class for each of the previous years. I make sure to show up for second period, when attendance is taken, but otherwise I begin each day by getting ready and rushing over to Tim's house.

Sometimes he's still asleep on the couch when I arrive. Which is all sorts of tempting. I want to pull back the blanket to see if he's got morning wood, or crawl on top of him and go back to sleep, or any number of fantasies. All I know is that, when he stirs and sees me, Tim always smiles. Afterwards I make sure he's got something for breakfast before I fetch fresh clothes for him to wear. From there it's usually a mad dash to get to school. Then the hours drag by until I'm free to see him again. At least Allison's car is back from the shop. I no longer need to drop her off, which means at the end of each day I can drive directly to Tim's house.

And it's so good when I'm there that I'm tempted to barricade us in. We always hang out in his father's den, often sitting on the couch together while watching TV. Tim is the kind of guy who gets sucked in by the screen. When he's watching something, I have to say his name a few times to get his attention. Which is great, because it means I can get away with staring at him, equally transfixed by what I see. So far I haven't found a single part of him that I'm not fascinated by. His ears, for instance, which have detached lobes, unlike my own. I want to nibble them gently before kissing him on the neck. I like the way his adam's apple bounces when he laughs, and the deep husky sound that emanates from his throat. I'm dying to touch his dark hair, which I've noticed is always styled by the time I visit in the afternoon. I choose to read into that, considering I'm literally the only person he sees as of late.

Krista hasn't been coming around. I've dreaded the possibility of her stopping by, or one of his other friends, but so far it hasn't happened. I made an offhand comment about that the other day. Tim merely shrugged and said, "I only want her to see me at my best." Which makes me wonder about his hair. Is he vain? Or does he want to impress me as well? If so, why? I'm wondering that now as I stare at him. I honestly have no idea what's on the TV screen. Tim finally notices, and as usual, I smile or laugh in embarrassment before looking away. Except in the corner of my eye, I could swear that he's still watching me. When I check…

Our eyes lock, and I feel like he's the one rummaging through my underwear drawer, but it's one-sided because I still can't read him. All I know is that it's intense. Tim doesn't look away. He's not smiling or making a silly face. Instead it's like he wants to take me right then and there. My entire body is reacting—my heart, my lungs, my cock… Then he lowers his gaze, his brow furrowing before he looks away, and it just about wrecks me, because it felt like a kiss that he changed his mind about halfway through. I want to touch his hand to get his attention again, or slide across the couch to be closer to him. The words that come to mind are either too clumsy or too direct to actually say aloud. Instead I focus unseeing on the television until a commercial with a catchy jingle comes on.

Tim looks over at me with transparent hope.

"I'm not singing to *that*," I tell him with a laugh. "Let's get our homework done, so we don't have to worry about it during the weekend."

Tim groans. "Mood killer!"

"Unless you have a better idea," I say, instantly backpedaling.

"Nah," Tim says easily. "Grab your backpack."

We have some of the same classes and teachers, despite being in different periods, so there's some overlap in the assignments. I've never been too fussed about my grades. I'm normally the kind of guy who does his homework at the last second, but I don't want to give the school an excuse to come snooping around. That's my job!

"So I was thinking," I say when we're both occupied with math problems.

"Uh-oh," Tim replies.

I smile before forcing myself to press on. "All this running around is kind of exhausting. What if I stayed the night?"

Tim shrugs. "Yeah, okay."

That was easy. "I don't think I could get away with staying both nights," I continue. "So I figured tomorrow would be best."

Saturdays are my favorite. We'll have the entire day together, that night, and the next morning. Twenty-four hours of non-stop Tim!

"Sure," he says, looking up from his homework. "We've gotta do something fun though."

"Like what?" I ask, hoping he'll suggest that we wrestle naked like the ancient Greeks used to.

"I dunno. This is your hometown. Show me something cool."

"Something cool," I repeat, already feeling like it's a tall order.

"Yeah. Whatever is fine."

I've imagined myself going on a multitude of romantic dates over the years. Surely I can repurpose one of them. "I'll think of something," I promise him.

I don't stay as late as I want to. Tim is confused that I can't spend both nights with him, which is flattering, or maybe indicative of how lenient his parents are. Although he often makes them sound strict. All I know for sure is that my own parents have to be carefully played. I don't usually feel that way, but at the moment, I feel protective of what Tim and I have together. Which is a bad sign because all we've got is friendship on his side and a blossoming crush on mine. So I spend Friday night where my parents can see me, and much of the next morning being sociable, all while trying to think of a plan so exciting that it will turn Tim gay.

I still haven't decided the next day, when I'm on the way to his place, although I have the options narrowed down. Tim doesn't demand an answer when I get there. Instead it feels like any other day. He's hungry and wants me to feed him, which of course I do. When he complains that he's out of jogging shorts, I start a load of laundry. Then I run him another bath and straighten up the living room while Tim is in the tub. I'm arranging the magazines on the coffee table when I notice the black book. The one I saw in his underwear drawer. I pick it up, assessing the heft. I'm grappling with the temptation to open the cover when he calls for me. Or more accurately, my services. But not in a hot way.

"I'm gonna need some clean clothes soon! The water is getting cold!"

"Then it's a good thing you married such a patient guy," I murmur before setting the book down and going to the laundry room. I scoop the clothes out of the dryer and dump them into a basket before plucking an outfit from the contents.

After delivering this to Tim, and trying to sneak a peek for my efforts—without luck—I take the rest upstairs to his room. I fold everything into stacks on his dresser and am puzzled when opening his underwear drawer, because the black book is still in there, even though I just saw it in the living room. I stare at it a moment before noticing the corner of another. I carefully begin removing folded underwear like an archeologist revealing ancient treasure. It soon becomes apparent that more than one black book is hidden there. Enough to line the bottom of the drawer, in fact.

They must be journals. Which would explain why pencils and pens were on the table downstairs, even though I put all that away yesterday after we finished our homework. I decide not to invade his most private of thoughts, but only because none of the books here will mention me. The journal downstairs is likely the newest. If he feels anything for me at all, that's where the evidence will be.

Tim is on the couch in the den when I return.

"I'm so bored!" he moans.

"Yeah, me too," I say, plopping down next to him. "I've been sitting around all day."

Tim winces. "Sorry. The house looks nice though."

"Thank you." My gaze moves to where I last saw the black book. Except now it's gone.

"I'm going stir-crazy," Tim continues. "I'm not used to being home this much. Let's go somewhere."

I sigh for dramatic effect before standing and offering my hand.

Tim ignores it. "I can get up on my own."

"Yeah, but that's not the point," I reply.

He looks at me funny before laughing. And proves *his* point by pushing himself up to a standing position without my help. "I'm seriously hyped," he says.

"You don't even know where we're going."

"Yeah, and I don't care. I need a change of scenery. And my left shoe." He looks at me with expectation.

"Not so independent after all," I say with a smirk.

All he does is smile, which quite frankly, would be enough to make me do his homework for the rest of high school, and his taxes for the rest of his life. I try to hide this behind a weary sigh. "Be right back."

I run upstairs for a single sock and grab one of his blue shoes when passing the entryway on my way back. I watch him put these things on before he announces that he needs to use the restroom. As soon as I'm alone in the den, I begin searching for the black book. Tim isn't very mobile. It couldn't have gone far. I just need to know if I'm wasting my time. I'll still help him until his parents get back, since I'm the one who knocked him into a ditch, and I'll keep being his friend. But I'll try not to feel as much for him if all he's written about is his new platonic buddy.

I'm shoving my hand between the couch cushions when my fingers hit something hard. The shape and size is right. Sure enough, it's the book I saw earlier! Before I can second-guess myself, I crack it open. The first page is bare, but the inside cover has the year written in one corner. I glance up to make sure I'm still alone before flipping through, starting from the back, so I can find the most recent page that isn't blank. When I do, ink fills the white space, wild lines zipping back and forth to form a sketch of a young man. I stare at a face so beautiful that I almost fail to recognize it as my own. I notice a few telltale details around the drawing of me, like the outline of a cabinet door, and remember the way Tim studied me while he was taking the first bath I ran for him. Was it for this? And is that really how I look to him?

"You know what I was thinking?" I hear Tim say from the hall, so I quickly shut the book and shove it between the couch cushions. "Instead of you having to cook or whatever," he continues when entering the room, "we can get dinner out. My treat."

"That would be great!" I say with burning cheeks.

He notices. "Everything okay?"

"Yeah. I just—" I try to think of something embarrassing enough to explain my blush. "—farted."

"Happens to the best of us," Tim says with a cackle. "I'll stay over here until the room clears. Unless you're ready to go."

"I am." My face continues to burn on the way to the garage. That's what I get for sticking my nose where it doesn't belong. The man of my dreams made me look beautiful in a drawing, and I responded with fictitious flatulence. If he ever sketches me again, it'll probably be cartoonish and involve a fart cloud.

"I'm so ready for this!" Tim says after we pull out into the street.

"Me too," I reply, even though part of me feels like making an excuse to park and go inside his house again, because I need more information. Maybe he draws everyone like that. Krista, Bryce, Stacy, and Darryl. The sketchbooks I saw in his underwear drawer might be filled with the faces of his family and friends. And maybe they all look hotter as sketches than in real life. Or maybe he really sees me that way. I glance over and catch him studying me, but he doesn't try to hide it. Instead he reaches for the stereo.

"Let's see who you're singing with today," Tim says.

I blush again, this time with a smile, because all that matters to me is who I am singing *to*.

CHAPTER SEVEN

We're nearing our destination when Tim turns down the stereo and sighs. "It's good we're doing this now. The party is almost over."

I glance in the rearview mirror but fail to spot any drunken guests in the backseat. "Are you kidding?" I reply. "The party is just getting started!"

He grins at this. "You still haven't told me where we're going."

"Why bother when we're almost there?" I'm eager to impress him, even though I don't have much of a plan. I can only hope that he'll be moved by nature's splendor. "And what do you mean the party is almost over?"

Tim makes a face. "I'm going back to school on Monday."

"Oh." My stomach sinks. I can already imagine how his friends will react when they find out about this. It won't take long before they turn him against me. "You could probably get away with staying home for another week," I venture.

"Nah. My parents come home on Wednesday. It'll look bad if I haven't been to school the whole time they were gone."

"I guess so," I murmur. "Unless I sprain your other ankle."

"No thanks!" Tim splutters.

I remain somber. "Are we still going to be friends?"

Tim's head swivels toward me. "Why wouldn't we be?"

I size him up before returning my attention to the road. "You're not worried about your reputation?"

He's quiet for a moment, which is all the answer I need, but he responds anyway. "That depends on what people are saying about me."

"What if they find out that you're friends with a gay guy?"

"I don't care," Tim replies. "I mean, the sort of thing my ex-girlfriend said, *that* mattered to me."

"Understandably," I say, "but how will you feel if people assume that you're gay? Because they will if you're seen with me."

"I'm dating Krista," Tim says. "Isn't that proof enough that I'm not?"

It hasn't been enough for me, and I doubt it will be for others. But if he's willing to take the risk, then so am I, because being friends with him will come at a price. When his buddies learn about us, they'll pay even more attention to me, and not in a nice way.

"Do *you* still want to be friends?" Tim asks suddenly.

The question isn't easy for me to answer honestly, since I want way more than that from him. So I settle for a different truth. "Just try and stop me!"

He grins at this, and I'm glad, because I'm in too deep to back off now. I can't stop thinking about the sketchbooks in his underwear drawer, and the painting on his bedroom wall. I liked him enough when I thought he was a jock. Now that I've seen the hint of an artist's soul… I'm not ready to put the L word on it yet, but it's safe to say that I'm infatuated with him.

"Oh wow!" Tim breathes.

We've just crested a long bridge and are high enough to see where the land gives way to water, a small city nestled up against the shore.

"Have anything like that where you come from?" I ask.

"Definitely not," Tim says, still in awe.

I notice his fingers twitch and wonder if he's fighting the urge to draw. I wish I could broach the subject without giving away that I snooped. Maybe if I start putting paper and pen in front of him, he'll be unable to resist and will reveal himself. I'm surprised he has any secrets at all. I didn't think he was the type. But it does give me hope.

We both need to use the restroom, so we stop in a touristy part of town and walk down a street filled with little shops. One of them is a gallery. Tim pauses to look in the window, but when I ask if he wants to go inside, he feigns disinterest. Is that what he's doing with me? Should I invite him in and find out?

"This is cool," Tim says, "but I want to see that water again."

"You've got it!" I notice how he picks up the pace on the way back to the car. "Your ankle seems to be doing better."

"Yeah!" Tim says happily. "It almost feels normal again. I'm tempted to stop using this dumb boot. But I won't," he quickly adds when noticing my concern. "I'm gonna follow doctor's orders. And milk it for all the sympathy I can get. Have you seen the way people keep opening doors for me? I might start wearing it all the time."

"I think it's the crutch more than the boot."

Which he currently has tucked horizontally beneath an arm. I worry about him not using it, but he really does seem to be doing fine without. Although when we drive to the shore, I insist he take it with him and am repaid when we begin to navigate sandy ground. Tim slips a few times, but the smile never leaves his face. I watch his gelled spikes tremble in the wind, the orange light from the setting sun making his bronze skin glow. I stop to take off my shoes, wanting to walk barefoot through the lapping waves.

"You're making me jealous," Tim says as he watches me pull off my socks.

"You still have one good foot," I reply.

"Yeah, I guess I do!"

He plops down on the sand next to me and starts undoing the laces. Soon we're walking side-by-side along the beach, his blue shoe dangling from my fingertips, since he needs his hands free for the crutch. Just one of them really. But like a faithful puppy, I kind of enjoy getting to carry his shoe around.

"I wish I could go swimming," Tim says longingly.

"I'll take you to a great water park sometime," I offer. "They have a wave pool, one of those lazy rivers, and a bunch of water slides."

"Sounds cool!" he says. "We should do that!"

Of course that would put us both in swimsuits. I'm not sure I have enough self-control just yet. "We should probably wait until next year," I say. "When the weather warms up again."

At the moment, the days are still plenty hot, but the nights are getting colder. I don't want summer to end. I wish we had met at the beginning of the season, when he first moved to town, so we could have had three glorious months together.

"We've gotta come back here too," Tim says, eyeing the water again.

"I'm sure you've seen bigger and better," I reply, picturing a tropical paradise. "Rich people's vacations must be amazing. My family spends most of ours camping in a big leaky tent that we all have to share."

Tim grimaces in sympathy. "Why don't you sleep in the private jet?"

I turn an incredulous expression on him.

"I'm kidding!" He tilts his head toward a washed-up fishing

boat that is further inland before hobbling toward it. "My family isn't *that* rich. And my parents never take me on trips with them. Even when I was a kid."

I imagine a little boy with a mop of dark hair and piercing silver eyes fending for himself in a large empty house. "Never?"

"Except for Mexico," he amends. "To see my grandma."

We've reached the boat now, or what remains of it. Only the stern is still intact, forming a sort of hard couch. The rest is scattered wooden slats bleached white from the sun, some singed black from fire, because it's clear that other people have used this as a place to hang out. I take Tim's crutch when he holds it out to me and wait for him to get settled before I sit next to him.

"I've never been out of the country," I admit. "What's it like?"

"Mexico City?" Tim asks. "Amazing! You've never seen so many colors in your life. Every inch of the place is filled with sounds and smells and people doing things." He shakes his head. "Words can't begin to describe it."

"You'll have to draw me a picture," I suggest, giving him an opening, but I'm not sure he even notices the bait, because Tim seems like he's been transported somewhere else.

"My grandma lives in Xochimilco, where they have these super cool canals with *trajinera* boats. Ever heard of those?"

"What are they called?" I ask. Mostly because I love how he slips into an accent when saying Spanish words.

"*Trajineras,*" he repeats, slower this time. "They're all long and painted up, sort of like those boats in Venice, but bigger and way more colorful. You can eat on them, or kick back and have a few drinks. Usually you get to hear live music, because mariachi bands are floating around on their own boats."

"*Muy bonito,*" I reply, hoping to impress him.

Tim looks surprised. "*¿Tú hablas español?*"

"Not very well," I admit. "It's one of my worst subjects. What about you?"

"It's one of my best," Tim says with a grin. "When I was growing up, my mom only spoke Spanish to me, and my dad only spoke English. Which was great, because I don't remember learning either language. *Soy muy afortunado.*"

"I have no idea what you just said," I admit, "but the words sound so much hotter coming from your mouth than my teacher's."

Tim makes a face. "Hotter?"

"Yeah," I say with a nod. "You could literally read a grocery list out loud in Spanish and it would turn me on."

Tim laughs. Then, with half-lidded eyes, he leans towards me and murmurs, "*Pan, leche, mantequilla.*"

"I've got literal goosebumps right now," I say, raising an arm to show him. "What did you say?"

"Bread, milk, and butter," Tim reveals.

I shake my head. "Doesn't sound as good in English. Go back to Spanish."

"And say what?"

"I don't know," I reply with a shrug. "Something nice."

I expect him to scoff. Instead his expression grows serious, concentration creasing his brow as he studies the horizon. When his eyes flick to meet mine, he says, "*Enséñame a volar, mi mariposa hermosa.*"

"Something *nice*," I repeat, scowling in return. "My Spanish isn't great, but I know what *mariposa* means."

Tim shakes his head in confusion. "It's not a bad word."

"Then why do your dumb friends keep saying it to me?"

His face lights up with realization. "Oh! It's like calling someone a fairy in English."

"Which I've heard plenty of times too," I complain.

"Yeah, but it's all about—"

"Oh thank god!" a new voice cries, startling us both.

A group of women is walking down the beach, one of them making a beeline for us. She sets down a cardboard container with an image of multi-colored bottles on the front before sitting on one of the wooden slats. "I can't walk anymore," she says, raising her feet in the air to wipe sand off them. Which brings them closer to my face than I would prefer. She reminds me of my sister. In fact, they all look older than us.

"Sorry," a wispy girl says quietly. "She's drunk."

"And you should be too," the first woman says, shaking the cardboard box and making the bottles rattle. "Help yourself."

"Really?" Tim asks, taking her up on the offer. He passes a bottle to me, which I open and sip from halfheartedly.

The others settle down around us, their ringleader sizing Tim up.

"You're cute!" she says. "I've seen you before, right? What fraternity are you in?"

"We're not—" I begin.

"Gamma Zeta Delta," Tim interrupts.

"Have we partied there?" the ringleader asks before deciding that they have. "We've partied there."

"I'm sure of it," Tim says, twisting the cap off his drink. "Cheers, ladies!"

They're happy to clink bottles with him. I'm not so thrilled, because the girls proceed to dominate the conversation while remaining fixated on Tim, which I can't fault them for. Only the wispy girl tries to engage with me, but I'm not feeling social because Tim is smiling broadly, laughing at their jokes, and telling funny stories of his own. In other words, he's flirting again. Like he did with the nurse at the hospital, despite having a girlfriend. Like he never does with me, even though he must know that I'd be receptive to it. Oh sure, I've caught him staring, but that's probably a visual artist thing. The next time I check his sketchbook—and I already know that I will—these four women will surely be in it. My mood darkens along with the sky. I'm tempted to walk away and see if he even notices. But I don't, because I still want him. Just give me this weekend before I'm forced to face reality. And get us the hell away from here!

"I'm hungry," I manage to interject into the conversation.

"Have another," the ringleader says, reaching for the cardboard box.

"We haven't eaten dinner yet," I say lamely.

"Oh right!" Tim says. "I promised my man here a meal."

"I'm hungry too," one of the women says. "Where are you going?"

"We have a reservation," I snap. "At a place that's hard to get into."

"Aren't you a fancy boy?" the ringleader says with a hint of a lisp.

I've never been in a catfight before but I'm ready to pounce. Lucky for her, Tim is struggling to get to his feet, and he's more important to me. I stand and hand him his crutch, leaving my unfinished drink in the sand.

"It's been a real pleasure, ladies," Tim says, smiling at a captive audience. "Feel free to stop by the fraternity anytime."

He's laying it on thick. And can get away with it, apparently, because we walk away to a chorus of, "I hope your ankle gets better soon! His eyes were so pretty! Did anyone get his number?"

My mood doesn't improve much, even when we put enough distance between us to no longer hear their voices. I feel foolish. And I only have myself to blame.

"That was fun!" Tim says.

"I didn't notice," I say evenly.

"Are you okay?"

"Never been better."

Tim slows in my peripheral vision. "For real, dude. What's wrong?"

"You wouldn't understand."

He grabs my wrist to stop me. "About what? Oh shit! You mean the *mariposa* thing? We got interrupted. The word changes depending on the context."

"It's not that," I say, my voice warbling. "You don't get what it's like to be gay."

"Then explain it to me."

He hasn't let go yet. Tim allows his crutch to fall to the side before pulling me down onto the beach with him. Only then does he release me. His expression is open and earnest, but for once, I wish he wasn't so handsome. I'm still irrevocably drawn to him, no matter how hopeless this has become.

"I always end up alone," I say, my throat so tight that it's hard to get the words out. "Which sucks, because this isn't a choice. I don't wrestle with temptation before deciding that I want to be into guys instead of girls. There's nothing to choose between. It simply feels, I don't know… *right*. People can hate me for that all they want. They can keep calling me names. But you know what the worst part is? Guys like you." He looks stricken, so I hasten to assure him that the opposite is true. "I really *really* like you, Tim. And I know it's never going to happen, but I pretend it will anyway, because it's better than nothing. Even though it hurts sometimes. All those women had to do was stop to get your attention, when I would *literally* do anything." I'm on the verge of tears that I barely manage to hold back, not wanting to cry in front of him. "None of this is your fault. It's mine. I'm sorry that I'm having a breakdown about this now, but I'm so freaking tired of being alone!"

"Me too," Tim says with a swallow.

"What's that supposed to mean?" I'm not angry. I'm pleading, because if there's any chance that we're alike, I need to know.

Tim's attention is on the ebb and flow of the waves, his expression impossible to read. "I'm not sure," he says at last. "But it's what I was trying to tell you earlier. *Enséñame a volar, mi mariposa hermosa.*" He turns toward me, his voice laced with emotion. "Teach me how to fly, my beautiful butterfly."

Tim leans closer, and I don't know how to react, or what to do, but those silver eyes hold me prisoner until his lips touch mine. I instantly come to life and shift to face him, not wanting to lose contact as our mouths press together. I feel his hand on the back of my head, taste the fruity remnants of the drink he had, and begin to burn from the inside like never before. I almost cry out in protest when he pulls back, his eyes searching mine with a newfound intensity. I can only hope he finds what he's looking for.

"You're not alone," he says. "You've got me."

I'm not sure what to make of that, but I'm not going to ruin the moment with a million questions. Instead I seek out his hand on the sand, praying that it wasn't merely a pity kiss. Or him being drunk. I'm reassured when he turns his hand over so our fingers can intertwine. Even though it doesn't last very long. "We're both so grimy," he says when shaking me off.

I laugh, my eyes wet with happy tears, and I can't help it. I have to tell him. "That was my first kiss."

"Really?" he asks, looking surprised. "What about all those guys you've been with?"

"There weren't *that* many," I say in my defense, "and none of them were interested in that sort of thing."

Tim scrunches up his face before he shrugs. "Their loss. You're a good kisser."

"You really think so?"

"Yeah. How'd I do?"

"It was the best kiss of my life. And the only one."

"Oh right." Tim grins before his face becomes somber. "Listen, I don't know what I'm doing. This is all kind of new to me."

"That's okay," I say. "We can figure it out together."

"I don't want to make any promises." Tim's expression is apologetic. "And I uh… have a girlfriend. So I probably shouldn't have kissed you."

"Then why did you?" I ask.

"I don't know." He stares at me a second before a smile tugs at his cheek. "I guess it just felt right."

My heart is about to explode out of my chest. I'm ready to marry the boy. Get me to a chapel!

"We can take it slow," I say in contrast to these thoughts. Mostly because I don't want to scare him off.

"Cool," Tim says.

A breeze blows across my skin, making me shiver with excitement rather than cold.

"You still wanna grab something to eat?" he asks me.

"On one condition," I reply while getting to my feet.

Tim manages to stand on his own. "What?"

"Say it again."

Tim is only puzzled momentarily before he puts on bedroom eyes, his voice husky and seductive. "*Enséñame a volar, mi mariposa hermosa.*"

Spanish has never sounded so good! I'm going to really apply myself at school and get an A in the subject. When I'm not busy with a class of my own, because I'll do exactly what he wants.

I'm going to teach Tim how to fly.

I wake up the next morning in his bed. Alone, unfortunately, even though I don't want to rush this. Not anymore. I want to savor every moment with him—let each day bring a new discovery. He doesn't seem to be in a hurry either. Tim hasn't kissed me again, despite having plenty of opportunities. After we had burgers last night at a fast food place, we drove home. I made him sing a duet with me along the way. His voice is terrible and he got most of the lyrics wrong, but that only makes me want him more. I like that he's not perfect. And that I have something special to offer him. He does too. I roll over, my gaze settling on the dresser drawers. I'm tempted to flip through his sketchbooks to learn more about him. Then I imagine Tim sitting on the edge of the bed with me while turning each page to reveal his heart. That's how it should go, so I'll wait.

While being a total creeper in other ways. I'm naked between sheets that haven't been washed since he last slept in this bed. And I love it. I roll back and forth restlessly, my boner refusing to subside as all sorts of fantasies parade through my mind. Eventually my stomach grumbles and I check the clock, surprised to see that it's closer to lunch than breakfast. I'll have to make an appearance at home or my mom will worry. Afterwards, I plan on coming right back over here.

I get out of bed and put on my old clothes. After stopping by the upstairs bathroom to relieve myself, I attempt to tame my hair and use some mouthwash—just in case—before bounding down the stairs with a grin. I'm nearing the den where Tim slept last night when an unexpected voice stops me in my tracks.

"But you still like… take it off to wash, right?"

"Uh… You don't want to know."

I inch forward until I can peek around the corner. Krista is sitting next to Tim on the couch. Even with their backs to me, I can tell her attention is on the boot that he often props up on the coffee table.

"You should at least get a second one," she says. "So you have a matching pair."

I roll my eyes, because it's a funny idea that I wish I'd come up with instead of her.

"Heh," Tim replies. "It's crazy padded on the bottom, so if I did, I'd feel like I was walking around on the moon."

He glances over his shoulder, as if he's looking for me. After we lock eyes, he tilts his head, indicating that I should retreat down the hall. So I do.

"Hey, let me get you something to drink."

"I'll go," Krista says. "You shouldn't have to get up while you're hurt."

I clench my teeth. She is *not* replacing me as his nurse!

"No, it's fine," Tim says. "The doctor says I have to stay active. Wait here."

"Aren't there drinks in that little refrigerator?" she asks.

"Nothing my parents want us to have," he lies. "Find something we can watch on TV. I'll be right back."

He certainly can maneuver well, despite the injured ankle.

I wait at the end of the hall until he sees me. Then I walk to the kitchen and wait.

"Hey," Tim whispers as he enters the room. "Sorry! She just showed up at my door."

"I can't imagine why," I grumble.

He makes a face. "I didn't ask her to."

"I know. I'm just surprised it took this long." I chew my

bottom lip while watching him remove two cans of soda from the refrigerator. I don't think either of them is for me. "Maybe you should introduce us," I suggest.

"What? Why?" Tim looks panicked by the idea. "Don't you know each other already?"

"Yes, but she doesn't know that we're friends." I swallow. "Or whatever."

Tim is shaking his head. "That's a bad idea!"

"How come?" My brow knots up. "You said yesterday that you didn't care if your friends knew."

"Yeah, but that was before…" He checks the entrance to the kitchen, making sure we're still alone. "You know."

"So we'll keep that part a secret," I press.

His expression is guarded. "We've gotta keep the whole thing a secret, Benjamin."

I frown at this. "How come?"

"Because my friends… my parents… they'll only get in the way."

"Of what?"

He sets the sodas on the counter and reaches for me, his touch cold from the refrigerated cans. "Us."

I wrap my hands around his to warm them again, which shouldn't take long with all the blood coursing through my heart. I can handle a secret or whatever, because he's given me what I needed. There's an *us* now. We'll figure out the rest later.

I lean toward him.

He laughs and pushes me away. "My girlfriend is in the next room! And I've got morning breath!"

"Good!" I say. "Maybe that'll scare her away."

"Speaking of which, I'm out of toothpaste downstairs. Can you run up and get more?"

"Nope!" I say. "Have fun with your girlfriend."

"But what if she wants to—"

"See ya!" I say, already heading for the door.

"Wait!" he calls after me. "One more thing."

I turn around, hoping for a hug, or even a stinky smooch. Instead he holds out his hand. "Give me back my damn keys!"

I pretend to be confused. "But how will I drive you to school tomorrow?"

His face contorts until I laugh.

"Will you call me?" I ask, wanting a little more reassurance. "When she's gone."

"Yeah," Tim says. "I'll call you."

I dig the keys out of my pocket and place them in his palm, the tips of my fingers brushing the side of his hand as I pull away. I barged into his life and have barely left since. Now it'll be up to him. I won't have a key to his front door anymore. He can lock me out if he wants. But judging from the affectionate way he ruffles my hair, I don't think this is the end. Not for either of us.

CHAPTER EIGHT

Allison drives us to school the next day, part of me wondering if it was all a dream. I don't have any souvenirs. No photos or handwritten notes to prove that some hunky guy kissed me. That hadn't felt necessary when I was driving around in his car. Now I wish I had something tangible to hold on to, because I'm worried that everything will revert to the way it was. Tim will be hanging out with the cool kids again. He's already told me about getting drunk at Darryl's house after school and some party that's coming up. I can't compete with those sorts of things. Tim doesn't really need a nurse anymore. He already has someone to kiss. I almost wouldn't blame him for ignoring me from now on.

And yet, when I see him and his friends walking down the hall, Tim's eyes meet mine and he winks before returning his attention to the girl on his arm. That's how it goes all week. Sometimes it's a subtle smile, or an eyeroll like he's miserable, but he always acknowledges me in some small way. We haven't seen each other outside of school. On the first couple of nights, his friends wanted to hang out with him, but he always calls me once he's home. I don't hear from him at all on Wednesday, when his parents are due back. I figure he's enjoying the family time. But on Thursday, when I see him in the hall—and yes, I now go out of my way to ensure that I do—Tim pretends to scratch the hair above his ear with a thumb before letting a pinky drop to his mouth, like he's talking on the phone. He wants me to call him! Or he'll call me. I'm not sure, but I practically push down on Allison's foot when she's driving us home after school. I dial his number as soon as we reach the privacy of my room but don't get an answer, so now I'm waiting while we hang out. Allison is wonderfully patient about how divided my attention is between her and the phone. Then again, she has distractions of her own.

"So this is the note Ronnie slipped me during class," she says, unfolding a torn-out sheet of notebook paper. Allison clears her throat. "It says: 'Would it be okay if I sit with you at lunch from now on?' And then there are options below."

"With check boxes?" I ask.

She nods. "Yup!"

"I love it. Let's hear them."

"'*Yes, I would love to eat lunch with you from now on.*' That's the first one. The second reads, *'Of course, that would be great, but you have to buy me lunch.'"* Allison glances up. "That's my favorite so far. The third option says, *'Maybe, I need to think about it, but I promise to answer soon.'* And then the fourth and final says, *'No, I want to break your heart.'"*

"Awww!" I say. "Choose that one!"

Allison laughs. "Boys *are* cute when they cry, so I'm tempted."

"Why doesn't he just ask you to be his girlfriend?"

Allison shrugs. "I don't know, but it's kind of sweet. I like being chased."

"I hope Tim feels the same way," I murmur. "So which option are you going for?"

"I'm not sure," Allison replies. "What do you think?"

"Let me see."

After she hands the note to me, I take out a pen.

Allison cocks an eyebrow. "What are you doing?"

"Do you trust me?" I ask.

"No, of course not!"

She lunges for the note. We wrestle around on the bed while negotiating.

"I don't want Ronnie to know that I showed it to you!"

"Why not? This is who we are. It's better he finds out now!"

"Then let me answer the phone when Tim calls."

"Are you crazy?"

"Are you?"

"Fine! It's a deal."

Allison stops trying to grab the note. Her hands are busy pinning my shoulders anyway. "You'll let me talk to Tim?" she asks.

"Maybe," I say noncommittally.

"Ben!"

I laugh. "Okay! Just don't say anything crazy."

"Just don't write anything crazy!" she shoots back.

She finally lets me sit up again. I move to the dresser so I'll have a flat surface to write on and check the option about him buying her lunch. Then I add a line to Ronnie's handwriting: *And you have to buy my best friend lunch too.*

Allison laughs when reading this. "Why?"

I shrug. "Better to find out now if he's a cheapskate."

"What about Tim?"

"He's rich. Wait until we're married. I'll make him buy us each a house."

"And one for his little girlfriend too," Allison retorts.

"She'll be ancient history by then," I say confidently.

"I like it." Allison consults the note again. Then the phone rings, her face lighting up. "My turn!"

"No!" I say, lunging for it.

Allison doesn't try to stop me. "You promised!"

"Did I?"

"Yes!"

I relent and grimace in anticipation while watching her answer my phone.

Allison puts on a professional tone. "Good afternoon. How may I direct your call?"

I can hear a male voice on the other end but can't make out the words.

"Benjamin?" Allison repeats. "I'm sorry, but it sounds like you do indeed have the wrong number. Oh wait! Do you mean Ben by chance?"

I'm already reaching for the phone, which she keeps pressed to her ear. "And who may I say is calling? Uh-huh. Let me see if he's available, because Ben is a *very* busy boy. You'd be surprised how many handsome men call him each day, Tom. Hm? What's that? I do apologize, *Tim*. Just a moment please."

I'm pretending to stick my head through a noose when she finally stops torturing me. I toss the imaginary rope aside and grab the phone.

"Hey!" I say breathlessly.

"Hey," Tim echoes while sounding uncertain. "Was that your mom?"

"No!" I say with a chuckle. "That was Allison, my best friend."

"Oh." The line is quiet a moment. "You don't go by Benjamin?"

"No," I admit. "Only you call me that." Allison is staring at me, but oh well. "And I like it."

"Oh yeah?" Tim says, the confidence returning to his voice. "What else do you like?"

"Want me to make you a list?" I offer.

"Tell me in person," he suggests. "Let's go for a walk later."

"When?" We haven't hung out since Krista nearly caught me at his house. I'm desperate to see him again.

"Eight."

It'll be dark by then, which is no coincidence, I'm sure. "Okay," I say without hesitation. "Should I come by your place? Or do you want to come here? I'll give you directions. It's not far."

The line is quiet again. "Do you remember where we first saw each other?"

"Do you?" I ask in surprise.

"I mean where you knocked me into the ditch."

Which is roughly the same place. I wonder if he knows that. "Yeah, of course."

"Let's meet there."

I smile into the phone. "Should I bring my Rollerblades?"

"No!" Tim says with a mad cackle. "Definitely not. See you then?"

"Yeah," I reply. "See you then."

I'm biting my lip when lowering the phone.

"Do you have to go?" Allison asks.

I shake my head. "Not until later. He wants to go for a walk. At night." I don't explain why, letting it sound romantic, rather than him not wanting to be seen with me. I'm honestly okay with either, as long as I get to be around him again.

"Thank god!" Allison says. "I need my Ben time."

"Not as much as I need my Allison time." Now that I have plans with Tim, it's easier to focus on her and simply have fun together, even though he makes frequent guest appearances in my imagination. I'm glad we'll be together in real life soon, because I have questions. The kind that can't be answered with multiple-choice checkboxes.

Tim is already waiting for me when I arrive at the park that night. Which is nice. I don't actually care if someone is a cheapskate, but if they kept me waiting, that would make me feel unvalued. That we're both early is a good sign. Especially considering that he's not fast on his feet at the moment.

"No crutch?" I ask, having noticed that he hasn't been using it at school.

"Nah," Tim says. "I'm not going to be in this boot much longer either."

'Have you seen the doctor again?"

"Nope, but I've been doing rehab every night. That's why we're out here." His gaze takes me in. "You look nice."

"Thanks!" I say, happy that he noticed. I freshened myself up before leaving the house and put on a dress shirt. I nearly took it off again, because we're going for a walk, not out to a fancy restaurant. But then I figured there's no sense in being with him if I can't be myself, so I kept it on, wanting the night to feel that much more special. He's wearing jogging shorts and a muscle shirt, as he often does, but that's fine with me. I'm practically developing a fetish for the combo. Besides, with the weather getting cooler, he won't be able to wear such skimpy clothes much longer, and I intend to soak up the view while it's still on display.

"You all right?" Tim asks as I continue to stare.

"I was just thinking the same thing about you," I say smoothly, while blushing like an idiot. "That you look nice."

Tim laughs. "I missed you."

"Oh yeah?" I ask, even though I'm certain he meant it as a joke.

"Yeah." His happy expression falters. "My parents are back."

His tone makes it sound like he's sharing bad news. "Were they upset about your ankle?"

Tim shakes his head. "They barely even noticed."

I study him a moment. "That's what we wanted, right?"

"Yeah, of course," he says dismissively. "I guess I just got used to having the place to myself." He opens his mouth as if to say more before closing it again. I'd pay top dollar to hear those words. Before I can offer, he tilts his head and starts walking in that direction. "Bryce did the craziest thing at lunch today."

"Did he?" I ask.

"Uh-huh. He's always asking if people are going to finish their fries, so I got an extra portion, just for him, and when he said it wasn't enough, Darryl offered his but only if he ate *all* of them. Like, the double portion he already had plus another. So then Stacy gets in on the action and offers hers—"

The story is fine. I just don't see what it has to do with us. That's the topic I'm most eager to discuss, but he's left me hanging since that kiss. And the words that had felt so comforting at the time have been impossible to figure out ever since.

You're not alone. You have me.

What did he mean exactly? That he supports me as a friend? I keep thinking about his disclaimers after we kissed, how he said he didn't know what he was doing and couldn't make any promises. That hadn't mattered in the moment. I was just so thrilled to have been kissed by him. But now I'm wondering if he was buzzing from the drink he had and only wanted to cheer me up. He sure had acted like there was more when not wanting Krista to see me at his house. He dodged my kiss right after, so I honestly don't know. But it's time to find out.

"That's funny," I say at the end of his story. "And gross."

"No kidding," Tim says with a guffaw. "He was still green at the end of the school day. I don't know how he managed to keep them all down."

"He's normally such a hot guy too," I say, despising the words despite them being true. "Don't you think?"

Tim turns a confused expression on me. "Huh?"

"Don't ever repeat this, *please*, but I think Bryce is hot. Haven't you ever checked him out in the shower?"

"He's on the football team. I play baseball."

"Right. What about your teammates? Ever been tempted to peek?"

"That would be social suicide," Tim replies, deftly dodging the question.

Unless he honestly doesn't get it. Maybe I need to be direct.

"Who do you think the hottest person is at our school?" I ask.

"Stacy!" Tim says instantly.

I make a face. "Not your own girlfriend?"

Tim shrugs. "Hey, I'm just being honest. Keep that between us, okay?"

Suddenly that *us* he spoke of previously doesn't sound as special. I want to be more than just his confidant that he experimented with briefly. "Okay," I say, forcing myself to be patient. "Stacy is the hottest girl. What about the hottest guy?"

I stare at Tim as he narrows his eyes, as if deep in thought. I'm dying to hear his answer.

"Me," he says, grinning broadly.

I groan. "Anyone besides you? Who do you think about when jacking off?" I hold up a hand when he starts to reply. "*Besides* all the girls."

Tim's mouth snaps shut. I wait out the silence, only to be rewarded with, "I don't know."

"How could you not? Oh. I guess you don't know everyone's names yet. What kind of guys catch your eye?"

He glances at me, which would be flattering if he said anything to confirm it. Maybe he thinks I'm fishing for compliments. Not that I would mind.

"Are you into guys at all?" I press. "Because you don't seem like you're pretending when it comes to girls."

"I'm not," he says. "I definitely like girls."

My stomach sinks. "But you're not sure about guys? Because I can't remember a time that I wasn't. Even back in grade school. I didn't know what sex was, but there were boys I wanted to be friends with because I liked how they looked. I just didn't understand why at the time."

Tim is quiet, my despair increasing with each step that we take. I'm walking in the dark.

"There was this one guy," he says at last. "Back where I used to live."

"Tell me about him," I say, stopping so that Tim will too. I want to be able to see his face when he tells me his story.

He looks uncomfortable before scratching the back of his head sheepishly. "It was uh… Carla's little brother."

"Your crazy ex-girlfriend?"

"Yeah," Tim says with a laugh. "Her parents were out of town, and she was in one of her moods. Carla loved tearing me down in front of her friends. She wasn't as bad when we were by ourselves, but for whatever reason, she always gave me shit when other people were around. Anyway, it was one of those nights. When she told me to go check on her little brother, I was glad to get away from her, so I went up to his room."

"What was his name?" I ask. "And what did he look like?"

"Cole. He wasn't so different from his sister. Skinny with the same black hair. I didn't think he was hot exactly. He was twelve or thirteen at the time. Way too young for me. I was already in high school. We had fun hanging out though. Enough that I decided to stay in his room, since he was actually nice to me. We played video games and listened to some music. Cole was cool. Like the little brother I never had. He'd noticed the way Carla treated me. He said she was crazy, and that he would never do that to me. Which seemed weird, but I rolled with it. A little too much maybe because…" His face contorts before he shakes his head. "He started looking at me funny and said, 'You can kiss me, if you want." Tim swallows and leaves it at that.

"So did you?"

"No way! Like I said, he was too young. *And* my girlfriend's little brother. Which I explained to him. So he started talking about how we could keep it a secret." Tim's eyes dart to mine and away again. "I kept thinking about that," he continues. "The offer, I mean. Like what would have happened if he was his sister's age, and I wasn't with her already."

"Yeah?" I ask, feeling hopeful.

Tim searches my eyes and nods. "Yeah. And you can, by the way."

"What?"

"You can kiss me," he says with a dopey smile. "If you want."

There's no question about what I want. It's the circumstances that concern me. "And you can break up with Krista," I reply. "If you want."

"Right," he says with a sigh. "I just figured, since we've already gone there, that it wouldn't make a difference. Like if she finds out that I kissed you, I don't think she's going to be worried about how many times it happened, you know?"

"Good point," I say before throwing myself into his arms. I didn't need convincing. I wanted an answer. Maybe this is it.

I don't hold back. Neither does he. I revel in his touch as we continue mashing our lips together. His fingers move through my hair before cupping my neck. His other arm wraps around me, pulling me closer. I love how his body feels against mine. I want him to squeeze me so tight that it almost hurts. Instead he takes a step back and glances around.

"I don't see anyone else out here," I say after doing the same.

He lets me kiss him again, but I can tell the moment has passed. His guard has been raised again. But not entirely.

"You," he says.

"What about me?"

Tim smirks. "You asked who I think about."

"Really?"

"Really." He glances around again. "Want to keep going?"

"Yes!" I say, stepping forward.

Tim laughs. "I meant on our walk."

"I knew that," I reply, playing it cool. "Just messing with you."

"Uh-huh." Tim has a spring in his step as we continue strolling. Or maybe it's just the padded sole of the boot. "We could make a habit of this," he suggests.

"The walking part?"

"All of it."

I think of Krista, but she's an easily banished ghost. "Okay," I say, not hiding how much I like the idea. "Sign me up! So is this going to happen every night? Even on the weekends?"

"Oh," Tim says. "I uh… actually have plans on Saturday. That party I told you about?"

"Right," I say, snapping my fingers. "I actually have *two* parties that day. I'll be way too busy for the likes of you." I've been worried about this, figuring that Tim's friends would expect more time with him. "What about Sunday?"

He cringes. "I have church in the morning."

"People still do that?" I cry aghast.

"My family does," Tim grumbles.

A Sunday afternoon is better than nothing. Until I come up with an inspired plan. "How about Friday?" I suggest. "You could stay the night at my place."

Tim thinks about it. "Yeah! That might work."

For him. I already know that I won't get a wink of sleep. But it's a price that I'm more than willing to pay.

CHAPTER NINE

Watching a sleek black sports car park in front of my house is surreal, especially when a super-hot guy gets out and flashes his pearly white teeth at me. Tim is the stuff of wet dreams. I stand and brush myself off, as if making myself presentable, while waiting for him to join me on the front stoop. I'd love it if he kissed me in greeting. Even just a smooch. Instead he seems increasingly apprehensive as he nears.

"Are your parents home?" he asks.

"Yeah," I reply. "They kind of live here."

He eyes the house as if it's haunted and asks, "Do they know much about me?"

"Only that I have a new buddy. You've got nothing to worry about."

"Yeah, okay," he says, not seeming comforted.

We go inside, and even though I know he'd prefer that I take him upstairs to the safety of my room, I lead him to the kitchen where my parents are talking. My sister isn't home, so this should be easy.

"Hey!" my dad says, pushing away from the counter and extending a hand. "You must be Tim!"

"Nice to meet you, sir," he replies dutifully.

I manage not to snort. My family isn't that formal.

"That's a nice firm handshake," my dad says, sounding amused.

My mom is making eyes at me but I'm doing my best to ignore her.

"So nice to meet you at last," she says, focusing on Tim. "Ben has told us so much about you."

"He has?" Tim asks with a flicker of worry.

"Just the embarrassing personal stuff," my dad teases.

"Nothing like that," my mom assures him. "Your family just moved here, didn't they?"

"Yes, ma'am."

"From where?"

I stand aside and listen to him repeat information I already know. Tim does well, loosening up as he tells a parent-friendly version of his life story.

"Have you had dinner yet?" my mom asks him eventually.

"That depends," Tim replies. "If your cooking is anything like your son's, then yeah, I've already eaten."

"Hey, I don't remember you complaining!" I shoot back.

"You've been cooking for him?" my mom asks in interest.

Uh-oh. "For us," I say. "When I spent the night at his house."

My mother's eyes are sparkling. "What did you make?"

"I just added some stuff to a frozen pizza," I say dismissively.

"Well we can do better than that," she says with a smile. "We're going to *order* pizza. What do you boys want on yours?"

"Pepperoni," I reply.

"I prefer sausage," Tim counters.

"I would have expected Ben to say that," my dad murmurs.

God I love him! Even though the joke makes Tim's face turn red.

We keep naming the toppings we each prefer, having to get rid of one or two we disagree on, but in general we've passed the compatibility test.

"I'm so glad you like pineapple," Tim says on the way upstairs.

"Pineapple for life!" I say in a deep voice before bumping fists with him.

I open the door to my bedroom and step aside, letting him go first. I stayed up late cleaning so everything would be perfect. There isn't much to see. I have a queen-sized bed that Allison loved teasing me about when I first got it. *When the queen rises from bed in the morning, does he put on queen-sized slippers before sitting on his queen-sized toilet?* She's just jealous. Her bed is only wide enough for one. My parents let me dream big. I was just starting high school when they bought it, and I honestly thought I'd be sharing it with a boyfriend long before now. And yet, here we are, four years later…

I watch Tim perform a similar inspection to the one I gave his room. I won't let him rummage through my underwear drawer (who would do such a thing?) but at least I'm there to answer any questions.

"Where'd you get this?" he asks, touching a small coconut that's been carved and painted to resemble a pirate's head.

"That was the guy before you. I used dark magic to shrink his head. I can't wait to add yours to the collection."

In truth it was a souvenir that I picked up on a family

vacation. No idea why, but I've been living with a disembodied head ever since.

"I like that," Tim says, nodding at a band poster on the wall. He touches it experimentally. "The original version was probably a screen print."

"A what?" I ask, walking over to join him.

"Like they applied each layer of paint separately," he explains. "See how there are only a few colors?"

"I never noticed before," I admit. "Are you into that sort of thing?"

Tim shrugs and moves to a group of photos I have taped to the wall. "Who's that?" he asks, pointing at Allison.

"My best friend," I reply.

"She's hot," Tim says in approval. "Who's the dork standing next to her?"

"Shut up," I say, pushing him playfully. "I wanted long hair. For whatever reason it just gets thicker, like a helmet."

"Huh," Tim says. "I've thought about growing mine out."

"You totally should!" I say, eying his silky-black locks.

"My dad wouldn't like it," he says dismissively. "Is that your sister?" he asks, pointing to a family photo.

"Yup." I'm braced for him to say that she's hot.

Instead his gaze is guarded when he turns to me. "That joke your dad made… Do your parents know?"

"About me?" I laugh. "Yeah! They've known for ages."

Tim sits on the edge of my bed. "How did that go?"

I remain standing so we're facing each other. "My mom was easy. She basically asked me, so she must have already suspected. Telling my dad was kind of awkward."

Tim swallows. "How come?"

I exhale. "Because he started talking about this gay guy he shared a dorm with in college, and how they messed around once, but it wasn't for him." I do my best imitation of my dad's voice. "'For me it was just an experimental phase, son, but I never had a better roommate, so I'm happy that you're gay like him.'"

I expect Tim to laugh. Instead he looks uncomfortable.

"I was traumatized," I assure him. "The thought of my dad messing around with another guy almost turned me straight."

"Is that a thing?" Tim asks.

"No! I'm stuck this way, believe me."

Tim shakes his head. "I mean an experimental phase. Do people really have those?"

I could kick myself! I don't want him to doubt what we have. I do enough of that for the both of us. Then again, I don't want to trick him into being anything that he's not. "My attraction to other guys is definitely not a phase," I answer, "but straight guys experiment, yeah. That's how some people figure out who they really like. Those other guys I was with, I don't think any of them were actually gay. They didn't seem interested enough."

Tim's brow is furrowed. "How did that work anyway?"

"They'd show me some porn and ask me to lend them a hand. Or they'd talk about how horny they were when getting into bed for the night and pretend to be asleep. If I didn't take the hint, they'd roll over and 'accidentally' rub up against me. Which was dumb, because all they had to do was ask." I stop talking, giving him the opportunity to do just that. I'd love to suck his cock. That's all I've fantasized about since we met. I'd be honored. Hell, I'd thank him for the privilege! Of course in my fantasies, he doesn't have a girlfriend.

"So those other guys weren't interested in doing stuff back to you?" Tim asks.

"If they were, they sure managed to hide it well."

The creases on his forehead deepen. If we ever do hook up, I probably just condemned myself to it being one-sided. I don't regret speaking openly. As much as I want his body, love is my true goal. I'm willing to risk it all, even the chance to sleep with him, to get what I really need.

For now, I want him to see how normal my life can be. I put on some of my favorite music. Songs that make me think of him, but I don't say as much. When I sing, the clouds blows away and he seems happy again. We watch a random show on the small TV in my room while eating pizza and play video games afterwards. When night has fallen, I suggest we go for a walk, but I don't pressure him to do anything romantic. Only when we stop in a tunnel of trees to listen to the insects hum do I lean against him affectionately. Tim turns toward me, cupping my face in his big strong hands, and this time it really does feel like an experiment. The kiss doesn't last very long before he pulls back to look at me, but in the darkness, his features are mostly lost in shadow. I don't know what conclusion he reaches. Tim suggests we keep walking. When we're back at my house, we watch a rented movie—a lighthearted comedy—because I don't want him to feel tortured around me. I'm willing to bear that burden on my own.

"Are you ready for bed?" I ask when he yawns during the credits.

"Yeah," Tim says. "If you are."

"Yup. Hey, do popular kids do sleepovers? I can't imagine you and Bryce having a slumber party."

Tim chuckles. "We don't call it that, but yeah."

"How would you guys say it then? Like when inviting each other."

Tim shrugs. "I don't know. I guess if we were hanging out and it got this late, I'd let my friend know that he could crash at my place."

"And would you share the same bed as Bryce?"

He makes a face. "You seem fixated on him."

"I'm really not. Make it Darryl instead, I don't care. It's been a long time since I've had a straight guy friend. I don't know how it works at our age."

Tim thinks about it. "Sharing the same bed is normal. Some guys prefer to sleep on the floor, I guess. My best friend back where I used to live always made us sleep head to foot. Like one of us would be upside-down."

"So you'd be sleeping with your feet in each other's faces?"

Tim nods.

"Gross! Why?"

He looks uncomfortable.

"Trust me," I assure him. "I've heard it all. Your friend thought it was less gay that way, didn't he?"

"Yeah," Tim confirms. "But I always thought it was dumb, because our dicks were still lined up. I guess it's only gay if you kiss." He looks exceedingly uncomfortable after speaking these words.

"I'm not sleeping upside-down," I tell him, "but I can use a sleeping bag and give you the bed if the vibe is getting too gay for you."

"Nah," Tim says. "It's cool."

I get ready in the bathroom, brushing my teeth for the third time that day. When I return to the bedroom, he leaves to do the same. I strip down to my underwear and T-shirt while he's gone and turn off the lights. All but the small lamp on the nightstand next to me. I'm sitting up in bed when he comes back. Tim shuts the door behind him and locks it. I try not to read into that. I honestly don't know if anything is going to happen, or if I really want it to, considering the circumstances. But I *am* sure that I won't be able to say no to him. Not tonight.

I watch as Tim strips off his shirt. He's facing me as he does so. And flexing, at least a little. I know what his muscles look like at rest. I've stared at them often enough. Although his biceps are so round that it can be hard to tell. He's watching me watching him and doesn't seem to mind. I experience a thrill when he grabs the waistband of his jogging shorts and they drop to his ankles. He's wearing a pair of black boxer briefs underneath. I'm already rock hard. I can't help it.

"I thought you couldn't get underwear over your boot," I comment.

"I don't sleep with it on anymore," Tim says, sitting on the edge of the bed.

As he loosens the strap, I study the curve of his toned back and those incredibly beefy shoulders that look so firm and warm. I wish I could pull him over me like a blanket and be smothered beneath all that muscle.

"Wanna see?" Tim asks, making my cock twitch.

He leans back. I'm so drunk on hormones that it takes me a second to realize that he's referring to his ankle. Which I am curious about. I shift in bed, keeping the covers on me strategically. I can feel the heat from his body as I slide closer and gaze down the ridges of his torso to the bulge in his underwear. Which doesn't seem abnormally swollen. That reminds me to look at the ankle he's holding up. It's the right size again, although still yellow and green with bruising.

"Sorry," I say with a wince.

"Huh? It's totally cool! I see the doctor on Monday. I think he's gonna let me ditch the boot."

"So it doesn't hurt anymore?" I ask while retreating to my side of the mattress.

"Nope. It's just a little tender."

Tim gets into bed. He stretches out with his back to me, which I try not to take personally.

"Good night," I say before switching off the lamp.

"G'night," he mumbles.

I remain facing him. Even in the washed-out gray of a darkened room, my eyes adjust enough to see how the blankets are only pulled up to his waist. I want to run the tips of my fingers along his back, maybe draw a little picture while asking him to guess what it is. Or even better, I'd like him to hold me. I want to kiss him some more, suck him dry, and whisper secrets to each other that nobody else knows. Nope, I'm definitely not getting any sleep tonight!

I listen to the sound of Tim's breathing instead, which doesn't seem to be slowing. I slide my hand across the sheets to the space between us, leaving it on the invisible border between our sides. I *need* to touch him. I won't. But I need it, really bad.

Tim rolls over to face me. The light from the window catches his silver eyes, which remain open. Can he see that mine are too? I remain perfectly still, but I don't try to hide that I'm watching him. If he wants me, I'm right here. Come and get it! Tim shifts and extends an arm until the tips of our fingers touch. I nudge him back playfully. He slides his hand over mine. I'm certain that he's going to move it beneath the sheets and finally accept what I've been offering. He doesn't though. Instead his fingers wrap around mine like we're wearing mittens. Then he squeezes. Tim's eyes finally close. Mine do not. They remain open until my fluttering heart slows to a steady beat that, I like to imagine, is in perfect harmony with his own.

I'm sitting across from Tim at the kitchen table the next morning as we wordlessly eat cereal together. Although plenty is communicated in the silence. We're all by ourselves, since we slept late. Tim keeps dunking his spoon into the bowl to capture little marshmallow and oat pieces. Then he'll bring the bite to his mouth and chew, all while fixing a smoldering gaze on me. Sometimes I laugh. Or blush. I'm happy to stare back in either case, my pulse quickening each time, because I think I love him. I don't know what else this could be. He's literally just eating cereal, but it drives me wild, my libido and heart in agreement that this is the guy for us. My mind still has a few reservations, but what does it know?

"I guess I should take off," Tim says.

"Are you sure you don't want more?" I ask, pushing the box of cereal toward him.

Tim smirks. "I want more."

He doesn't touch the cereal.

My mouth is hanging open as he stands and stretches, the bare skin of his stomach revealed in a teasing flash.

"Should I walk you to the door?" I ask.

"I think I can find it on my own," Tim says. Then he shrugs. "But okay."

"When will I see you again?" I ask when we're standing in the entryway.

"Sunday night?"

"Works for me!"

"Cool." His eyes dart to the living room. We're alone. He doesn't kiss me though. Instead he ruffles my hair. "See you around, Benjamin."

"See ya," I say breathlessly as he walks out the door.

I'm rinsing our bowls in the kitchen sink when my mom joins me.

"Has your friend gone home?" she asks.

"Yeah," I reply. "He just left."

"What a handsome young man." The seemingly innocent statement is laced with meaning.

"He is," I admit, turning to face her. "I'm crazy about him, Mom."

"That's wonderful!" Her smile becomes less certain as she studies my face. "Isn't it?"

"He has a girlfriend."

"Oh." She sounds genuinely disappointed for me. "So he's not…"

I press my lips together and shrug.

My mom leans against the counter. "Remember what I used to say when putting a bandage on your knee? You should. I had to often enough. You were such a clumsy boy."

"I still am."

"Do you remember though?" my mom presses.

I nod. "You always said that pain is our body's way of letting us know when something is wrong."

"The same is true for our hearts," she says, rubbing my arm affectionately. "Love is a good thing, even when it's unrequited. But if it starts to hurt…"

"I'll come ask you for a bandage," I promise her.

"You do that, darling boy. Now tell me everything!"

I blanch at this request. "No way!"

My mom puts on a wounded expression. "Someday, when you're a parent, you'll realize how much it hurts when your own child refuses to share his thoughts and feelings with you." She sighs dramatically. "I guess I'll have to keep relying on Allison for details."

"Ha ha!" I say before peering at her in suspicion. "You guys don't *really* talk behind my back, do you?"

"What choice do I have?" she says, still playing it up.

"Fine, fine," I say with an eye roll.

We sit at the kitchen table, and I tell her everything. About my feelings for him, at least. I don't mention that we've kissed, or that I skipped school to take care of Tim after putting him in the hospital. My parents aren't *that* understanding. But I do try to impart how amazing I think he is… and how special he makes me feel.

My mother's words are prophetic. I feel the first sting of love when going for a walk with Tim on Sunday night. He's distant. I'm not sure why. Something could have happened at the party he went to, like his friends making fun of gay people, which would remind him that this isn't an easy path. Or maybe while at church he sat through a hellfire and brimstone sermon about the sin of homosexuality. God forbid anyone listen to their own heart. I wait until we're undeniably alone and shrouded in darkness before I reach for his hand. Tim jerks away at my touch.

"Hey," I say, trying again.

He stops walking. I lean toward him, hoping for a kiss.

Tim takes a step back.

"Is everything all right?" I ask.

"Yeah," he answers, turning his face away.

"Are you okay?"

"I'm fine."

His tone is firm. And final, so I let the subject drop. I don't want him to feel like he's having an existential crisis whenever he's around me. I want him to be happy.

I try to keep things upbeat during the next couple of weeks, even though a chill remains in the air, but the October weather isn't to blame. I feel like he's leaving me behind, which is demonstrably true, since he walks faster now. We don't stroll leisurely like we did before. As soon as Tim is able, I'm sure he'll go back to running, and I might not be able to keep up.

Sometimes we don't go on walks at all. Like when it's raining, or when his friends keep him occupied. On rare occasions he'll kiss me again with the desperate hunger of someone who has been deliberately starving themselves. The fleeting physical contact is all that keeps me anchored, because his words are too ambiguous. I go over them repeatedly when we're apart and can twist every utterance into exactly what I want to hear, or just as easily make it mean the opposite. All but the magical phrase he spoke to me in Spanish. Tim *asked* me to teach him how to fly.

Unless he wrote that line for some girl who came before me.

For now, all I can do—besides obsessing over him every waking second—is wait for each night to come. When I'm lucky he'll call and I'll step outside, my pulse quickening in anticipation, like it's doing now.

I hear a *thump thump thump* that takes me right back to the end of summer. Tim appears from around the corner wearing his trademark outfit of jogging shorts and a muscle shirt, the blue shoes restored to both his feet. He's smiling as he speeds toward me. I open my arms as if to catch him, which makes Tim laugh.

"You're running again!" I say.

"Yeah," Tim pants as he comes to a halt in front of me. "This is the first time I let myself since the accident."

"And?"

"It feels good!" he says, grinning broadly. "Just in time too." He rubs a hand over his chest and stomach. "I was getting soft. Don't you think?"

"I don't know," I say while staring openly. "I'm getting hard."

He laughs instead of grimacing. That's a good sign!

"So does this mean we're not going on walks anymore?" I ask.

"Up to you," he says. "Think you could keep up with me on your skates?"

"No, but I have a birthday soon. Buy me a bike."

"With training wheels?" Tim asks.

"If you want to be on the safe side, yeah! For tonight, let's keep it simple."

"All right."

Tim gets behind me and starts pushing, forcing me into a run. He's in a goofy mood. I let him drive me like a horse until we've reached the trees. Then I slow to a steady trot. "Neigh!" I cry when he pushes on me again. "This horse wants a divorce!"

He looks confused.

"It made sense in my head," I tell him. "I was playing with the onomatopoeia."

"Sounds contagious," Tim says. "Sort of like *Popocatépetl.*"

I snort. "What?"

"*Popocatépetl,*" Tim repeats. "It's my favorite volcano."

This makes me laugh even harder. "Who has a favorite volcano?"

"I do," he says shamelessly. "I got really into them in junior high after writing a paper for an assignment. The next time we went to Mexico, I made my parents take me there."

"One more time," I say, wiping at my eyes. "Please."

"It's a cool place!" Tim says, starting to sound defensive. "The second-highest peak in Mexico, in fact."

"Yeah, but what's it called?"

Tim rolls his eyes but humors me. "*Popocatépetl.*"

I bump shoulders with him until he smiles again. "What do you like about it?"

"The view is amazing. You feel small and insignificant in front of something so massive. And the raw power inside that can create or destroy… I dunno. It's like getting a glimpse of the paint God uses."

I study him, becoming more somber as I do.

"What?" he asks.

"You're one of my favorite people," I tell him, already bracing myself for rejection.

Instead he just smiles.

"Hey!" Tim says as we keep walking. "I have an early birthday present for you."

"Yeah?"

"Yup. My parents are going out of town again."

"Perfect!" I say, my head whipping back and forth. "Where's the closest ditch?"

"I don't want to repeat the *whole* experience!" Tim says with a mad chuckle. "But I did like it."

"Me too," I admit. "How long will they be gone?"

"Just the weekend." Tim smirks. "Wanna have a slumber party?"

"Yeah!" I say, eager to resume my housewife dreams. "I can't stay the whole weekend though."

"Pick a night," he tells me, "and it'll be yours."

"Saturday," I say instantly. "What are we going to do?"

He shrugs. "Whatever you want."

"Ha ha! I don't think you mean that."

"Try me," he says, stopping and turning.

I lean forward and feel like I'm teetering on the edge of a cliff until I feel his hands on my shoulders and his mouth on my lips. That's part of flying, I suppose. You have to trust that someone will catch you if you fall.

CHAPTER TEN

Eating in the school cafeteria has been a different experience for the past week. Ronnie paid the price of admission. He bought lunch for Allison and me, but only on the first day. We might be crazy, but we're not mean. He also brought a friend along with him. I've shared a few classes with Leon over the years. He's a white guy with dreads, which is unusual, but the stoner voice helps sell the look. He usually gets to the table before Allison and Ronnie do—like now—but I find him easy to talk to. Leon has a keen interest in music. He's part of a band that only has two members, him and Ronnie. I also enjoy rocking out with my best friend, so that's enough common ground to keep conversation flowing. We're debating who the most overhyped and underappreciated artists are when the others finally show up.

"Can I tell them?" Ronnie says with a crooked smile. He used to have grungy dreads and wore nothing but Jamaica-themed T-shirts. Now his hair has been cropped down to twist braids that reach the top of his ears, framing a face with strong features that are undeniably handsome. His skin is a shade lighter than Allison's. They make a striking pair. "Or I guess I could tell my best friend," Ronnie continues, "and you could tell your best friend?"

"Considering that they're sitting next to each other," Allison says, taking the seat across from me, "I think we can get it done in one."

"We're going on a date!" Ronnie declares. Loud enough that people look at us from surrounding tables.

Allison doesn't seem embarrassed by this. I can tell she's proud as she unpacks the lunch she brought from home. Ronnie has started bringing his too, probably so he doesn't lose any time with her when waiting in line. Or maybe he's been saving up for the big date. I can't help but feel a little jealous. I would love it if Tim announced to the entire school that he was involved with me. I wonder if he even thinks of it in those terms. I sure do. I'm *involved* with him. I love how tawdry that sounds, like an affair. Which I guess it technically is.

"Where are you guys gonna go?" Leon croaks.

"I was thinking we could play some minigolf and—" Ronnie

begins to say before he glances at Allison. "Actually, it's ladies' choice."

I smirk. She's got him trained already. "Minigolf sounds fun," Allison says. "And you know that really expensive steakhouse that everyone eats at for prom?"

"Yeah?" Ronnie says, looking slightly panicked.

"There's a great barbeque place across the street. It's takeout only, but there's a park nearby."

"Whatever you want!" Ronnie says breathlessly.

"Although the steakhouse does have a nicer restroom," Allison murmurs as if uncertain.

I can tell she's toying with him.

"What about you?" Leon asks me. "Got any hot dudes on the line?"

"I wish," I say. "Why? Are you interested?"

"If I was into guys, you'd be the first to hear about it," Leon replies easily. I'm glad he's so accepting. Ronnie too. I know that's important to Allison. She dropped a couple of her previous suitors when they turned out to be homophobes. I'd do the same if Tim made a racist comment. I'd talk to him about it first, because human beings say all kinds of stupid things they don't really mean, but if he stuck to his guns, that would be the end of it. "I was thinking you could come by the garage sometime," Leon continues. "Allison says you've got one helluva voice."

"You should have heard her rocking the mic the other day," Ronnie says with transparent admiration.

"If you think I can beat that," I tell him, "then you'll be sorely disappointed."

"I was thinking more of a duet," Leon interjects.

"With me?" I bat my eyelashes. "Are you *sure* you're not interested?"

"I dunno, man. Maybe I am!"

I can tell that he isn't, but I like that Leon has a sense of humor about it. He suggests different songs Allison and I could sing together, which starts a discussion that lasts the rest of the break. Even while on a mostly unrelated topic, I can tell how much Ronnie likes her. He hangs on Allison's every word and sometimes smiles at her for no reason. I've had some of those moments with Tim, but I hope that—eventually—we won't have to rely on the shadows as much.

— — —

I'm fresh out of the shower and putting on a newly bought shirt when the phone rings. I decide to ignore it, since I most definitely have plans. Not only did I go shopping for clothes in preparation for my weekend with Tim, I also got a recipe from my mom that's supposed to be foolproof (ha!) and went to the grocery store with her to pick out ingredients. I'm going to make shrimp scampi on a bed of angel hair pasta. Which sounds *way* too difficult, but my mom assures me that it's not. Best of all, wine is one of the ingredients, and there will be leftovers we can drink with the meal. Tim will be excited. I'll be drunk on love. And apparently, the stupid phone isn't going to stop ringing, so I finally answer it.

"Hey, Benjamin!" Tim says, sounding upbeat.

"Hi!" I breathe in return. "I'm just about ready."

"Oh," he says, shooting me down with a single word. Then he swiftly dispatches me with two more. "About that…"

My body tenses. "What?"

"I messed up."

"You got the date wrong or something?" I ask, slowly sitting on the bed.

"Worse. I let it slip that my parents are going out of town. Everyone knows."

I shake my head. "So?"

"So my friends expect me to throw a party."

"Tell them that your parents are really strict."

"Doesn't matter," Tim replies. "They're not here. Listen, I'll make it up to you. The next time they're gone, I'll make sure that nobody but you finds out."

"What about tonight?"

All I hear is white noise in response. So much for my early birthday present.

If I was smart, I'd hang up on him. But I don't really want that. I'd rather find a way that we can still be together. "Can't you pretend to get food poisoning or something?"

I can hear the inhalation of his breath as he hesitates. "I feel like I owe them."

"Fine," I say with an eye roll. "What if I come over afterwards?"

"I don't know. It'll probably be really late."

I try to swallow my pride, but it gets stuck in my throat. "What if I come over now?"

"I wish. Darryl is on his way so we can pick up a keg from a guy he knows."

"I'll come along," I suggest, already knowing that it's impossible.

I listen to more white noise.

"What are you doing on Sunday?" he asks.

"Washing my hair."

He laughs, the stupid idiot. I was being sarcastic, not charming!

"I'll call you when the coast is clear," he says. "Better stay away until then. Okay?"

Now it's his turn to listen to silence.

"Benjamin?"

"Sorry," I say. "My mom is shouting for me. Gotta go."

I hang up before he can say something that makes me feel good in the moment but leaves me confused later. I obsess over his words anyway while seething. He wants me to steer clear, and I get why, but I don't know if I trust him anymore. What if Krista made him a better offer? Is that why he's been so hot and cold with me lately? Are they getting closer, even though I keep sneaking behind the curtain between scenes to kiss him?

While locked in my room, I run through the entire gamut of emotions. Anger. Jealousy. Sorrow. And last but not least, love, because if Tim called me back to say that he changed his mind, I would forgive him. I'd never mention it again if it meant we could be together.

But I don't know if that's possible anymore. Maybe it never was.

I end up cooking dinner with my mom. She can tell that something went wrong. If the canceled plans weren't enough, I'm sure my face gives it all away. I can read hers just as well. She's trying to stay positive, not wanting to see me sad, but it's hard to feel cheerful when I sit down to eat with my parents on a Saturday night. Alone, because my sister—like my best friend and probably everyone else—is on a date. I wish I did have Leon's number. I'd rather hang out with him and get stoned.

"Tastes great, son!" my dad says encouragingly.

"It really does," my mom chimes in. "Great job!"

"It's even better than when she makes it," my father adds.

My mother's eyes narrow. "What's that supposed to mean?"

My dad squirms for a moment before deciding to stuff his mouth full, so he can't respond.

I manage a half-hearted smile. "Mom did most of the work anyway."

"And next time, when you do it all on your own, you'll have experience," she replies.

"I don't know if there's going to be a next time," I say, like a great big downer.

The table is silent until my mother slaps it. "I know what we're missing," she says with a twinkle in her eye. "The wine!"

"Wine?" my father repeats, perking up.

She has my attention as well.

"Why don't you help your father?" my mother suggests. "Bring three glasses back with you."

My dad and I hustle to the kitchen. The rest of the meal is a lot more enjoyable. Especially when we get a little buzzed and start laughing over old memories. We each take turns telling stories. Karen isn't there to defend herself, so I dredge up the time she got diarrhea at a theme park and started screaming for them to let her off the rollercoaster so she could use the restroom. But not before the ride had already begun.

"I swear to god," I tell my parents, laughing so hard I can barely see through my tears, "when we went through the loop-de-loop, she let one rip… and it lasted exactly as long as that loop!"

"Just be glad she managed to hold the rest in," my father says in sympathy. "Those g-forces can wreak hell on your bowels."

"It definitely reeked," I reply.

"They really need to stop selling chili dogs at theme parks," my mother says with a shudder.

They invite me to watch a movie with them, and usually I wouldn't be against the idea, but I have more stewing to do in my room. My mom sends me off with the rest of the wine. It's only half a glass, but I drink so rarely that I already feel like I've gone on a bender. I put on some music and try to feel cool about getting drunk. By myself. On a Saturday, when just a few blocks away, there's a party raging. Supposedly. I think again of my theory that Krista and Tim have been getting closer the more distant he becomes with me. He's willing to lie to other people. Maybe I've been getting the same treatment. I'm probably just his backup plan on days when he's not getting enough attention from her. I bet there's not a party at all.

It wouldn't be hard to find out. I could walk by his house. That will either prove my theory or put it to rest. I down the rest of the wine and grab my shoes. After leaving my house, I shiver and zip up the light jacket I'm wearing. Nervous anticipation turns to dread as I reach his street. The thud of heavy bass and a scattering of cars outside his house banishes my worst fear. Curiosity swiftly takes its place. I can't imagine Tim with his friends. I've seen glimpses at school that don't reveal how they truly interact. Does he have a preference when it comes to Darryl and Bryce? What do they talk about either way? Or maybe Tim spends most of his time with Krista. He doesn't say much about her around me. Are they together now?

I'm not learning anything by standing across the street from his house. Screw it! How hard can it be to peep in a window? I don't even try to be subtle. I make a beeline across his yard, where I learn just how difficult it can be, because there are bushes in the way that don't seem like a serious obstacle until I'm crammed between them. I stand on my tippy-toes, trying to look through the living room window, but the sill is higher up and I'm still too far away.

"What are you doing?"

I spin around and discover two guys watching me from the yard. I don't know their names, only that I've seen them around school before.

"Uh…" I reply. "Nobody answered the door so I was going to knock on the window." There! A perfectly reasonable explanation!

"Hey," one of them says, peering at me funny. "Don't I know you?"

Of course they do! I'm the local homosexual. And if they figure out I was trying to watch a party I wasn't invited to, I'll be a humiliated homosexual.

"I am the new exchange student." I say while emerging from the bushes.

"From where?" the first guy asks.

"Lichtenstein!" It's the first country that comes to mind. Who says they don't teach anything useful in school?

"Oh," the first guy says, seeming appeased. "Do they have beer in Whatever-stein?"

"Lichtenstein!" I repeat. "We have the most wonderful beer." And we speak with Swedish accents, apparently, because for some reason, I've slipped into one. "All the happy children are allowed to drink it once they are ten years old."

"Really?" the second guy says. "That's awesome!"

"And delicious!" I add.

"Well come try some of *our* beer," the first guy says. "You're gonna love it."

"Oh." I try to think of a good reason to leave when they just saw me going to great lengths to (purportedly) get inside, but I've painted myself into a corner. "That would be very nice!" I brush leaves and twigs off me as I walk with them to the front door.

"Hey, is Lucky-stone near Amsterdam by chance?" The first guy asks. "You know what they sell there, right?"

"Women and weed!" the other guy cries before they high-five each other. And then they high-five me. Maybe I should run with the new persona. I've never felt so accepted! And so out of my element as we go inside. A few dozen people are there, if not more, all shouting to be heard over the music while guzzling from red plastic cups. I might have pulled a fast one on my new friends, but someone here is sure to recognize me. And know me by reputation.

"Uh-oh!" I say to my companions in a Swedish accent from Lichtenstein. "I must go upstairs to make a pee-pee now."

They laugh and tell me to come find them later. As soon as they head toward the living room, I crane my neck to see past them, but there's no sign of Tim. I do, however, notice Bryce's massive form towering above the masses, like a lighthouse that takes pleasure in wrecking ships, so I dart down the hall toward the den. I keep my head down along the way, pretending to be preoccupied by something cupped in my hand. Why didn't I put on a disguise before I left? Not like a fireman's costume or anything silly, but a hat and a hoodie and bandages to wrap around my damn face, because I just passed Stacy, and I swear her head turned to follow me.

A couple of guys are walking in my direction, and they

definitely know my name, so I stoop to pick up an empty plastic cup on the floor until they pass. And hey, now I look a little more natural. I can pretend to drink from the cup and partially obscure my face, but only in an emergency, because I don't know whose lips have been on the rim.

I finally reach the den. I must be psychic, because Tim is exactly where I imagined him. The same place I saw him sitting so many times before. He's on his dad's leather couch, his eyes closed as he slowly—and intimately—kisses Krista. My stomach sinks as I park myself in a corner to watch. My timing wasn't fortunate. I didn't just happen to catch them smooching. They're full on making out. She pulls back to say something. He gently brushes the hair out of her eyes and says something back. Then they resume kissing. He doesn't make an excuse, or take a drink so his mouth is unavailable. He just keeps kissing her. Longer than he's ever kissed me.

I'm a fucking idiot. I really am. I wish I could rip the heart out of my chest and stomp on it, right in front of everyone. *You win!* I would scream. *I'll never find love. Are you happy now? Or do you want to kick me while I'm down?*

Sadly, I think I know what their answer would be. I stare a second longer before I turn and leave the room. I don't want to be here. Ever again. I'm not as cautious on my way to the front door. Not until I reach the entryway and I hear Bryce's booming voice.

"You get drunker if you chug upside-down," he's saying.

"Yeah, yeah," Darryl replies, jostling him so he'll keep walking. "Just show us in the backyard instead."

They'll soon be between me and the front door. I might be able to make it, but it would be like diving in front of a semi-truck. I also don't want them to force me deeper into the house toward the den, so I turn and take the only other avenue available to me. I go up the stairs, certain that at any second one of them will call out and demand to know what I'm doing there. I make it to the top, and when I glance back, I see Stacy in the entryway talking to a red-headed cheerleader. Great.

I go to Tim's bedroom and try the door, but it's locked. I figure people are messing around in there, so I try his parents' room next, more willing to hang with Jesus than the assholes downstairs. That door is locked too. I press my ear against it and don't hear anything. Nobody responds when I knock. Tim must have taken precautions and locked the bedroom doors upstairs. I used to do the same with my room to keep my sister out when I wasn't at home. Such internal locks are super basic and ridiculously easy to pick. All anyone needs is a flathead screwdriver, but what I always do is hide something above the door on the frame. I return to Tim's bedroom and feel around up there, and sure enough, I'm rewarded by a flat metal key. I pop the lock, return the key to its hiding place, and let myself inside.

Being surrounded by Tim again—to feel so close to him, and yet so distant—is heartbreaking. He's somewhere beneath my feet. Less than a minute's walk would take me to him, but he might as well be a million miles away. I notice a ball cap. Tim probably has a hoodie in his closet. I could put on both, keep my head low, and make it out the front door. But I don't want to leave. Not before saying goodbye, in my own way, so I lock the door behind me. Then I walk around his room, touching his things with a lump in my throat. I open his underwear drawer and grab one of the sketchbooks, flipping through the pages randomly, but it hurts to see the beauty he's capable of. We could have been amazing together.

The bed is made. A plush rabbit nestles up against the fluffed pillows, its fur worn thin from too much love. Tim must have had it since he was a child. I sit on the edge of the mattress, which brings me closer to his scent, and the temptation is irresistible. I kick off my shoes, grab the plush rabbit, and curl up with it in my arms. I know I need to leave. Tim will probably invite Krista to his room before the night is through. I can't be here, but it's so hard to let go. He was the closest I ever got to making my dream come true.

My chin trembles as I fight against tears, but a few break loose anyway. They soak into his pillow as I mourn everything that will never be. With my eyes closed, I try to imagine an entire life for us: going to college, beginning our careers, saving up for a house, getting married, adopting children and raising them together… I would have liked to grow old with him.

I'm groggy from the wine and washed out from feeling so much. I've always considered myself a fighter, but not tonight. I'm tired. And I ache for him, even now. I drift off without meaning to, my dreams haunted by visions of Tim. Sunlight sets his silver eyes aflame. His lips press against mine, over and over again. Eventually, in a husky voice that makes my skin tingle, he says, "Sorry, Benjamin." I feel his arms wrap around me. "I'm so glad you're here."

I take solace in these fantasies. Too much, as it turns out, because when I open bleary eyes, daylight is warming a square of the mattress where my hand rests. I must be half-awake, because the remnants of the dream haven't faded completely. I can still feel him holding me from behind and hear his slow breathing, each exhalation accompanied by the scent of stale beer. Which seems a little *too* detailed. I shift and feel his arm tighten around me possessively. My eyes shoot open. This isn't a dream! I fell asleep in his room, and now…

My heart flutters in excitement. I remain perfectly still, not wanting to wake him. He must have stumbled into his room last night while drunk and crawled into bed with me. I've wanted him to hold me like this for so long. My body reacts. I'm used to morning wood, but this is more like *petrified* wood. And I don't think I'm alone, because something hard is pressing against my butt. As exciting as that is, I like the feel of his hand even better. Where his arm wraps around my torso, the tips of his fingers are trapped between the mattress and me. I wish I'd taken off my clothes before getting into bed, so our bare skin was touching. Of course I hadn't intended to fall asleep. I was trying to leave him.

When I think back on the evening, it's the cold shower I need, and a timely reminder that nothing has changed. I give myself a little more time regardless, wanting to take this memory with me when I go. His chest swells against my back each time he inhales, making me sigh before I finally gather up my convictions and place my hand over his to move it away. I listen to him gasp and murmur words of confusion as I sit up. I don't look over my shoulder, certain that it would make me weak.

"Hey," Tim breathes. "Good morning."

I feel his touch on my back before I stand, his fingers sliding off. The stuffed rabbit drops to the floor. I pick it up and finally glance in his direction. Like me, Tim fell asleep on top of the covers. Although he stripped down to his underwear. He's got a great big boner that I'll be fantasizing about for the rest of my lonely existence. I just hope his future wife appreciates it as much as I would have. Tim smiles and reaches for me. I place the plush rabbit in his hands.

"Captain Bunbun!" Tim exclaims. "Did you sleep good?"

His eyes flick to mine. I'm not sure which of us he's talking to, but I don't plan on responding either way. Instead I notice a trail of discarded clothes that leads from the bed to the door. I begin picking it all up so Tim can get dressed, mostly so my willpower doesn't crumble.

"Here ya go," I say, setting the wad of clothes on the mattress.

Then I turn my back to him and stare at the painting on the wall, my sorrow increasing, because there's something special about it. He has real talent, but it'll probably remain locked behind a door with everything he truly cares about—a stuffed rabbit, for instance—so he doesn't have to suffer the mockery of others.

"Are you okay?" Tim asks.

I can hear shuffling fabric behind me.

"When did you get here?" he tries. "I don't remember seeing you at the party."

I continue to stare at the painting, a tsunami of color splashing against a solid gray wall. Maybe I can do this. If I steel myself, and try to be more patient, I can help him finally break through the barrier.

"Did anyone else see you?" Tim asks casually.

Or maybe it's hopeless. I shake my head, turning to face him at last. He's dressed in yesterday's clothes. Even wrinkled and rumpled, half-awake and confused, I'm tempted to fall to my knees and beg him to open his heart to me. One last try. I turn around and consider the painting again. "I really like this," I say.

"You do?" Tim asks, walking over to join me.

"Yeah. I've got a thing for rainbows." I look him in the eye. "Who's the artist?"

Tim shrugs, his brow furrowing up briefly. "What's your favorite color?" he asks.

"Orange," I tell him, not seeing what that has to do with anything.

"That's unusual," he replies.

"Yeah, well, I'm not like other boys."

Tim is avoiding my gaze while chewing his bottom lip. If he can't admit that he's got an artistic side, then he sure as hell won't be able to deal with coming out. If he even likes guys at all. I'm tired of the guessing game. I sit on the edge of his bed to put on my shoes.

"Are you taking off?" Tim asks, sounding concerned.

"Yup."

"Do you want to stay for breakfast?"

"No."

I get up and walk to the bedroom door, having to unlock it to let myself out. After ducking into the neighboring bathroom to relieve myself, I return to the hall to find Tim waiting for me. "I gotta go too," he says, shifting from foot to foot, "but I don't want you to leave yet. Okay?"

I roll my eyes and sigh.

"Please?" he says.

I try to shake my head, but the stupid thing nods instead.

"Thanks," Tim says, pushing past me.

He doesn't even shut the door, like he wants to make sure I won't abandon him. Which is just pathetic enough to keep me standing there, even though listening to him pee is all kinds of awkward. And it makes me think about what I saw straining against his briefs. Ugh! Forget it. I walk down the stairs, intending to wait by the front door, but I slow on my way down.

"Hey!" Tim says, hustling after me.

He also slows and then stops to stare. The living room is trashed. Red plastic cups and empty cans are everywhere. An open pizza box sits face down on the carpet. The whole house smells like cigarette smoke. The white couch has been tipped over onto its back, the pillows and cushions scattered around the room.

"Oh shit!" Tim says, leaping down the rest of the stairs. "Oh fuck, oh fuck, oh fuck!"

I watch him start stacking cups before he gives up and goes to the couch to lift one end.

"Can you help me?" he asks with a pleading expression.

I clench my jaw a few times. Then I walk over to join him. Judging from the blankets thrown over the couch, someone wanted to build a fort. Which is fortunate, because one of those blankets is wet with beer, but it managed to protect the couch.

"You got lucky," I say after we right it and take a step back.

"Lucky?!" Tim repeats incredulously.

I shrug. "I don't see any stains."

"Yeah, but just look at this place!" he says, working himself up into a panic. "How bad is the rest?"

I'm curious enough to follow him through the house,

carefully stepping over more garbage along the way, until we reach the den which is even worse. None of the furniture has been knocked over, but the room is trashed. The wet bar has been raided, the refrigerator door left open. A bra hangs from the antlers of the mounted head on the wall. Tim resumes swearing while darting around the room to pick things up, but he makes little progress before some other freshly discovered mess distracts him. Eventually he becomes so overwhelmed that he stops and stands in the middle of it all, his shoulders slumping.

"My parents are going to kill me," he whimpers.

"When do they get home?" I ask.

"Not until the afternoon. Around three, I think."

I check the nearest clock. It's eleven in the morning. Tim follows my gaze and swears again.

"What am I gonna do?" he asks me.

If I could stop myself from caring so easily, I wouldn't be here now.

"We need trash bags," I say while mentally kicking myself. "A lot of them."

A flicker of gratitude eases his features before panic takes hold again. I follow him to the kitchen where shards of broken glass are soaking in a puddle. I avoid the mess and go to the fridge, glad there are still a few cans of cola inside, because we're going to need the energy. We each guzzle one down, pausing on occasion to burp.

"Okay," I say, setting an empty can next to the others. "Let's do this."

We work for the better part of four hours. Tim orders a pizza when we get hungry, although we don't sit down to eat. We take bites in between everything else we need to do. I put on music while picking up trash, partly to keep myself going, but also because I don't want to talk to him. We're often in separate rooms anyway. Like when I check the downstairs bathroom and find puke in the sink. "You're needed in here," I call as Tim passes by.

"Aw man!" he says when joining me.

"I'll keep working on the den," I tell him. "Have fun!"

My mom has always doled out chores to the rest of us, so I'm used to the work, but it's a lot. Everyone who was here had a complete disregard for the state the house was left in, which really gets my back up. Even when things start to look normal again. Tim tries to say something to me as I'm vacuuming, but the noise is too loud to hear him clearly, and I sure as hell don't feel like stopping for some chitchat. Instead I scowl and keep moving the machine back and forth until he takes the hint and wanders off. Although I run out of convenient excuses eventually.

"I think we're good!" Tim says, joining me in the den.

I'm stretching to reach the bra hanging off an antler. Tim pushes himself up on his toes and swipes it easily. "I wonder who this belongs to," he murmurs.

"Krista, probably," I snap.

"Nah," Tim says, holding the bra up to his chest. "Wrong size."

I clench my jaw. "I saw you kissing her."

"What?"

"Last night." My hand trembles as I point at the couch. "You were sitting right there."

Tim looks in that direction and swallows. "Oh."

"Oh?" I repeat. "That's it? After kissing me on all those walks we went on? You don't have anything else to say?"

Tim furrows his brow. "She's my girlfriend."

"So what am I?" I ask, pounding on my chest. "Just some game that you're playing?"

"No!" Tim says, taking a step toward me. "I like you, Benjamin. For real."

I laugh without humor. "Obviously! That's why you ditched me so your asshole friends could come over and trash your house. Where are they now, huh? How come Krista isn't here cleaning up this mess? If they're so much more important to you than I am, then where are they?"

Tim looks pained. "They aren't more important than you."

"Prove it!" I say. "Drive me to school on Monday. Walk with me down the hall. Sit with me at lunch. Tell them all who your new friend is."

Tim swallows. "It's more complicated than that."

"Of course it is," I snarl, shaking my head. "Let me make it nice and simple for you: We're done! Whatever the hell this is, I want out!" I'm already turning to leave.

He tries to grab my wrist, like he always does, but I yank my arm away. "Don't touch me!" The words come out sounding wounded rather than defiant.

"Benjamin," he says, his voice warbling, "please don't go."

"Are you sure you want me to stay?" I ask, nodding at the clock. "Your parents will be home soon."

A hint of fear betrays his silver eyes.

"Call me if you ever grow a pair," I growl.

My heart is thudding in my ears, making it impossible to hear his apology. But that's just another fantasy. He's not sorry. It's time to wake up. I leave his house and walk down the street, my hands clenched into fists in an attempt to stop them from shaking. My legs feel unsteady, my breaths short and shallow. I don't want to do this. I hate it! And yet, I also know that I can't turn back. I have too much pride.

I get so lost in my thoughts that I'm surprised to have made it home already. As soon as I push through the front door, my mom appears out of the kitchen, her concern turning to anger.

"Where were you?" she demands. "I went up to your room this morning and you were gone! Your bed wasn't even slept in!"

"I stayed at Tim's house," I reply, moving for the stairs.

My mother blocks my path. "And you couldn't have told us before you left? Or at least called this morning so I would know that you're safe?"

I scowl at my feet.

"Answer me!" my mother insists. "You're in big trouble, young man!"

I look up at her, ready to vent my anger, even if it's at the wrong person. I open my mouth but all that comes out is a squeak. Then my face crumples and I begin to cry. When I feel my mom's arms around me, I don't resist. I let her pull me into a hug and continue to weep while she whispers soothing words that promise everything will be all right, even though I don't see how it ever could be again.

CHAPTER ELEVEN

I do my best to move on, when in truth, I spend the first few nights waiting for Tim to call. I figure that losing me, even as a friend, would mean something to him. All evidence points to the contrary, but I never could take a hint, so for the first time since our falling out, I search for him between classes. When we pass each other in the hall, he locks eyes with me, but I don't hold his gaze. Instead my attention darts down to where Krista has herself wrapped around his arm. Then I look away, because clearly nothing has changed.

I don't seek Tim out after that. Not even in the parking lot when climbing into Allison's car. I prefer to focus on my best friend, whose newfound joy is contagious. Her date with Ronnie went really well. I refuse to feel jealous about that. Had the weekend played out differently for each of us, Allison would be happy for me, despite her own disappointing result. So I make sure to smile when Ronnie brings her flowers on Wednesday and am enthusiastic when he becomes her favorite subject. I don't have to fake it. He's a good guy and is treating her right. That's what we both deserve.

Despite the temptation, I don't feel sorry for myself. I got to kiss one of the hottest guys in school. Repeatedly! That was worth bruising my heart a little. And even if it wasn't, I have supportive parents, an awesome best friend, and a birthday coming up. I'll be eighteen soon. My life as an adult is about to begin. Next year I'll be off to college and can try again. There's bound to be a special guy out there for me somewhere.

And yet, when I'm lying in bed each night, it's impossible not to dwell on the one I almost had. I'm still haunted by how it felt to be held by Tim. When I jack off, my thoughts always drift to him. I try to make my fantasies carnal, like it was with those other guys. I rewrite my history with Tim so I was giving him blowjob after blowjob without any feelings involved. Which only works until I come. That's when emotion seeps in from around the edges. On good nights, I fall asleep before they can. On others, I alternate between anger and sorrow in a futile attempt to keep love at bay.

I keep reminding myself to focus on the positive. My big day finally arrives and is especially nice since this year it falls on a Saturday. When I go downstairs for breakfast, everyone treats me like a prince. Even my sister, since those are the rules. We take birthdays *very* seriously in my family. My mom slides a card across the table to me, which is unusual, since I normally have to wait until the relatives show up to open presents. I can already tell that it's loaded with cash. Way more than I've ever gotten before.

"You're eighteen now," my mom explains. "This will be your last birthday at home."

"You told me the same thing," Karen grumps.

"We love having you here," my father assures her.

"I'm not pushing you out of the nest," my mother says to me. "You're welcome to stay. But I've always known that you're a flier."

Her choice of words makes me feel a pang of sorrow. I don't feel like a butterfly these days. I'm more like a cocoon that someone knocked off the tree. Allison calls as breakfast is winding down to wish me a happy birthday, which is sweet but silly, since she'll be coming over in a couple of hours and could have told me then.

"Are you sure about tonight?" she asks.

"Absolutely," I say without hesitation.

My birthday is close enough to Halloween that the two holidays often blend together to some degree. Like in the third grade, I asked everyone to wear their costumes to my party, mostly because I couldn't wait to put mine on. This year I thought it would be fun to go to the haunted houses downtown. The plan was for it to be just Allison and me, but when she casually suggested that Ronnie could go with us, I readily agreed. And when the subject came up at the lunch table, I invited Leon too, figuring the more the merrier. If I could do high school over again, I'd form my own clique of freaks and geeks. We outnumber the popular kids ten to one. That's not a bad blueprint for life actually. If all the minority groups joined together, they would be the new majority.

Not ready to run for president just yet, I take a shower, get dressed, and put on my favorite tunes until it's time to go downstairs and make an appearance. I've always felt like the black sheep of the family, but I do like my relatives, despite our differences. Once the party is in full swing, I'm in high spirits. We're only waiting for my grandma to show up so we can cut the cake and open presents. When I hear a knock, I rush to respond.

"Nana!" I cry happily when throwing open the door.

The smile slides off my face. Tim is standing there with a hangdog expression. He's holding a wrapped gift that's flat, rectangular, and so tall that the bottom edge rests on the tip of his blue shoes. I'm amazed by how quickly the joy drains from me as pain bubbles up to take its place.

"Hey," Tim says, sounding muted. "Happy birthday."

"What are you doing here?" I ask, stepping onto the porch and pulling the door shut behind me.

Tim swallows. "I wanted to give you this."

I barely glance at the gift. "Anything else?" I ask.

Tim shrugs. "I guess I wanted to say—" His eyes widen as the door behind me opens again.

"Oh!" my mom says in surprise. "Tim! How nice of you to stop by! We were just about to have some cake. Come on in!"

"*Mom*," I stress in a way that I hope communicates just how awkward the situation is.

"That's okay," Tim says.

My mom isn't listening. She's looking at the street, where my grandma has just pulled up. "Finally! Ben, honey, let your father know that we're almost ready. I'm starving!" She smiles at Tim. "Get inside and make yourself at home." And with that, she moves past us to greet her mother.

Tim waits until we're alone before he says, "Can we talk? About everything. Please."

"Sure," I say, using my foot to push open the door behind me so he gets a good view of how many people are there. "If you don't mind waiting. I'm sure Allison would love to finally meet you. A couple guys from school are coming by later. It'll be fun."

I expect him to make an excuse and flee. Instead he clenches his jaw a few times before nodding. "All right."

I scoff at this. "I'm not going to swear them to secrecy. People might find out that you were here."

He struggles with this before nodding again. "Okay."

I stare in disbelief. Then I step aside. "Right this way."

Allison's eyes practically bug out when she notices who's

trailing along behind me, but she quickly puts on a friendly smile. "This is an unexpected surprise," she says, a hint of a question in her gaze when she glances at me.

I'm not sure how I feel about him being here, so I shrug. "Allison, this is Tim."

"Hey," he says, grinning in a way that's smarmy. "I've heard so many good things about you."

"Name three," she replies.

That catches him off guard. Allison will keep Tim on his toes while I'm busy. I have to greet my grandmother, and once I have, I'm ushered toward the table of presents so I can begin opening them. Most people blow out their candles first. Not us. We were always too impatient as kids, so it's become a family tradition to do it in reverse. I get things I want and some stuff that I don't, but the sentiment is appreciated either way. To be honest, most of it barely registers. After unwrapping each gift, I express my gratitude before my attention returns to Tim. At first he seems uncomfortable, often engaged in conversation with my relatives, but eventually he loosens up and seems more like the guy I know. At the moment he's chatting with Allison. I'm dying to know what they're talking about. I'll get a full report later, no doubt.

"All right, everyone," my father says. "It's time for cake!"

"Not yet!" my mother cries, gesturing at Tim to come closer. "We have one more present."

"That's all right," he says dismissively. "It can wait."

"Don't be silly," she replies. "Bring it here."

Allison gives him a little push. Tim's face is red as the whole family turns toward him. The present is about three feet tall. I keep thinking it's the painting off his bedroom wall, but it looks too big. He pulls out a chair to set his gift on the seat, so I'll have an easier time tearing off the paper. I waste no time in doing so, revealing wild strokes of thickly applied paint. The colors vary, most of them warm, but orange is the most dominate. Especially the heart in the center, which blazes with a fiery passion. Beautiful, but also kind of lonely, until I notice the edge of blue behind it outlining another heart in its shadow. Tim's eyes are guarded. Mine are wet with emotion, because whatever his intent, it's an acknowledgement of how intensely I burn for him. And perhaps is a promise that I'm not alone.

"Isn't that gorgeous?" my mother enthuses. "Did you paint it yourself?"

"I hope so!" my sister interjects. "I can't imagine anyone paying money for it."

"Karen!" my mother scolds before shaking her head helplessly. "Where did we go wrong with you?"

"She's always had a critical eye," my father says. "Not many people do."

"There's your answer," my mother murmurs to herself.

"It's gorgeous," I whisper to Tim.

"Really?" he asks, as if he truly doesn't know.

I consider the canvas again and am so moved that I have to wipe at my eyes. "I love it."

He smiles in relief and opens his mouth again, as if there's more he wants to say, before he glances around self-consciously.

"Later," I promise him.

Tim's face lights up, like he just received a gift of his own. I place the painting out of harm's way. Then I turn my attention to my father, who carries a cake toward me while everyone sings. When they reach the end of the song, I wait. Allison belts out an extra verse all on her own, like she does each year, and it's stunning. Especially after the untrained voices of my relatives. Everyone breaks into applause.

"Okay, okay," I say over this. "She's great, but let's not forget whose special day this is!"

I wink at Allison before filling my lungs with air. You only get one birthday wish a year. I always make sure to spend them wisely. My eyes move to Tim, and I don't try to hide how I feel. *Him*, I think. *That's all I want.* I focus on the candles and blow them all out on my first try.

"Great job!" my dad says. "What did you wish for?"

"You really need to ask?" I hear Allison quip.

"Don't tell him!" my sister says. "If you do, it won't happen!"

My relatives debate over the rules of such things as the cake is sliced. I'm with Karen. Wishes have to remain a secret or they won't come true. Maybe Tim thinks so too. God, I would love to be his wish!

"Are you happy?" my mother asks when placing a festive paper plate in front of me. The question is weighted with more meaning than usual. She knows what I've been going through.

"I'm really happy," I croak before laughing at myself. I didn't expect the day to be so emotional.

"I'm glad, darling," my mom says, kissing the top of my head.

I don't get much time with my friends while eating. Too many relatives want to remind me that I used to be a small squirming creature who pooped himself. They assure me it was only yesterday. Thankfully, they are wrong.

"I just adore this!" my mother declares eventually. She's standing next to the painting while smiling down at it. "Honey, why don't you have Tim help you figure out where it will go?"

I instantly shoot to my feet. "Good idea!"

Tim seems to agree. His smile is subtle, although still uncertain, as he makes his way over to me.

"Where do you want it?" he asks.

"In my bedroom."

Allison snorts. I try to glare at her but can't, since my face is already occupied with a grin. I attempt to temper my joy on the way up, because our issues haven't been resolved. I like that Tim showed up on my birthday, and I absolutely adore the painting, but he made me cry. Not on purpose. I won't hold it against him. But I also won't forget the reason why, since not much has changed.

"What do you think?" Tim asks as we enter my room. He holds the painting up to an empty space near my closet, seemingly without irony.

I shake my head. "I was thinking over here," I say, leading him to the opposite side of the room near the headboard of my bed. I sleep on my side, and I like the idea of the painting being the first thing I see in the morning. And the last thing I look at each night. Although that might be a bitter experience, depending on what he has to say.

"The light is nice here," he comments while trying the spot out. "Does the sun hit this wall?"

"I don't think so," I reply.

"Cool. If you grab a hammer and nails—"

"Tim?"

"Yeah?"

I sit down on the edge of the bed. "Let's talk."

"Oh." He swallows and sets the painting on the floor so it rests against the wall. "Okay."

Tim sits next to me, but not close enough that we're touching. We're both silent for a moment. I keep trying to think of the right question, but they all feel too needy, so I'm glad when he speaks first.

"My family isn't like yours," he says. "Not even close." He gnaws his bottom lip, his brow furrowed as he glances at me and then back down to his feet. "I think I was a mistake."

"Oh," I reply. "If it makes you feel better, I was too."

"Really?"

I nod. "My parents wanted to wait another year before having a second kid. I'm surprised they wanted more at all, but I guess Karen couldn't talk back then, so they didn't know how bad it could get."

"No kidding," Tim grumbles.

"So anyway, they weren't expecting me. I bet that's the case with more people than we realize."

"Probably," Tim says. "The difference is, my parents didn't want children at all. I overheard them talking about it to another couple a few years ago. You haven't seen them together. My mom and dad, I mean. They only have eyes for each other, which sounds great, unless you're on the outside." He glances at me with a guilty expression. "My mom loves me. Don't think she's a bad person, because she's not. I have a lot of happy memories, but nothing like what I saw downstairs. We're a small family. My mom's relatives all live in Mexico. I haven't seen my dad's side since I was little, so that whole family vibe…" He shrugs. "I don't really know what it's like."

"Being an only child must be different," I say. Karen and I were often at odds with each other, but we still teamed up when it came to all the fun stuff that kids like to do.

He shrugs. "I guess. It would've been nice to have a brother or sister around."

As much as I like learning more about him, there's something I need to know. "What about us?"

Tim sighs. "That's what I'm trying to explain. When my ex-girlfriend said that I raped her, it really messed with my mom. I could tell. She always claimed she believed me, but you know how it is. Part of you wonders anyway. And she probably imagined it, even if she didn't want to." He grimaces before continuing. "My mom is really religious. A diehard Catholic. If I was like you, she'd think I was going to Hell."

I scoff at this. "If there is a god, I refuse to believe he's that much of a jerk."

"Doesn't matter if it's true or not," Tim says, shaking his head. "She'd believe it anyway. Her own son, burning in Hell for all eternity. I don't know how she'd sleep at night. The allegations already put her through so much. That was the worst part, knowing that it hurt her."

"What about your dad?" I ask.

The color drains from his face. "He hardly said a word to me. Like he thought I was guilty. Or maybe he was pissed at me for upsetting my mom, I don't know."

"So if he found out that you're dating a guy?"

"He'd disown me," Tim says. "I know what he thinks about gay people but uh… you don't need to hear any of that."

I consider what he told me. Tim has one parent he doesn't want to distress, and another he doesn't want to alienate. That's a tough position to be in. I can give him credit for that, but it doesn't answer my most pressing question. "You don't have to put a title on it but… Do you like guys?"

Tim seems to struggle within himself. He studies his feet. Then he glances up at the painting before turning toward me. "I don't know. But I like you."

What few barriers remain come tumbling down. When he leans toward me, I meet him halfway. Tim presses his lips to mine, his hands on either side of my face as he inhales deeply through his nose. Then he pulls back, his eyes pleading with me to understand. And I think I do. Enough to forgive him and try again. Except…

"What about Krista?"

Tim's expression is apologetic. "It's going to look weird if I refuse to date anyone. Krista doesn't want much from me. She's a virgin and plans on staying that way until she gets married. All we've ever done is kiss, and I like that because… I don't want my mom to have doubts, you know? About any of it. If she sees that I'm with a different girl and there aren't any accusations." He shakes his head. "I don't want her to think I'm a fucking rapist. And it'll keep her from wondering about the rest too."

"That you've made out with another guy?" I shrug, like it's not a big deal. "That sort of thing happens on a dare. Or is it going to go further than that?"

"I want it to," Tim says, his eyes searching mine again. "Don't you?"

"Yes," I admit. I can't pretend otherwise, even to make him squirm. "How's this going to work?"

"I don't know. We can figure it out together."

I'm setting myself up to get hurt again. I can hear Allison in the back of my mind, warning me. She's soon banished to the depths of my imagination. I want this too much. But I'd be a fool if I didn't test the waters before leaping back in. "My friends and I are going to the haunted houses later on," I say casually. "Come with us."

Tim hesitates. "We need to be careful."

"It's downtown. And a big city. I've never seen anyone from school there before. Or at least I didn't notice them, because it's always crowded."

His brow furrows up again.

"And it's my birthday," I press.

If he can't take one small step for me, then I don't see how we'll ever dance together.

"Okay," Tim says. "You've got it."

He places his hand over mine. I notice traces of orange paint beneath his fingernails. My heart is bursting with joy. Those birthday wishes sure are powerful!

"If I grab a hammer and nails," I say to him, nodding at the painting, "will you do the rest?"

Tim smirks. "If you want something hung, I'm your man."

I've already seen enough to know he's not kidding. And I really *really* like the idea of him being my man. I don't know if this will work, or where any of it will lead, but I can't wait to find out!

CHAPTER TWELVE

After Ronnie and Leon show up, Tim offers to drive us all downtown. Which scores more points with me, because his car is recognizable. He seems tense until we leave the town limits, although he relaxes again when I find a song on the radio that Allison and I can sing together. Leon is thrilled by our performance and begs us to join his band. I tell him that I'll need to see a contract first.

Once we've arrived and are waiting in line, it's interesting to see how Tim interacts with the other guys. He tries talking about sports but doesn't get very far. Then he switches to cars. Ronnie is a little more interested than Leon, although the two friends mostly talk to each other. I've got my hands full with Allison, who keeps trying to get details out of me when the others aren't listening. That leaves Tim as the odd man out. I attempt to get us all talking as a group by pointing out some of the more interesting costumes people are wearing.

"That guy looks like a mad scientist on his way to a job interview," Ronnie comments.

"He's dressed up as Warhol," Tim replies.

"Hey, you're right!" Leon says. "That dude was crazy. I know the tomato soup thing is super passé, but he did some wild stuff."

"You mean his pee paintings?" Tim asks.

Ronnie makes a face. "Wait, what?"

"He had a bunch of guys pee on copper plates," Tim says. "So it would oxidize and create patterns." He glances at me self-consciously. I nod in encouragement. The other guys are grinning. "It's true!" Tim continues with more confidence. "Or sometimes he'd have dudes ejaculate instead, like his own take on Jackson Pollock."

"Those are the dribbly paintings, right?" Ronnie asks.

"Yeah."

"I've got a great book about underground art at home," Leon croaks. "I've even tried my hand at it."

"Oh yeah?" Tim asks in interest. "In what way?"

"Graffiti mostly," Leon replies. "And some airbrushing."

Tim perks up. "You've got one of those?"

"An airbrush? Yeah. I got it for Christmas one year. My mom was trying to wean me off the spray cans." Leon blinks. "Not that

I was huffing paint or anything. I think she wanted me to find a more legitimate medium to work in."

"Next time tell her that it's all valid," Tim says. "Piss and come especially."

The other guys howl with laughter. Allison rolls her eyes. And even though Tim doesn't volunteer that he paints, I like that he's found common ground. Maybe he'll realize that he can hang out with a different—and in my opinion, better—group of friends.

The haunted houses are a blast. I love suspending my disbelief and getting freaked out. Nothing ruins the fun like someone bravely marching through it all. So I am both amused and relieved that Tim is so chicken. Almost every single scare has him jumping and shouting in terror. I'm worried he's going to die of fright. Although he sure seems fine when we're feeling our way through a pitch-dark maze. My hands slide along the walls as I guide the group. Tim's hands are on me. Sure, a lot of that is him clutching at me in terror, but I still like his touches, no matter the reason. When we reach a dead end and the others turn around, Tim does not. Instead he pins me against the wall. I feel his mouth on my neck, which is new. I'm getting seriously turned on by his kisses until a group of girls bumps into us with a shriek and I feel his teeth instead.

"Sorry!" Tim says as we set out to find the others. "I swear I'm not a vampire. Are you okay?"

"Yeah," I reply. "I'm just glad you weren't going down on me."

"Although *you* don't scare as easily," he murmurs. "So if we really wanted…"

Oh, I want to! Just not here.

I shrug innocently when we catch up with the others and Allison gives me a knowing look. We survive the harrowing experience, pile into Tim's car again, and grab a bite to eat before heading back to town. I'm standing in the driveway while watching Ronnie's SUV drive away when Tim's hand brushes against my own.

"I've got something else for you," he says. "One last birthday present."

I watch as he undoes the ball chain necklace he wears. Tim tugs to pull it free of his shirt, revealing the attached house key. "I felt bad about making you stay away when my parents were gone last weekend." He moves closer to me, the necklace drooping between each hand. "So with this, you can come see me whenever you want."

"Even when your parents are home?" I tease.

"Yeah," he says, fastening the chain around my neck. "But only when they're asleep. Like tonight."

He seems serious!

"Tonight?" I repeat.

Tim nods. "Uh-huh. They're heavy sleepers." His face is close to mine, a playful smile on his lips. "All you have to do is let yourself in and sneak up to my room. They're usually in bed by ten, so any time after eleven is safe."

"What if I get caught?" I ask.

His eyes twinkle. "Aren't you a professional gay stalker?"

"I mean, I haven't gotten my certification yet, but basically."

"You've got this." Tim takes out his car keys. "I'll see you later." He glances around before kissing me. Just a light smooch, but it promises more.

I stared dumbfounded as he gets into his car. Tim is driving away when I shout, "Or you could just spend the night here!"

Probably. I'm not sure how my mom would react, now that she knows I have feelings for him. The idea of sneaking over to see him is hot anyway. I don't think he wants to stay up all night talking. Although I wouldn't mind that either. Still, it pays to be prepared. I go inside, make an appearance for my parents, and retreat to the bathroom to freshen up. Then I sit on my bed and stare at the painting he gave me while wishing time would match the rapid pace of my heart. When the hour draws near, leaving is easy. I'm on home turf. I know everyone's schedule and which stairs squeak the most. It's when I navigate the silent suburban streets that I become nervous. Tim's house is dark. The porch light isn't on. None of the windows are glowing. Which I guess is a good sign, since it means his parents have gone to bed. My hand is shaking when I try to slide the key into the lock. I get it after a few false starts. Then I swallow, hold my breath, and turn the knob. The door makes a noise as it swings away from the frame. Just a small sticking sound that probably isn't very loud, but I go rigid anyway, not daring to move until I'm certain that I haven't alerted anyone.

As bad as I want him, this is a *terrible* idea! What will I say to his parents if either of them catch me? I can't think of a single excuse to explain why I'm slowly locking the door behind me and creeping toward the stairs. Scaling them is twice as intimidating. If his mother caught me in the entryway, I could dart into another room and maybe escape out the back. On the stairs, she'll have plenty of time to turn on the lights and get a good look at me. I stop halfway up, my palm sweaty on the handrail. I still don't hear anyone. Tim's bedroom door beckons, the promise of sex enough for me to abandon my reservations and creep the rest of the way. I'm eager to get inside to safety, my attention darting to his parents' bedroom door.

Which begins to open!

I quickly turn the knob to Tim's room and shove my way inside. The interior is dark except for a window that overlooks the backyard. Moonlight illuminates an empty bed. I'm thinking of diving beneath it, although maybe it would make more sense to get under the sheets and pretend to be Tim. Where is he anyway? I leap onto the mattress and claw at the comforter, attempting to cover myself, which doesn't go well, so I grab a corner and roll, turning myself into a human burrito. The light flicks on. I clench my eyes shut like a little kid who thinks it'll make him invisible. Then I hear laughter.

"Not bad," Tim says loud enough to wake the whole house. "But I think you could use more practice."

I sit up and blink against the light. Tim is leaning against the doorframe while smiling. "Your parents!" I hiss.

"Are out of town," he replies.

I groan and toss a pillow at him, which he easily catches. "You suck!"

"So do you," Tim replies. "That's the rumor at school at least."

"You're not finding out tonight!" I growl. "You almost gave me a heart attack!"

"You'll live," he says, taking something out of his pocket. "You did good though. I didn't hear a thing. I wouldn't have known you were here if I wasn't watching for you through the upstairs window."

"I am *never* doing that again!"

Tim shrugs, flipping open a metal lighter and flicking it to make a flame appear. "Up to you."

I crumple up my brow in puzzlement. "What are you doing?"

"Setting a mood." Tim walks to his dresser to light candles that definitely weren't there before. I recognize them from the dining room table downstairs. Glancing around, I notice a motley collection of candles gathered from around the house. "I don't know what you're so upset about," he continues. "You were paying people to scare you downtown just a few hours ago."

"Yeah, but I knew that was fake," I say with a laugh.

He smiles and goes to the light switch to flip it off, leaving us in a warm orange glow. Tim turns to assess the room. "Are you into this?" he asks.

"Very!" I say breathlessly.

"Cool. It's still your birthday. What do you want me to do?"

I stare for a second. "Anything I want?"

He nods. "Yeah. Name it."

"Take off your shirt," I say, sitting up with my back against the bed's headboard.

"It's nothing you haven't seen before," Tim says while complying.

True, but his meaty pecs and rounded shoulders are a combination that gets me every time.

Tim tosses his shirt aside. "Now what?"

I bite my bottom lip before answering. "Flex for me."

Tim laughs. He puts on a show, doing the classic bodybuilder poses, which is funnier than it is sexy. So I get up and go to him, placing a hand on his bicep.

"You like that?" he asks.

"Yeah," I say, already hard.

Tim's eyes are smoldering as his hands move to his jeans. "Wanna see the rest?"

My jaw drops before I nod eagerly. I sit on the end of the bed to watch. Tim deftly steps out of his jeans. The boxer briefs are bulging in the front. Tim hooks a thumb behind the waistband and teasingly lowers them inch by inch, revealing a tuft of black pubic hair and the base of a big fat sausage. I'm so dizzy with excitement that I might need smelling salts!

"Damn, it's starting to hurt," Tim says, abandoning this game. "Here goes nothing!"

More like everything! The underwear slides off his hips as his cock springs out. I'm impressed by its thickness, especially when it bounces and continues to swell. He's got a nice set of balls on him too, but I'm mesmerized by that python, which is the same brown as the rest of him. Including the head? I'm puzzled by that, but only at first.

"Wait, are you uncut?" I ask, barely able to contain myself.

"Yeah," he says, sounding self-conscious. "Is that all right?"

"Are you kidding?" I get to my feet so I can take a closer look. "I've always wanted to play with one of these!"

Tim laughs. "You've never seen one before?"

"Nope! Not in person."

"Girls get freaked out by it sometimes," Tim says. "But I've always liked it." He takes hold of himself and pulls, the foreskin rolling back to expose a fat rosy head. When his fist moves in the opposite direction, the skin slides forward to cover him again.

"That's amazing!" I say, practically drooling over it.

"Wanna try?" Tim offers.

I treat the question as rhetorical. Of course I want to try! I wrap my hand around steaming hot meat and begin to pump. He makes a guttural sound, like it feels good.

"How do I stack up?" he asks.

"You're big," I say before tearing my eyes away so they can meet his. "You've never checked out other guys before? Like in the locker room?"

"Well, yeah, but we don't walk around with boners. That's not how it works."

"It does in my fantasies." I begin to get to my knees before he catches me by the elbow.

"Hold up," he says.

I shake my head in confusion. "What?"

"You skipped a base on your way to a home run." He pulls me close for a kiss.

I'm surprised, because that's not how it worked with the other guys. None of this is. The only piece of me they wanted was my mouth. And I guess he does too, but in a way that makes me feel loved. I kiss him back, pressing my body against his, but it's impossible to ignore that something is poking me.

"Please?" I ask when leaning back.

"Hey, it's your birthday," Tim says with a cocky grin. And a great big cock that is soon in my face as my knees hit the carpet. I make the foreskin slide back and forth, so I can see it in action up close. I'm intrigued, but I'll have to continue my research later, because I can't wait any longer. I lick the head of his cock, intending to tease him, but his precum tastes so good that I engulf him with my mouth. All the way to the hilt.

"Damn!" Tim says. "I've never met a girl who can do that!"

Which makes me all the more eager to compete. My lips are tight, my tongue firm against the underside of his cock as I retreat to the very tip. Then I go deep again, having conquered my gag reflex long ago. Tim gets into it, putting his hands on either side of my head and thrusting. All I have to do is hold on for dear life as he continues to grunt, his nuts slapping my chin a few times.

"Fuck, dude!" he says, pulling out completely. "I'm close!"

"That's fine," I say before opening my mouth again.

"Yeah, well, I'm not ready." He reaches down to grab my arms and pull me to my feet. "I wanna see you naked."

"Really?" I ask.

"Yup." Tim puts his hands on his hips. "Show me what you've got."

"Okay."

I unbutton my shirt, already puffing up my chest as it's slowly exposed. He's going to be so disappointed! But maybe the candlelight and shadow will work in my favor. After my shirt comes off, I do my best to flex and make myself look bigger.

Tim laughs. "Relax!"

I exhale and let my arms go limp. It's useless anyway. "I should probably start lifting weights or something," I mumble.

"I kind of hope you don't," he replies. "I'm not into muscles. Skinny is way hotter."

"Even when it comes to guys?"

Tim nods. "Yeah. I like that I can see your ribs."

Words that I never imagined hearing, but boy are they welcome! I don't starve myself or anything. I just have a high metabolism. Tim moves close. He places his palm on my flat stomach, moving it up to my chest, where his thumb brushes against one nipple and then the other.

"They're so pink!" he says, like it's a good thing.

This makes me laugh, but he doesn't seem to mind. I guess we all have our kinks.

"Take your dick out," he says, "so we can compare."

I've got nothing to be ashamed of, but it's an intimidating

request, because he's got me beat in every category and I don't want him to be disappointed. I'm not used to a guy taking an interest in me like this. I unzip my pants and pull down my underwear.

"Damn," Tim says. "You're pretty all over."

"Pretty?" I repeat, but not incredulously. I like the sound of it.

"Yeah," he says, putting a thumb on the base of his cock and pushing so it's horizontal to the floor.

I do the same. Then we park them next to each other, where the obvious becomes even more apparent.

"Mine's bigger," he says.

"Fatter for sure," I reply. "You've only got an extra inch on me."

"Still bigger," he repeats. "I like that."

"So do I," I assure him. "And since you win the contest, you should get the prize."

I kick off my jeans and crawl backward into bed. "Come here," I say, reaching for him.

Tim crawls on top of me and attacks my lips again. I kiss him back before grabbing his hips and pulling. When he looks down at me in confusion, I pat the mattress on each side of my chest. "Put your knees here," I tell him.

Tim finally gets it and grins. Soon that magnificent cock of his is fucking my mouth, and I decide to remain there for the rest of my life. I've found my purpose and my place!

While gripping the headboard, he looks down at me. "I'm close again," he says.

My mouth is too full to talk. All I can do is nod in encouragement. He picks up the pace, and when he growls, I make sure not a single drop is wasted. Even when he tries to pull out, I strain my neck to take him back in.

"Okay, okay!" Tim laughs before rolling off to the side. "Holy shit! That was incredible!"

"Yeah," I agree after swallowing. "I'm up for a repeat. Anytime you want."

"Be careful what you wish for," Tim says. "I'm a horny dude."

"I can handle it," I assure him.

Although I'm not entirely sure what to do with myself. A lot of the guys I've been with would pretend to fall asleep. Or make an excuse, like how their parents would be home soon, before getting dressed. Tim simply flops onto his back while panting. Normally I wait a few minutes and then excuse myself to use the restroom, so I can finish myself off. I guess that works.

"I usually last longer," Tim says.

I smirk at this. "Prove it."

"I will," Tim says, stretching and sitting up. "Next time."

"I can hardly wait," I say, swinging my legs over the side of the bed so I can stand. I don't manage to fully before Tim grabs my hand.

"Where ya goin'?" he asks while pulling me back into bed.

"I was about to get dressed."

"No way!" he rolls on top of me and pins me down by the shoulders, a wicked grin on his face. "I wanna see you come."

"Okay!" I say enthusiastically before reaching for myself.

He knocks my hand away and traps my cock in one of his strong fists. Then he begins pumping. "Weird!" he says. "It feels different than mine."

"Uh…" I say, my body already writhing in pleasure.

"How do you jack off without foreskin? Everything's so tight."

"Lube helps," I suggest.

"Oh right." He stops long enough to spit into his hand. Then he wraps his hand around my dick again, this time loose enough that his palm can slide across my skin. "Does that feel good?"

I whimper in response.

Tim shifts and starts licking one of my nipples, which pushes me close to the edge.

"I usually last longer too," I gasp in warning.

"Not with me you don't." Tim is grinning from ear to ear while locking eyes with me.

I bite my lower lip before my cock starts convulsing and doesn't seem to stop.

"Holy shit!" Tim says with a chuckle. "Do you always come that much?"

"No," I say, looking down. I start laughing too. "Definitely not!"

His hand is so soaked that he does a flinging motion, hot drops splattering my torso. "Now I know where Warhol got the idea," he says.

We both laugh. Tim grabs his T-shirt so I can clean up. He uses his underwear for the same purpose, wringing his hands with it. He seems to have no intention of getting dressed again, which is fine with me. He tosses the soiled clothing to the floor and crawls into bed.

"Will you hold me?" I ask.

"Hell yeah!" he says, sliding in behind me.

We shift and adjust until I fit into the contours of his body. His forearm is pressed against my chest, a hand wrapped around the shoulder near my neck. I feel him smooch the back of my head.

"Where's the key I gave you?" he asks.

"In my jeans. How come?"

"Don't lose it. I wanna do this again. How does every night sound?"

"Like we'll get caught."

"Yeah, I guess you're right. But during the weeks when it's hard to see each other, this is how we'll deal with it. Okay?"

I swallow and nod, wanting to tell him how I feel. But he's already given me so much, so I keep it simple. "This is the best birthday I've ever had."

"It's not over yet," Tim says with a yawn. "Can you sleep here tonight?"

"Yes." I refuse to consider the consequences. I'm willing to pay any price to remain here with him.

Tim seems to feel the same way, the arm around me constricting. Asking for it would be greedy, so I won't... But if I had one more wish to spend, I'd make this night last forever.

CHAPTER THIRTEEN

I waited so long for someone to love. Now I'm making up for lost time. Two weeks have passed since Tim and I started having sex. I'm so horny for him that it's crazy. No one I messed around with before can compete. I only found a couple of them attractive. Mostly it was the excitement of getting to touch another guy that appealed to me. Everything is different with Tim. All he has to do is smile to get me in the mood. Or sometimes he'll whisper in my ear, making my skin tingle. *Wanna mess around?* He showed up at my house the other day, sauntered over to the couch, and sat back with a seductive smirk. I literally ran around to lock doors and pull curtains shut before kneeling before him. And it's never one-sided. He seems just as interested in me.

I can't get enough. Tim stayed at my place for another sleepover, my parents none the wiser. Now I'm actually glad I cried in front of my mother. She thinks I'm wallowing in unrequited love, when in truth, my heart is soaring through the sky. And sometimes creeping through someone else's house late at night. I've done that a few times now, certain that I would be caught on my way up to Tim's bedroom, but somehow that only makes it hotter. This whole sneaking around thing is kind of fun!

Usually.

While sitting at our table in the school cafeteria, it's hard not to feel envious at times. Allison and Ronnie are officially a couple. They always sit on the same side, their bodies touching in little ways. I watch Allison lean against Ronnie after he says something funny and notice how he continues smiling when she sits upright again. The guy next to me has dreads and smells faintly of cannabis. As likable as Leon is, I can't help imagining what it would be like if Tim was sitting there instead. I'd feed him one potato chip after another, or let my hand go wandering beneath the table, or ask him to describe everything I'm eating *en español* just to hear the delectable accent he always slips into.

"Do I have something on my face?" Leon asks, sounding worried.

I realize I've been staring at him and feign concern. "Yeah, but I think it's supposed to be there." I reach up to touch my nose. "Oh god… I have one too!"

Leon laughs. "We have to get stoned together, my man. You're a riot!"

The compliment is appreciated, but if Tim was sitting with us, I could be racking up points with him instead. I can't stop thinking about him during lunch, so after the bell rings and we leave the cafeteria as a group, I give in to temptation.

"Mind if we take a quick detour?" I ask, slowing at the next corner.

"I've gotta swing by my locker," Leon says. "See you guys later."

I watch him bump fists with Ronnie, who would follow Allison into the desert without so much as a thimble of water, if that's what she wanted. I'm on high alert as we wander down a hall lined with science classrooms that none of us attend this period. The traffic flowing toward the cafeteria is what interests me. The school has alternating lunch breaks. Tim and his friends should be heading there now, if we haven't already missed them.

Ronnie says something to me, but I miss it since I've just spotted Tim, who is flanked by Bryce and Krista. As usual, she's wrapped around one of his arms. That's okay. He'll make eye contact with me and nod, or more likely risk a naughty smirk, considering we just messed around the night before. Except this time, he's more distracted than ever. Krista seems excited about something.

"Really?" she asks, letting go of him. "This weekend?"

"Yeah," Tim says, his smile faltering when he finally notices me. "Of course."

"Hooray!" Krista shouts, bouncing around like a rabbit before using the extra height to kiss him. "You're the best boyfriend ever!"

His eyes dart toward me and away again before he focuses on Krista, who wraps herself around his arm. If I had a crowbar, I'd pry her off and chase her down the goddamn hall. I can feel my face burning as we pass Tim and his friends. My own are silent, but only at first.

"I thought he was your boyfriend," Ronnie says, seeming genuinely confused.

"Shut up!" Allison hisses, swatting him on the arm.

"It's okay," I mumble, my face still flushed. "We haven't made it official yet."

"Oh." Ronnie clearly has more questions, but a nudge from Allison makes him stifle them.

I can only assume that she'll fill him in later. Which is fine. Even though I told Tim that I wouldn't, I did actually swear Ronnie and Leon to secrecy. They were cool about it, when I explained that he hadn't come out yet. Of course I failed to mention that Tim has a girlfriend. I don't like dwelling on that. Allison, on the other hand...

"Are you sure about this?" she asks when we're alone.

"About what?" I ask innocently while watching Ronnie walk away.

"Ben!"

I sigh and turn toward her. "Yes, I'm sure. Krista is just for show. She's not *really* his girlfriend."

"Try telling her that," Allison retorts.

"I would love to."

"I mean it! If she's his girlfriend, what does that make you?"

"The guy he's sleeping with," I say, intending for it to sound important. But once the words slip out of my mouth, I can't ignore how damning they are. "That means more than some silly title."

"I know it does to you," she says, not needing to twist the knife. I've already gotten the point. Her tone softens. "I'm worried you'll get hurt. That's all."

"I'm okay," I promise her. "Really," I insist when she continues to look concerned.

"Okay," she says before hugging me. "I'll see you after school?"

"Yeah."

We go our separate ways, but her words remain with me. *If she's his girlfriend, what does that make you?* I can't stop thinking about that as the day continues, especially when I return to the same hall for my physics class. I take my seat next to Danny, who keeps glancing over at me while we wait for the teacher to show up.

"There's a comic book convention this weekend," he says suddenly.

"Oh yeah?" I ask, grateful for the distraction.

"Yeah. I have a flyer." He starts digging through his backpack, his bouffant ginger hair wobbling on top of his head. "Wait until you see everyone who'll be there," he says while searching. "I'm going to get so many autographs. Look!"

He pulls out a crinkled flyer that includes a list of names, but none that mean anything to me. "That'll be cool," I say politely.

"You could go too," Danny says with an eager expression.

I hesitate, unsure if he's asking if I want to go with him, or if he's just excited and wants me to know about the convention. "I already have plans this weekend," I say with a grimace that he's welcome to interpret as apologetic.

"Oh." Danny seems crestfallen, making me wonder if he has any friends. "What are you doing?"

"Going on a date," I reply, mentally replacing myself with Krista so I was the one who leapt around Tim gleefully while proclaiming him to be the best boyfriend ever.

"With another guy?" Danny asks.

I take a deep breath, preparing myself for his reaction. He's obviously heard about me, like everyone else at school. Once I confirm the rumors, he might say something rude. Or worse, he might clam up and stop talking to me. Not that I look forward to these little chats, but being rejected sucks, even if you're not particularly fond of the other person.

"Yeah," I reply. "I'm going on a date with another guy."

"What's it like?" he asks.

Which isn't one of the usual responses. "Which part exactly?" I ask.

"Going on a date," Danny says hurriedly. "I've never been on one."

"Oh." I think about it. "Me neither. It'll be my first time."

Danny scratches his nose with such intensity that I expect the freckles to start flaking off. "Who's the other guy?"

"He goes to a different school," I say. "You've never heard of him."

"That makes sense." Danny takes the flyer back but doesn't put it away. "Do you ever watch this?" he asks, tapping the title of a sci-fi show. "It's really good!"

He launches into a lecture that is cut short when the class begins. I try not to feel sorry for people, because beneath the sympathy are assumptions that might not be true. Danny never having gone on a date, for instance. A lot of people would pity him for that, when in truth, he might be better off. I'm not sure, because love is more complicated than I ever imagined. Explosions are exciting, but nobody in their right mind wants to wander through a minefield. Allison sure seems to think I'm venturing into dangerous territory. And yet, I can't resist taking a few more steps, no matter the consequences.

I'm never quite sure when I'll see Tim. His plans vary so much that there isn't a single day I can count on. Usually, if he's available at all, he'll call and casually say something like *"I'm going for a run"* or *"Are you going to be home later?"* That tells me where to wait. Which is why I'm here, standing next to a playground in the middle of the night. A chilly breeze shakes the branches above, sending leaves spiraling down to keep me company.

The wind goes still as Tim appears, jogging toward me with a lopsided smile.

"Hey," he says when slowing to a stop. His head whips around to make sure we're alone. Only then does he lean in for a kiss. When I feel the heat radiating off his body, I'm tempted to cling to him.

"Do you go jogging the whole year?" I ask. "Because in a few months, you're going to find a snowman waiting for you instead. One who looks a lot like me."

"You're cold?" Tim takes my hands in his. "I bet I can warm you up again."

"Oh yeah?" I ask, already feeling a flush.

"Yeah."

He glances around once more before leading me across the grass and deeper into the shadows, where we resume kissing. I want nothing more than to run my hands down the impressive muscles of his torso to the prize in his shorts… But I can't help wondering if that's all he needs from me. Especially when he gets the rest from Krista. I place my hands on his chest to push him away. The firmness of his pecs doesn't help my resolve.

"Let's do something else," I suggest.

"Like what?" he asks with bedroom eyes.

I shrug. "Let's swing."

Tim scrunches up his face. "With who?" he asks, before glancing toward the playground. Then he laughs. "Oh right. Yeah. Okay! Race you there!"

He sprints across the playground. I give chase, despite knowing I can't win. I'm just happy that he's willing to have other sorts of fun with me. Soon we're seated on the swings, kicking and stretching to gain height. Tim really goes for it, nearly parallel with the ground at one point. I slow to watch, his body a brown and blue blur that streaks past me on occasion.

"Think I should jump?" he shouts.

"Yeah!" I respond. "That way I get to drive you to the hospital again!"

"Oh right."

His pendulum swings become shorter and shorter until we're idly wobbling next to each other.

"If I wasn't worried about my ankle," he says, "I totally would have jumped."

"I believe you," I reply, mostly in the hope that he'll never feel the need to prove himself.

Tim is grinning. "That was fun. I haven't been on a swing in ages."

"I'm a good time," I say leadingly, but the bedroom isn't my goal. "You should take me out on the town."

"You mean like a date?"

"Hey, now there's an idea!" I try to sound upbeat, although a little vulnerability escapes into my voice when I add, "Don't you think it's long overdue?"

His brow furrows up. "We've been on a date before."

"We have?"

"Yeah! When you took me to the beach. We kissed, I busted out some smooth lines about you being my butterfly, and we had dinner."

"That's your take," I say, fighting down a smile. "From my perspective, you said stuff in Spanish that I misinterpreted, some sorority girls crashed the party, and then I had a meltdown. Although I did like that kiss."

"Yeah?" he asks, pushing against the ground to swing closer.

I lean away so he can't reach me. "Where are you taking Krista this weekend?"

Tim rolls his eyes, but not at me, as it turns out. "Some vegan place. It sounds gross. And then afterwards, I have to see some chick flick that's supposed to be super sad. Why would anyone want to feel that way? I don't get it."

At last, a level playing field! "I was thinking a steakhouse. And afterwards there's that big movie about drag racing."

"For real?" Tim says, perking up. "Everyone else saw it when my ankle was jacked up. Bryce says it's really good."

"How about Saturday then?"

His grin falters. "That's when I'm taking Krista out."

"So reschedule," I say with a shrug.

"But I promised." At least he has the decency to look conflicted. "How does Sunday sound?"

"Like I'd be sloppy seconds," I say, shaking my head. "Friday night?"

"Darryl is having some of the guys over, but I could bail on them."

Thank goodness! Krista is bad enough. My ego would never recover if he chose his straight buddies over me. Again. "So we're on?" I ask.

Tim changes tactics. He grabs the chain of my swing to pull me closer. "We're on," he says, just before our lips meet.

Crisis averted. He might belong to her still, but only technically. As he takes my hand and leads me back toward the shadows, there's no doubt that he's mine.

"Sometimes I feel like your mother," Allison says as she buttons up my shirt.

"I can't imagine why," I reply while watching her work.

We both know that I'm capable of dressing myself, but the gesture is affectionate and the feeling is mutual.

"What do you think?" she asks, taking a step back so I can see myself in the mirror.

I'm fully capable of choosing the outfit I want to wear, but Allison has better taste than me, and tonight is important. My first real date! I'm happy with my appearance. The burgundy dress shirt she helped me shop for looks dressy but casual, thanks to the unbuttoned collar and dark-blue T-shirt beneath. My jeans are a similar navy hue, and I have a pair of maroon sneakers that are really going to bring it all together.

"Tim's going to forget that Krista exists," I say, running a hand through my freshly trimmed hair.

"He should've already," Allison replies. "I would have."

"Thanks," I say, giving her a hug, even if it means risking a few wrinkles. She's more than worth it. "Now go away. Tim will be here in ten minutes and I don't want him to know my secret."

Allison snorts. "That you were going to wear a suit jacket before I intervened?"

"A vest," I correct. "I thought it would be cute."

"It was," she murmurs. "Like a monkey playing cymbals. Is he picking you up from here?"

"Yeah."

"Can I watch from the front window?"

I laugh. "You're actually *worse* than my mom!"

Allison smiles. "Does she know yet?"

"She suspects." I check the clock. "Do you think I should wear cologne?"

"He strikes me as the type who will wear enough for the both of you."

I move past her to put on the maroon shoes, my pulse picking up in anticipation. Then we go downstairs to wait by the door.

"Do you think he'll bring you flowers?" Allison asks.

"I hope not," I reply. "It's not like my grandma died or something."

"Boys are so weird," she says, shaking her head.

We both perk up at the sound of an engine. I peek through the widow and see his car pulling into the driveway.

"This is it!" I turn to my friend. "Do I look okay? No booger in my nose?"

"You're perfect," Allison assures me. "Have fun!"

I give her another hug and slip outside. Tim is standing next to his car. He's wearing a black dress shirt with the sleeves rolled up over his thick forearms, which works for me, because I can already imagine groping them while we watch the movie. The jeans he's wearing end in black sneakers which look new, judging from the stark white laces.

"Hey," I say casually when approaching.

"Hey," he replies. Tim walks to the passenger-side door. Then he glances around before opening it for me. I can imagine Allison adding and subtracting points. "You look nice," he says.

"Thanks," I reply, hoping she was able to read his lips. And speaking of his mouth… "No kiss?"

Tim laughs. "Get inside. Then we'll see."

"All right."

He doesn't keep me waiting. Once Tim is in the driver's seat, he leans over. If she's watching us kiss, I hope Allison can tell how real this is. She thinks he should break up with Krista before we go any further. I agree for the most part, but compared to all the sex we've had recently, a date seems positively innocent.

"Do you know where we're headed?" I ask.

"Yeah," he replies, reversing out of the driveway. "I even made a reservation."

I'm tempted to roll down the window and shout *"He made a reservation!"* just so Allison knows how awesome this night is going to be, but I manage to restrain myself.

"I like the color combination you're wearing," Tim says, glancing over at me again with a certain intensity that I associate with his artistic side.

He's still tight-lipped about such things. I refuse to pry, since I figure that when he finally opens up, it'll be a sign that he trusts me. So for now, we're at a standoff. "You look great in black," I reply, loving the way it matches his hair and makes his brown skin pop.

A smile tugs at his cheek. He reaches for the stereo, which he often does after picking me up, so he can hear me sing. But he turns it back down again before I have a chance to start.

"Uh..." he says, easing off the accelerator. "Krista lives around here."

"Great! Let's stop by and say hello."

He manages a halfhearted chuckle. "Would you mind leaning your seat back? Like all the way?"

"What for?" I ask before it clicks. "Wait, you don't want to be seen with me?"

He grimaces. "It'll be hard to explain why we were driving around together."

"Not if you're honest."

"For real," he says. "What would my excuse be?"

"That's what I keep wondering when sneaking into your house at night."

"C'mon," Tim insists. "Her street is just ahead!"

I roll my eyes, unbuckle my seatbelt, and lean over until my head is in his lap. The center console is relatively flat, but still not comfortable to drape myself over.

"That's a way better idea," Tim says, shifting his hips.

"I thought you'd like it," I grumble. The truth is, I do too. It's the situation I hate.

"While you're down there…" Tim says leadingly.

"Not a chance!" I growl. "You're lucky I don't bite it off, you jerk!"

"Sorry, Benjamin," he replies.

"Are you though?"

"Yeah." His tone is soft. "I really am."

His fingers weave through my hair, and it feels so good that my anger abandons me. I love his touch too much. But I do muster a little more indignation. "How long am I supposed to stay down here?"

"Just until we're out of the neighborhood," he says.

He continues to stroke my hair, making me weaker by the second. By the time the coast is clear, I almost don't want to sit up. When I do, I'm surprised by the direction we're heading.

"I think you took a wrong turn," I say. "The steakhouse is the other way."

"We're going to a different one."

I check my mental map. The steakhouse is part of a chain, and there isn't another until the next town over. "Why drive so far?" I ask, despite already knowing the answer.

"Do you really want to be interrupted by anyone we know?" he asks.

"I guess not."

"Cool," he says, turning up the volume again. Then he smiles at me in expectation.

Those pearly white teeth are my kryptonite. I sing, the music filling me with everything I feel for him. He's right. I don't want anyone to intrude on our night together. When it's just us, the rest of the world ceases to exist. I'm more than willing to retreat into our private universe, although it does feel different this time, since we won't be entirely alone.

That becomes especially apparent when we enter a busy restaurant. Tim squirms while standing in line to talk to the woman behind the podium, the area around us lined with people waiting to be seated. When we're shown to our table, it's in the corner by a window.

"Here you go!" the server says cheerfully.

"Uh…" Tim says, not yet sitting. "We were supposed to have a booth."

Which are high-backed and provide much more privacy.

"I'm sorry," the server says, "but it's a busy night and our booths can sit up to six."

She places the menus on the small square table. "Someone will be with you shortly," she says before rushing off.

Tim eyes the chairs before his attention moves to the crowded dining room and then the window, where a group of people are walking by outside. This is getting ridiculous. "Oh for fuck's sake!" I snap. "You sit here." I pull out the chair with its back to the dining room. Then I plop down in the chair closest to the window. "If anyone sees you on their way in," I say, "I'll dive beneath the table in shame. Happy?"

Tim is quiet as he sits. I'm still fuming.

A waiter comes by to take our drink orders. Then I glare unseeing at the menu.

"Sorry," I hear Tim say. "It's just that…"

I lower the menu. His expression is glum.

"Wasn't any of this stuff hard for you?" he asks.

"What stuff?" I ask, my tone still clipped.

Tim shrugs. "You know."

He won't even say the word. Which does bring back a few memories. I sigh and set down the menu. "I was happy when I finally figured it out, but when my so-called friends bailed on me, I tried to go back to the way things were. I thought if I didn't let anyone see me being gay, then the rumors would die down. So if I saw a hot guy—in real life or even on TV—I would look away. I tried to change the way I walk and talk, thinking that it wasn't macho enough or something. I stopped singing, pretended to take an interest in sports, and was absolutely miserable."

Tim leans forward, hanging on my every word, and I feel a burst of sympathy for him because I can tell that he relates. "So what happened?"

"I figured something out." I reply. "Something really important. Do you know what's worse than people hating you?"

He shakes his head. "What?"

"Hating yourself."

Tim leans back, and I nearly laugh when he asks, "Are you sure?"

"Yes! Absolutely. I can't control what people think about me, but I do get to decide how I feel about myself. So when I made the choice to be who I really am, I got one of my best friends back. Me."

I expect him to roll his eyes. Instead he takes a deep breath. "Did it take you a while to—I don't know—accept it all?"

"Yes," I admit. I don't think he's trying to make a point. Tim seems genuinely curious. I remind myself that we've only known each other for a couple of months. This is still new to him. Granted, he's got me as a guide, and we've gone further than I ever could alone. But maybe I've been dragging him along to get to all the good stuff I've yearned for, like sex, without giving him the same foundation I built for myself.

"What's more important to you?" I ask. "Being happy or making other people happy?"

Tim thinks about it. "I honestly don't know."

"That's okay," I assure him. "Let's flip it around. What matters more, your mom being happy, or your mom making *you* happy."

"I want her to be happy," Tim says instantly.

"Good! How do you think she would answer the same question?"

"She'd want me to be happy," he says before hesitating. "But I don't think she'd understand."

"Understand what?"

"Why I would risk going to Hell."

That makes it more complicated for sure. I didn't have to worry about religion being an obstacle with my family. His guilty expression makes me wonder if it's also an issue for him. "Do you believe that?" I ask. "Do you think you'll go to Hell for being gay?"

"I'm not gay," Tim says. "I like girls."

Oof! We really do have a long way to go. Maybe he's bisexual, which is fine, but I've never heard him use the word to describe himself. "Do you think you'll go to Hell for lying with another man?" I ask, intentionally paraphrasing the Christian bible. "Or that you deserve to be put to death?"

"That wouldn't be my choice!" Tim splutters.

"What about me?" I press. "I'm not turning back from this. If you got to play god for a day, what would my fate be? Would you strike me down in wrath? Or turn me straight?"

His handsome features wince in sympathy before he shakes his head. "No. I wouldn't change you for the world, Benjamin. I like you too much."

My heart is thudding, but I don't get to respond, because we're interrupted by the arrival of our drinks. We explain that we need more time, and as Tim's gaze repeatedly seeks me out from over the menu, I decide that he does too. For now, I'll try to be a little more patient.

So when we get to the cinema and he suggests I find us some good seats while he waits in line for popcorn and drinks, I don't call him on the reason why. And when he joins me in the back row and takes note of every person who walks into the theater, I don't bother pointing out that most people in our school have already seen this movie. In fact, I don't think it'll be showing for much longer, since most of the seats remain unoccupied. When the movie starts, we have the entire row to ourselves. Tim relaxes visibly. Then he groans.

"I hate previews," he says. "They always last so damn long."

"Agreed," I reply, cringing at the terrible music. My attention wanders to one of my favorite views. Tim has a great profile. His nose is strong and angular, like a Roman sculpture. The rest of him is nicely chiseled too. I love the way his chest presses against the dress shirt. I'd like to follow the trail of buttons, undoing each until they reach his jeans, and I wouldn't stop there.

I lean close to him and whisper, "How fast can you come?"

He looks over at me in shock. "What?"

"How long would it take?"

He shrugs. "On my own? Like, if I'm in a hurry?"

"Yeah."

"A few minutes."

"What about right now?"

He stares at me. Then he laughs. "You're crazy."

"I'm dead serious. Whip it out."

He looks around, seeming to realize just how alone we are. Groups of people are scattered in the rows ahead of us, but none of them are likely to notice, even if they all stood suddenly and turned around. Tim starts scrabbling at his jeans to get them open. Once they are, he looks around once more before lifting his hips and pulling the front of his underwear down, letting the elastic band rest beneath his balls. I'm pleased to see that he's already at full mast. I start with my hand, feeling apprehensive about the unseeing audience. Nobody catches the scent of spontaneous sex, so I slide out of my seat and position myself between his legs before I take him in my mouth.

From then on, all I can think about is earning my reward. I'm vaguely aware of the previews going by. I can get myself off in a few minutes too, so if I'm not mistaken, he's taking his time and enjoying himself. When one of those loud demos that highlight the theater's sound system starts to play, his hand pushes down on my head as his hips begin to buck. I taste the salty sweetness of his come and refuse to let a single drop go to waste. I'm still slurping greedily a minute later as he quietly whimpers and attempts to push me away.

"Benjamin!" he hisses at last, pleading with me to stop.

I swallow and return to my seat. Then I take a sip of soda, batting my eyelashes at him innocently as I suck on the straw.

He laughs, and when the movie's opening theme starts to play, leans close to whisper, "Need me to return the favor?"

"Nope," I say, shaking my head with a smile. "I'm happy."

For more than one reason: I'm on a date with my dream guy. I feel like we understand each other better, thanks to the conversation we had at dinner. And I absolutely loved getting to blow him. There's another perk too, one that didn't occur to me until now, but as I watch him grin and toss a kernel of popcorn into his mouth, I know that Krista won't be able to compete. Not in a million years.

CHAPTER FOURTEEN

Allison and I take turns sighing dreamily as we drift down the hallway to my next class. We're both falling in love. The symptoms are all too obvious: drawn-out exhalations, random giggles, and spontaneous declarations that are completely off topic.

"Tim walked me to my door after our date," I say without being prompted. "And he kissed me, even though the porch light was on."

"Aww!" Allison says, clutching at her heart. "That's so sweet!"

"Yeah," I say with a guffaw.

We take turns sighing as we round a corner.

"Ronnie wants a big family," Allison informs me out of the blue.

"What he's *really* saying is that he wants to have lots of sex," I tease.

"Hey, he's good with kids!" she says, shoving me playfully. "You should've seen him at the park we went to. When a little boy scraped his knee and started crying, Ronnie ran right over to cheer him up. He didn't even hesitate."

"That *is* hot," I admit.

"He's got a younger brother and sister." Allison smiles. "I've been trying to think of what we'll call our kids."

"Tim is a great name for a boy," I suggest.

"Uh-huh. And if we have a girl, I'll name her Krista."

"Shut up!" I laugh while checking our surroundings. "We have to be careful. She's in economics with me."

"That's right!" Allison says. "Oh my god, that must be awkward."

I shrug. "We sit on opposite sides of the room."

"And on the same guy's lap." She sticks out her tongue.

"Not true," I reply with exaggerated confidence. "He only comes to *my* hive when needing honey." I drop the act. "And um… I still haven't sat on anything."

"Me neither," Allison admits. "But lately I've been thinking that Ronnie might be the one."

My mouth falls open. "Are you going to sleep with him?"

"Not anytime soon," Allison replies. "But he sure is sweet. I'm thinking of introducing him to my dad."

I wince at the idea. "Are you sure? That's never gone well before."

"I know," she says with a grimace.

Her dad is very protective of her. When it comes to other guys, at least. I still remember the time she got in trouble for sneaking out and ended up with circular bruises on her arms from where he grabbed her too hard. That sort of thing keeps me up at night. Allison claims that he only gets like that when he's been drinking too much, but his benders seem to happen with increasing frequency.

"It'll be okay," she says, noticing my concern as we stop near my classroom door. "Ronnie is a charmer. He'll win my dad over."

"Just have him take you on a date to the zoo first," I suggest.

"Why?"

"So he can practice taming a lion. The meanest, hungriest one they have."

"My dad is more like a grizzly bear," Allison says before nudging me. I follow her gaze to where Krista is walking with a group of cheerleaders. She detaches herself from her friends, all smiles until she has to walk past us into the classroom. Krista's expression sours as she brushes at the side of her hair and uses her hand to intentionally block us from view.

"Ugh!" Allison says when we're alone again. "Do you realize that there's only one degree of separation between your lips and hers?"

"Don't remind me," I mutter.

"Maybe it's time for an ultimatum."

I shake my head. "It won't mean anything if I force it. He just needs more time."

"He'll get a swift kick in the butt from me if he's two-timing you both," Allison says.

She's not trying to rain on my parade. The concern we feel for each other comes from the heart. I feel a little irritated anyway after we hug and say goodbye, because experience has taught me that Allison is usually right. Although being with Tim feels so good that I'm willing to delude myself. I guess that's been the theme since the beginning. And it sure has paid off! More than I ever expected.

I take my seat and zone out while staring through a drizzle-speckled window. The gray day begins to match my mood. Most of the teacher's lecture is lost on me as I imagine not having to share Tim with anyone. No beautiful blond cheerleaders or regressively religious parents. I make him an orphan in my mind, one who needs all the love he lost replaced by a single person. I could do that for him. If only he would let me. Wait, what if I already don't give him enough? Maybe he needs Krista more than he lets on.

"Once everyone has chosen a partner," the teacher says, "discuss which topic you'd like to report on for this project and let me know."

Everyone around me is standing up. I literally have no idea what I'm supposed to be doing, other than choosing a partner. Which gives me an idea. I push away from my desk and hustle over to Krista, who remains seated, like she expects people to come to her. Anyone but yours truly, judging from the way she leans left and right in an attempt to see past me.

"Hey," I say while intentionally blocking her view. "Let's be partners."

Krista stares at me in disbelief. "You can't be serious!"

"Why not?" I challenge.

"Because you're—" She makes a *pfft* noise and rolls her eyes. "You wouldn't understand."

She tries to see past me again. I glance over my shoulder and notice a girl approaching while looking uncertain. "Too late!" I inform her.

"No it's not!" Krista says, getting to her feet. She tries to push past me.

I keep getting in the way, making it seem like an accident. "Oops! Sorry about that. You go left and I'll go right. No, *your* right, not mine." We keep dancing like this until Krista snaps.

"Would you stop!" she cries.

"Is everything okay?" the teacher asks.

"Yeah," I say, turning around. Everyone else has paired up already. Krista must have noticed too, because I hear her groan behind me. "We were just trying to figure out where to sit." I pivot to face my new partner. "So… Your place or mine?"

Those words come to haunt me. I'm standing outside Krista's house after school. I had no idea how involved the project would be. Now I understand why she was so averse to working with me. I figured it would be the sort of project we could get done during class. Had I known we'd need to spend this much time together, I would have steered clear. Still, I *am* curious. Tim has probably stood exactly where I am now, his finger pressing the same doorbell.

I size up the house while waiting for someone to answer. A butler maybe, because the place stinks of money. The yard is huge with lush landscaping, the abnormally tall windows of the steeple-roofed house gleaming in the dwindling sunlight. When the door swings open, Krista looks even smaller than usual against the backdrop of a massive entryway. She pokes her head out to look up and down the street, as if mortified by the possibility of someone seeing me. Which makes her a better match for Tim than I care to admit.

"Hi!" I say, finally drawing her attention.

"Hurry up and get inside," she snaps.

I can't help wondering if I'd be more likely to excuse her behavior if she was a hot Latino guy. Or if I was into girls, because she's undeniably pretty, even when scowling. I catch a glimpse of a large living room deeper in the house and can hear a TV blaring with the *beep boom bang* of a video game.

"Hurry up and kill him!" a juvenile voice yells. "Your energy bar is low!"

"I'm trying, I'm trying!" a squeaky voice shouts back.

"C'mon," Krista says, stomping toward a curved staircase. "Let's go to my room."

"Why yes, I would like something to drink," I say sarcastically while following her.

"What? Oh. I have my own fridge. You can have something from there."

"Fancy, fancy," I murmur under my breath.

I thought Tim's parents were rich, but their house isn't so different from mine. Sure the rooms are larger and more extravagantly decorated. And my dad certainly doesn't have his own den or wet bar. But this house is in another league. I crane my neck to peer into each room we pass, knowing that Allison will want details. That, and I'm shamelessly nosey.

When we finally reach her room, my eyes need to adjust to an onslaught of pink. The bedspread, curtains, rugs, lampshades, chairs, and even the wallpaper are all various shades of the color. With some lavender thrown in to break it up a bit. The entire room is ridiculously girly. And I kind of love it.

"We'll have to work in here," Krista says, walking over to a large white desk. "My step-brothers are way too annoying to get anything done downstairs."

"Step-brothers?" I repeat. Perhaps because I expected perfect people in a perfect house to have perfect lives.

"Yes," she says a little tersely. "My mom got remarried a few years ago. *Again.*" Krista squats next to a mini-fridge. "I've got water and unsweetened iced tea."

"Oh. Uh… Water is fine. Hey, is that a private bathroom over there? Or just a really big closet?"

"Both," Krista replies, handing me a bottle of water.

"Thanks."

"Pull up a seat," she commands before sitting at her desk.

I glance around and notice a chair in the corner that is basically a round cushion on a folding stand. The fabric is fuzzy. I can hardly wait to try it. I drag the chair over to her desk and sink into pink plushness.

"I hope you understand this stuff better than I do," Krista says, pulling out her copy of the economics book.

"Let's find out," I reply.

That's what we do for the next half hour, which feels surreal, because every so often I'll glance around and be reminded of whose room I'm in. And who she's dating. Especially when I notice a photo taped to the wall that's surrounded by red construction paper hearts of various sizes. From here, all I can see is dark hair and bronze skin. I'm certain it's a photo of Tim. I'm desperate to look at it up close.

"Ugh!" Krista tosses her pen down in frustration. "I still don't get it. I feel so stupid!"

This is my chance to get revenge and make her feel crappy about herself, like her little gang has done to me for years. Although I don't remember Krista calling me any names. She's made it clear that I'm beneath her notice, but then again, she treats Allison the same way and probably most other people too. So maybe it's nothing personal.

"Inflation is a very confusing concept," I assure her.

"This is why I wanted to work with Marcy instead of you," Krista complains. "She's practically a genius."

"I'm sure we can figure it out together," I say. "What part is tripping you up?"

"All of it!" Krista scrunches up her face. "If inflation is such a big problem, why don't companies lower their prices? They're just being greedy!"

"You know what? I think you understand it just fine."

Krista blinks. "Really?"

"Yeah! Rich companies expect consumers to pay more, but workers don't automatically get a raise when inflation happens."

"Doesn't that mean people can't shop as much?" Krista asks.

"Yeah. But I guess the big corporations would rather squeeze money out of the people who still have any left."

"That's so lame!"

"I agree. Now we just have to figure out a way of demonstrating it to the class."

Krista rubs her temples. "My brain is fried. Let's take a break."

"Okay."

I stand and stretch before casually ambling over to the photo I noticed earlier.

"Who's this?" I ask, as if he didn't already occupy my every thought and dream, because it is indeed Tim, flashing that gorgeous smile of his while leaning against a tree. The weather must have been warmer when the photo was taken. He's wearing a sleeveless shirt, his bulging biceps on full display. I don't possess a single photo of him. I'm already tempted to steal this one.

"That's my boyfriend," Krista says, her tone changing completely. I can hear the smile in her voice. "Timmy."

"Timmy?" I repeat incredulously.

"What's wrong with that?" she demands.

I turn to face her and shrug. "Sounds too much like a little boy's name. Especially for such a hot guy."

"Oh my god!" Krista says, placing a hand over her chest as if scandalized.

"What?" I ask with a chuckle. "Don't pretend to be surprised. Your friends remind me that I'm gay all the time. And anyway, I stand by my claim. Tim is way hotter than most guys at our school. Starting with those eyes."

"Aren't they gorgeous?" Krista enthuses. "I could stare into them all day."

"Does he let you?" I ask in genuine curiosity.

"Of course! We do everything together." She blanches at her own statement. "Wait, that sounds dirty."

"There's nothing wrong with sex," I say, my mouth going dry. I need to know if they're sleeping together, because according to him, they most definitely are not. "It's perfectly natural."

"That's *not* what I meant," Krista says. "I only mean, when we're together, that he's so…" She doesn't find the words to describe him, which is fine, because I'm not sure I could either. "I really love him," she finishes with a halfhearted shrug. "I'm just scared to tell him that."

This whole conversation is way too relatable. "How come?" I pry.

"Because he's a boy. They hate that sort of thing."

"I don't."

"Yes, but you're not *really* a boy."

"Gosh, thanks," I say without a hint of irony.

Krista peers at me curiously. "But you understand how guys think. Don't you?"

"I have some experience, yeah."

She nibbles the nail of a delicate finger. Then she walks over and sits on the edge of the bed, angling her body toward me. "Can I ask you a question?"

"I have a feeling you're going to anyway."

"It's about boys."

"That's literally my favorite subject," I say gleefully, grabbing my bottle of water and joining her on the bed.

"Okay. How soon do they expect a girl to…" She trails off.

I hazard a guess, "Have sex?"

"Yes," she says, seeming relieved. "How long will a boy wait?"

"As long as you make him. It's completely up to you."

"It's just…" Her blue eyes are vulnerable when considering me. "Can you keep a secret?"

"Yes," I say without promising that I will.

"Lately he seems… I don't know. Off."

"Really?"

She nods. "He's still nice to me. But I can tell something is wrong."

"What makes you think that?" I ask as casually as possible.

"He used to kiss me a lot more. Now he only does that when I ask him to. And when we go on a date, he seems bored. So I was thinking of showing him my boobs."

I'm taking a sip when she says this and water nearly shoots out my nose. "Sorry!" I gasp. "Swallowed wrong." I clear my throat. "I don't think you should."

Krista shakes her head. "How come?"

"Because that's not a good way to make someone like you. Trust me, I've been there. Personally, I'd only show my boobs to a guy who likes me for who I am." I briefly consider my past. "Unless I was really excited to show him my boobs and didn't care if he liked me or not."

She crinkles her petite little nose in disapproval. "You're even weirder than I thought you would be."

"You get what I'm saying though, right? Having sex with a guy won't make him like you if he doesn't already. He might enjoy the sex, but that's not what you want. Or at least, not the only thing you want."

"But what if I lose him to a girl who is willing to put out?"

I shrug. "Good riddance. When you imagine your dream guy, is he the sort of person who pushes you to have sex before you're ready? Or is he willing to wait until the time is right for both of you?"

She still seems uncertain. I almost feel sorry for her. Especially when I glance around the room again, because there isn't a single painting on the wall. I bet she doesn't know about Tim's artistic side.

"Most guys expect you to do *something*," Krista says.

"Then fake it," I suggest, attempting to lighten the mood. "Blow up a couple of balloons and shove them up your shirt. Let him squeeze those instead."

"That's it!" Krista says, leaping to her feet.

"I was kidding!"

"I know." She rushes over to her desk and opens a drawer. When she turns around, something made of latex is dangling between two pinched fingers, and thank goodness it isn't a condom. "Balloons!" Krista declares. "We can use them in our presentation. That's like… literal inflation!"

I laugh. "Great idea! Let's get back to it."

I stand and glance at the photo on her wall once more. Tim

is smiling at me like I did a good job of safely navigating the conversation. So why do I feel the stirrings of guilt?

I'm sitting cross-legged on Tim's bed while biting my bottom lip in anticipation. When he called to tell me his parents went out to dinner, I came running. Tim ordered pizza for us, which we ate at the dining room table, candlelight and all. The vibe was more goofy than romantic. I'm just so happy when I'm around him that it makes me giddy. He seems to be in a good mood too, considering that he's currently humoring my request.

"Hurry up and come out of the closet!" I shout.

"Almost ready," is his muffled response.

I'm staring at his closet door when it finally swings open. The breath catches in my throat as Tim saunters out dressed in a baseball uniform. The shirt and pants are navy fabric with white piping. Red socks pulled up to his shins match the half-length sleeves of the undershirt. The uniform does exactly what I'd like to do by gripping his body.

"This is from my old school," Tim says, pulling at the front of the shirt, "so it's a little small. I must have gotten bigger."

"You and me both," I murmur, shifting my legs out from under me to make room for my swelling erection. "So are you a pitcher or a catcher?"

"I'm definitely a pitcher," Tim says firmly, picking up on the innuendo.

"Are you really?" I ask while trying to visualize him out on the field. "Like for real. Or does everyone on the team take turns throwing the ball?"

Tim stares at me. Then he laughs. "You really don't know?"

"Maybe I'm just testing you."

"Uh-huh. No, we don't take turns. I'm mostly a center fielder."

"So you're somewhere in the middle?" I say leadingly.

Tim doesn't take the bait. "It's because I'm the fastest guy on the team. Just wait until you see me play. I'm the king of stealing bases."

"So how come you're not in track and field?"

I catch the longing on his face before he manages to hide it away. "My dad is into baseball."

"And he expects you to follow in his footsteps?"

Tim looks even more uncomfortable. "Nah. He never played."

"So he's living through you vicariously? That's even worse! My dad loves stage magicians, but he doesn't expect me to start pulling rabbits out of my hat."

Tim shrugs, as if it doesn't matter.

"What about college?" I press.

He rolls his eyes. "Don't remind me."

"You're going to keep playing? Isn't that when it gets serious?"

"Not if I don't get a scholarship," Tim says, standing up a little straighter. "I haven't yet. On purpose."

"Really?"

"Yeah," he says with a chuckle. "My dad will still expect me to try out, but I'll probably blow that too. I don't want to make a career of it, you know?"

I perk up at this news, encouraged that he was going against his parents' wishes before we met. Although not enough to enroll in a sport he actually cares about. "So what do you really want to do?"

His eyes dart to the wall, in the direction of the painting, before returning to mine. "Track and field might be cool, like you said."

"Yeah, but for a living?"

He shrugs again. "What are you gonna do?"

I prefer it when I get to ask the questions. "I enjoy singing, but I'd hate to be famous."

"How come?"

"Call it a hunch," I say wryly, "but I don't think I'd like total strangers knowing who I am."

"Because of the gay thing?"

"Because people are assholes," I retort. "Myself included. I love celebrity gossip. Hey, maybe that's what I'll do! I like to write."

"Oh yeah?" Tim says, sounding genuinely interested. "Like stories and stuff?"

"Yup! Or song lyrics. None of it is very good."

"Can I see some anyway?"

Suddenly I understand why he's so tightlipped about his art. "Yeah, but only if you promise to hang on to your baseball uniform, even after you stop playing."

Tim looks confused until a slow grin unfurls across his face. "You like how it looks on me, huh?" he says, puffing up his chest.

"Yes," I admit. "The few times I watched baseball, all I paid attention to were the butts and bulges."

"Don't be too impressed," Tim says, grabbing his package to adjust it. "Those guys were wearing cups. Mine's all real, baby."

"On second thought," I say while staring openly, "maybe I'd rather see you *out* of that uniform."

"I might need some help," he suggests with bedroom eyes.

I slide out of bed and kiss him while unbuttoning the jersey. I wish he didn't have the undershirt on so I could see his muscles. I pull up on it, exposing his abs. Tim is already working at his pants. As soon as the top button is undone, I slip my hand inside his underwear, feeling the hot firmness of his cock… and another pang of guilt. I try to ignore it by kissing him again, but when he pulls back to grin at me, it reminds me too much of the photo on Krista's wall.

"Maybe we should go for a home run this time," Tim says.

I pull my hand out of his pants. "I would, but your wife is watching us from the bleachers."

"Huh?"

"Krista," I say.

Tim snorts. "She'll never find out."

"Yeah, but *I'll* know," I say, no longer hiding the guilt I feel. "If we're going to keep doing this, I think you should break up with her."

Tim eyes me before shaking his head. "You know why I can't do that."

"Because of your parents. Have they ever met her?"

"No. But they've heard her talking to me on the phone and stuff. They know she's real."

"Perfect. Then you don't need her anymore. Let them think you're still dating, even after you aren't anymore."

He rolls his eyes. "It's not that simple."

"Sure it is. What do you need her for?"

"How about prom photos? My mom is obsessed. She didn't get any last year, for obvious reasons. My parents are going to think it's weird if I don't go with the girl I've been dating all year. Unless you want to throw on a wig."

I'm tempted to laugh, but it's actually a valid point. "So we'll invent a reason for you guys to break up before then."

"Or I could just keep dating her," Tim says, his brow furrowing. "That way it's bulletproof."

"Yeah, but she's…" A real human being. Working with her on the project backfired. It was easier not to care when I still had a two-dimensional impression of Krista. I can't pretend to actually like her, but I know now that she bleeds when pricked.

"What?" Tim prompts.

"Krista is going to be really hurt if she finds out about us. Lying to your parents isn't nearly as bad as cheating on someone, right? I'm not being judgmental here. We're both doing this to her."

Tim's forehead creases in thought. Then his eyes go wide when we hear a distant rumble.

"Oh shit!" he says, tearing at his clothes to take them off. "My parents are home early!"

"I don't think we have time for a quickie," I say while watching him undress.

He doesn't laugh. "They won't understand why I'm wearing my old uniform. And you've gotta get out of here!" The rumble stops for a moment, but it won't be long before the garage door goes down. Which is a shame, because that's what I was hoping to do.

"Use the front door," Tim says, attempting to push me out of the room. The pants around his ankles make him stumble. "Fuckin' run!"

"All right, all right," I say, distracted by the jock strap he's wearing.

We hear the garage door rumble again.

"Or maybe you should hide instead," he says. "Get in the closet."

"Not for anyone!" I snap. "Even you!"

I open his bedroom door and listen, hearing muted voices, but they don't sound close. I've still got time. "Better tell them you just got back from a jog," I say to Tim, since he's looking hot and flustered. "In case they hear the front door."

And with that, I take the stairs two at a time and see the light in the garage switch off as I'm sprinting across the driveway.

I'll come back later tonight to finish what we started. Although when I slow to a walk on the next block over, the idea doesn't sit right with me. I still want his body. And his heart. That hasn't changed. But something has to, because I can no longer pretend that Krista's feelings don't matter.

CHAPTER FIFTEEN

I'm standing in front of my economics class with Krista at my side. I'm doing most of the talking, like we planned. A few days ago I stopped by her house for a trial run. The photo of Tim was even more alluring than the first time, because I haven't seen him since we talked about everything. It's only been a couple days, but it feels like an eternity. I force myself to focus on the presentation before I start saying his name over and over again or something crazy.

"The more that inflation continues to swell," I tell the class as Krista slowly blows up a balloon, "the less purchasing power money has. If workers demand higher wages so they can continue to feed their families and pay their bills, companies might raise prices even higher to compensate. If this cycle continues unchecked, it gets really bad, because it can lead to hyperinflation." Most of the class is watching Krista now while grimacing in anticipation of the inevitable explosion. "That means prices could double every single day, like they did in Germany in the early twenties. And if that happens, the entire economy goes—"

POP!

Most people jump in their seats, even though they knew it was coming. Some of them laugh nervously. I'm thrilled with Krista's timing, but she hasn't said the next line like she's supposed to. When I look over at her, I notice her chin trembling. I tear my eyes away and decide to cover for her.

"That's why it's important for governments to—"

"Waaaaaaah!"

The pathetic wail is coming from Krista, who covers her face and rushes from the room, the door slamming shut behind her.

"Er…" I say, looking to the teacher for help, but she seems just as confused. All I know for sure is that this presentation is a big part of our final grade. "That's why it's important for governments to enact fiscal policies," I continue, "like instituting price controls or raising interest rates. Because it's easier to deflate a balloon than it is to put it back together again."

"Very nice!" the teacher says. "Would you like to check on your partner?"

"Uh…" I glance at the classroom door with unease. Don't they have school counselors for this sort of thing? Then again, if the reason she's upset has anything to do with Tim… "Sure," I say. "Be right back."

I leave the classroom and find Krista sniffling in the hallway. She looks up at me sullenly before scowling. "Is everyone laughing at me?" she asks.

"No. I think they were surprised, that's all." I walk over to her and raise a hand, intending to pat her on the shoulder reassuringly, but it feels so wrong for us that I end up placing it on the wall. "What's going on?" I ask while leaning casually, like an adult trying to be cool.

"It's Timmy," Krista says, wiping at her eyes. "I don't know what to think anymore!"

I shift and rest my back against the wall, which feels less awkward. "What happened?"

"He came to see me last night and…" She swallows before continuing. "We were in my room."

I'm hanging on her every word. What if he broke up with her? It'll be so hard not to smile!

"We were making out—" she continues, which is a real gut punch until she adds, "but he didn't seem into it. So I took off my blouse, and he looked like he was interested in seeing more, so I undid my bra…" Her chin starts to tremble again. Then she shakes her head while glowering at me. "Why am I telling you any of this?"

"I just have one of those faces," I say. "So anyway, how did he react?"

"He stared for a second. Then he said I should put my clothes back on. I felt so rejected!"

I'm both relieved that it didn't go further, and sympathetic to her pain, because he really bungled it. Tim should have complimented her first or maybe felt her up a little. Then again… "Sometimes guys aren't ready," I tell her. "Everyone assumes we are, because we're so obsessed with sex, but it's not always true. So it would be like if he whipped his thing out and asked you to touch it."

Krista blinks. "Do you think I should have offered?"

"No!" I say, wishing she would have listened to my advice in the first place. "But if you didn't feel like touching his wiener, that wouldn't automatically mean that you don't like him or don't find him attractive, right? Maybe he doesn't know what to do with a girl's boobs. I sure don't!"

Krista laughs and wipes at her nose. "You think that was it?"

"Probably. He wouldn't be your boyfriend if he didn't think you were hot. There has to be some other reason. I don't think it's you."

"So what should I do?" she asks.

I press my lips together, not wanting to heal a relationship that I'd like to see fall apart. But this would be a bad way for it to end. "Talk to him about it," I say.

It's good advice that I plan on taking. I need to talk to Tim, as soon as possible, because this mess has only gotten worse. I assure Krista that nobody thought it was funny that she ran from the room. Then I suggest we return to class, because I can't handle getting any friendlier with her. The situation is already too weird, but with any luck, it'll soon be over.

Tim's car is parked between streetlights, the interior dark except for the dashboard, which creates just enough of a glow for me to see the outline of his impressive body. And how handsome he looks. Tim's hair has gotten longer. He's brushing it to the side now instead of gelling it into spikes. The dark hair resting on his forehead makes his silver eyes stand out even more. I give in when he leans over to kiss me, even though I promised myself not to do this. I wanna suck him off and go back to my place so we can cuddle.

Instead I gently push him away. "Have you talked to Krista today?" I ask.

"Yeah, of course. I saw her at school."

He leans toward me again. I press my back against the passenger-side door, the discomfort making it easier to resist him. "Did she tell you what happened during our presentation?"

Tim shakes his head. "She hasn't said much about it at all. Only that…"

"What?"

He grimaces, as if I won't like it.

"Trust me," I assure him. "I'll be fine."

"She said that you're nerdy enough that she'll probably get a good grade."

I roll my eyes and question why I care about her feelings at all. But even if I decided that Krista deserved to be cheated on, it wouldn't make me feel better about the situation. "She had a breakdown," I inform him before launching into the details. Including everything she said in the hall.

Tim leans back in his seat with a groan. "When she flashed me, I panicked!"

"Yeah, but what did you *want* to do?" I press.

He looks uncomfortable.

I resist a sigh, already suspecting the answer. "I won't get mad," I assure him.

"She has gorgeous tits," Tim says. "I wanted to touch them but…" He glances at me. "I thought it would upset you."

I feel a surge of affection for him. He resisted cheating on me! Then again, I'm the guy he's already cheating with. "This is getting crazy."

"Yeah," Tim says. "I'm not sure what to do." He considers me wearily. "I know you want me to break up with her—"

"Not now!" I splutter. "At least, not so soon after what happened. That'll raise all sorts of questions. But you do need to come up with a reason why you didn't want more from her."

"Like what?"

I think about it. "Your family is Catholic. Tell her that you're really religious or something."

Tim's eyebrows shoot up. "Think that will work?"

"It does on me," I grumble.

"What's that supposed to mean?"

"That I know you struggle with it."

He shakes his head. "No I don't."

"Really?" I ask evenly. "Answer one question for me, and be honest."

"Fine."

"Are you straight?"

Tim's shrugs. "Yeah."

"Then what am I?"

"The exception to the rule," he replies so quickly that he must have comforted himself with the thought previously.

I don't believe it though. Not at all. It's a great big world. Surely there's another guy out there besides me who would do it for him, and that makes him bisexual.

I shift in my seat so I'm facing the front again, sad, guilty, and confused. Why is this so difficult for him? We must feel the same way. Or maybe not, considering how much he still hides from me.

"Benjamin," Tim says. He places his hand on my chin, turning my face toward his. Then he kisses me again, his gaze intense when he pulls back. "Isn't that all that really matters?"

"Yeah," I admit. I can live with his denial. I can help him figure it all out. I can wait until he's ready to open himself to me completely… "But not with her in the picture."

He leans back. "What are you saying?"

"That we have to stop. For now." I hate the words. Enough that I take his hand, even though it sends mixed signals. "We can still hang out. But we can't…" I make myself let go of him and don't attempt to talk around the lump in my throat.

"Her mom invited me over next week," Tim says with a sigh, "for Thanksgiving. And you said I shouldn't dump her so soon after—"

"Fuck what I said!" I swallow against rising emotion. "Just break up with her. As soon as you can. Okay?"

Tim presses his lips together. "You were right though. I don't need another breakup to explode in my face. I was looking forward to that dinner too, because my parents have plans of their own."

"You can come over to my house," I tell him. "You can hang out with me and my friends if yours reject you. It'll be fine. Just get it over with."

Tim's face twists up. "First you say I shouldn't dump her, and now you're cutting me off if I don't! Make up your goddamn mind!"

"Fine." I huff a few times, trying to calm myself down. "I want you to leave her."

Tim is already shaking his head. "I don't see why anything has to change."

"Because it hurts!" I snarl. And for once, I'm not talking about Krista's feelings.

I cross my arms over my chest and stare out the window on my side of the car. I don't trust myself to look at him.

"Are you mad at me?" I hear him ask.

I think about it and sigh, because he didn't do this to me. I walked into the situation willingly. "No," I say hoarsely. "You don't want to know how I feel about you. It'll only make it more complicated."

I feel his hand on my leg, squeezing affectionately or possessively, I don't know which. But I like it. I place my hand over his and let it linger there a moment. Then I release him and reach for the door.

"Hey! Where are you going?"

I finally look over and see concern in his eyes, but I don't know if it's for me or his reputation. Not that it matters. Of all the things I'd like to say to him, goodbye isn't one of them. "We'll catch up some other time."

I push against the door and stumble out onto the sidewalk, bundling up against the chill while already missing his heat.

I don't usually consider myself a gloomy person, but it's hard not to feel down after the high of getting to be with my dream guy. Everything has gone back to the way it was before I met him, like I awoke from a dream or maybe a fevered delusion. We haven't seen each other since we talked about Krista. I've been purposely avoiding Tim, because being around him would come with unbearable temptation that I would surely buckle under. And really, would that be so bad? So I felt a little guilty and slighted at times. At least we were together. Now all I feel is sorrow.

I'm so starved for him that I decide to deviate from my usual route at school. Seeing him will make the hunger worse, but I'm willing to risk it. And yet, when we do cross paths, I quickly lose my appetite. Krista is clinging to Tim's arm, like she always does. That's not surprising. When he notices me… Tim looks forward again, his gaze steady, as if I don't matter to him. I stop and stare, waiting for any sign that I'm wrong. He doesn't wink or smirk like he used to, or give any indication that I should call. Tim breezes by with his friends, and I'm left wondering if I made a mistake.

I'm still not sure the next day, but when my best friend picks me up in the morning, I learn that love has been wreaking havoc in both our lives.

"Finally!" she says the second I'm in her car. "I've been dying to talk to you!"

"Sorry," I reply. "I had my phone turned off." I hadn't wanted to hear from Tim while simultaneously hoping he'd come over uninvited. Speaking of which… "How come you didn't stop by?"

"Because I'm grounded," Allison says. "I couldn't have called you anyway. My dad broke my phone."

Her face is so drawn that I instantly forget my own troubles. "What happened? I thought you were hanging out with Ronnie."

"I was," Allison says. She places a trembling hand to her forehead before returning it to the wheel. "We messed up. You know how I usually have him drop me off down the street?"

"Uh-oh." I can already see where this is going.

"We weren't thinking," she continues. "Well actually, I *did* think about it when Ronnie parked in front of my house, but then he got out in a hurry to open the door for me. Which was so sweet that I didn't want to tell him to get back in and keep driving."

"Your dad saw," I interject, not able to stand the suspense. "Didn't he?"

Allison nods, her expression strained. "He caught us kissing. It was so bad, Ben! My dad was drunk and came hollering out of the house. Ronnie started walking over to him, like he was going to introduce himself, until my dad threw a whisky glass. He didn't get Ronnie, but it did hit his car."

"Oh shit! Was the damage bad?"

"I don't know. Ronnie got back in and drove off, thank god."

I look her over, searching for any sign that she's been hurt.

Allison notices. "I'm fine. My dad just yelled. A lot."

"But why?" I ask. "Because you're dating someone?"

She shakes her head. "It's because I was sneaking around."

"Which is your dad's fault. He always flips out like this! Actually, this is even worse than how he usually reacts."

"I know," she says with a swallow. "No way is Ronnie gonna keep seeing me. You should have seen his face."

"Poor guy," I say with a grimace. "And poor you. How long are you grounded for?"

"The rest of the month," she says with an eye roll. "I don't care. I just hope he doesn't scare Ronnie away." We slow at a stop sign, Allison glancing over at me. "I *really* like him, Ben."

As her best friend, I feel like saying that she shouldn't let anything stand in the way. And maybe I would have told her that a few months ago, but I'm not so sure anymore. On the rest of the ride to school, we discuss how they could continue to see each other secretly, but it's a dangerous game. Her dad will detonate if he catches them a second time. I'd be surprised if Ronnie is willing to try anyway. He wouldn't be the first guy her dad has chased off. So when I'm sitting at the lunch table with Leon later that day, I'm puzzled when Allison and Ronnie show up together while smiling.

"How's it going?" I ask casually.

"Good," Ronnie says, bumping fists with Leon before sitting down.

"Really?" I ask, not hiding my disbelief.

"Ben knows what happened last night," Allison explains.

Ronnie doesn't seem to mind. Nor does Leon seem confused. Best friends are for confiding in, after all. Although words aren't always necessary. I detect a hint of panic when Allison's gaze meets mine.

"Everything will be fine," Ronnie assures us. "I'm going to introduce myself to her father. Which is what I should have done in the first place."

Allison's eyes are pleading with me now. I don't think she wants me to hold back.

"That's a terrible idea," I say.

"How come?" Ronnie asks.

My eyes dart to Allison again, whose lips are pressed together, but she nods.

My tone is incredulous. "You really need to ask?"

Leon backs me up. "He did ding your car, my dude."

"He scratched it," Ronnie says dismissively. "You can hardly tell."

I scoff at this. "Yeah, but he was aiming for you!"

Ronnie appears hesitant, but he shrugs it off. "It's not like he's going to punch me in the face for knocking on his door, right?"

I shrug.

"He's not *that* bad," Allison says. "And maybe he wasn't trying to hit you." That doesn't mesh with what she told me just hours ago, but I hold my tongue, wanting to support her. "My dad has good aim," she continues. "He's a golfer."

Ronnie perks up. "Hey, my dad plays golf too! That's already common ground. I'm sure it'll be fine. And anyway, I don't blame him for being pissed. I've been sneaking around with his daughter. He probably thinks I'm a sleaze bag. That's why I've gotta introduce myself to him."

I'm not sure which stance Allison wants me to take, but she's more than capable of speaking her own mind, so I leave him with a warning. "Just make sure you choose a good time," I say, silently adding, *like when he's not drunk.*

"I'm gonna stop by after school today," Ronnie says.

I practically choke on a bite of sandwich, but I manage to swallow. "Maybe you should wait until he's not as upset."

Ronnie shakes his head. "Right now he's got the wrong impression of me. I wanna change that before it solidifies or whatever."

He's a handsome guy with a good heart. I'll leave flowers on his grave.

We move on to other subjects, but once fifth period rolls around, the potential showdown is the foremost concern on my mind and on my best friend's lips.

"You have to help me!" Allison pleads, dragging me into a secluded corner of the choir room.

"I was trying to during lunch!" I retort. "The boy is suicidal."

"I know," Allison says with a sigh. "But he's so sweet that I honestly think he's got a chance."

"Those gorgeous eyelashes of his aren't going to impress your father."

"Which is why I need you to be there." Allison grabs my hand, as if worried I'll flee in terror at the suggestion, and I might have if I didn't love her so much.

"Me being there will only make it worse. Your father hates me."

"He does not," Allison says. "He was always nice to you when we were kids."

That's before his wife died. He's a different person now. Allison doesn't need to be reminded of that. She needs her best friend.

"All right. What do you want me to do?"

Allison exhales and visibly relaxes, as if her problems are already solved. "Just be there when Ronnie shows up. My dad is less likely to freak out with someone else around."

That didn't stop him from chucking a whisky glass across the front yard, but I hold my tongue.

At the end of the school day, she drives us back to her place, where I try my damnedest to pretend that I'm not about to witness a disaster. We're sitting in the living room when her father arrives. He's a bald man with broad shoulders and a stern brow.

"Hi, Daddy!" Allison says, rising to give him a hug.

His beard bristles when he notices me. "You're grounded. What's he doing here?"

"Practicing for choir," Allison says. "Do you want to stay and listen?"

"Sure." He's always appreciated his daughter's talent. I'll give him credit for that. "Be right back."

We watch him walk toward the kitchen.

"How much longer until Ronnie gets here?" I murmur.

"About twenty minutes," Allison whispers back.

Long enough for her father to get a drink or two down. Springing this on him is a mistake. I'm so certain that I stand up.

"Where are you going?" Allison hisses.

"Keep a lookout. I'll be right back."

I feel unsteady on my feet as I walk to the kitchen. I'm not worried that I'll get my ass kicked or anything crazy, but the man has a short temper. I put on a friendly expression. Her father spins around when I enter, a bottle of something on the counter next to him.

"We need to wet our whistles if we're going to sing for you," I say, going to the cabinet where glasses are kept.

He watches me with his arms crossed. I set the glasses on the counter. An ice cube tray is next to the bottle, which is a convenient excuse to interact. "Do you mind?" I ask before reaching for it.

Her father steps aside to make room for me.

"Listen," I say. "I know I'm not your favorite person—"

"Alli should be spending time with other girls," he interrupts.

That came out of nowhere! For me, at least. I'm guessing it's been on his mind for quite some time. "A gay guy is the next best thing," I say with a smile that isn't returned. "Anyway, I want you to know that I feel just as protective toward Allison as you do. Because I love her."

He swirls his glass and takes a sip, his face impassive.

"So if this new guy she's been seeing was a jerk, or bad for her somehow, I wouldn't stand for it. He's not though. Ronnie is a good guy. We've known him since grade school. He really likes her."

"I bet he does," her father says without warmth.

"I mean it! That's why he's coming over in a little while to introduce himself to you."

"He's *what?*" her father snarls.

"It's important to him," I hurry to add. "Ronnie wanted to before now, but Allison made him wait until she was sure about him. She doesn't rush into anything. She's too smart."

"Could have fooled me," her father grumbles. "Allison isn't allowed to see anyone right now. She's grounded."

"I know. I told Ronnie to hold off until she wasn't, but he's worried about making a good impression. So please, just give him a chance. It's important to her."

Her father finishes his drink and sets the glass on the counter. Then he tromps toward the living room. I wince, certain that I've made it all worse. I quickly fill two glasses with ice and water before following. By the time I get to the living room, her father is sitting there quietly while listening to his daughter sing. She smiles and nods, like she wants me to join in, so I do. I'm not full of myself, but when we harmonize, it's truly beautiful. Even he can't deny that, judging from the way his features soften. Although they harden again a couple of songs later when the doorbell rings.

"That'll be Ronnie," I say, mostly so Allison won't pretend to be surprised about his arrival.

I take her hand as her father gets up to answer the door. Then we rise and follow along behind him.

"Hello, sir," we hear. "I'd like to apologize for the way in which you met me yesterday. My name is Ronnie, and I care very deeply about your daughter."

Allison lets go of me to stand next to her dad. I move to a different angle so I can see Ronnie, who is dressed like he's going to church, including a button-up shirt, slacks, and tie. Ronnie extends a hand. I hold my breath until Allison's father shakes it.

"I realize that Allison is grounded," Ronnie continues, "and that I haven't made the best impression. But once you see fit, I'd like a chance to introduce myself properly. Maybe we could go out to lunch with my dad, who is an avid golfer like you are."

"Oh yeah?"

"Yes, sir."

"Where does he play?"

"Rolling Hills Country Club."

Her father grunts. "That's a tough one to get into."

"I'm sure he'd love to have you out there," Ronnie says with a smile. "Maybe you guys could show us how to play. Your daughter already kicked my butt at minigolf." He clears his throat and puts on a more somber expression before adding, "Sir."

Allison's father snorts, as if amused. Then he shifts to the other foot. "Did your car get damaged?"

"It's hard to say," Ronnie replies in good humor. "I've put so many dents in it myself. But uh, not recently. My parents made sure I bought an older car while I was still learning to drive."

"You paid for it yourself?"

"Yes, sir! I started bagging groceries when I was fourteen. Now I work at the new burger place on Fifth Street. I'm usually there on the weekends and after school, if you ever want to stop by. Just ask for me by name. For now, I won't trouble you any longer." Ronnie looks at Allison. "Always nice to see you," he says with a smile. After nodding respectfully at her father, he turns and walks away.

We're both holding our breath as the door is shut.

"You can keep practicing until dinner," her father says. He eyes me a moment before returning his attention to her. "After that, no visitors and no phone calls. Understand?"

Allison hugs her father in response. She waits until he's left the room before doing a little dance.

"Did I tell you or what?" she says in excitement. "Ronnie is the last of a dying breed. A true gentleman!"

"You didn't need me here at all," I say wryly.

I'm not selfless. I'll tell her about the role I played eventually, but that isn't important now, when she's so high on love. I remember how that felt. At the moment, I've got the junkie shakes. I can't imagine Tim declaring his intentions to my parents. Or even to me in private. Sure, he showed up at my door on my birthday, but he did so wanting to be alone with me. Which was enough at the time. After seeing Ronnie in action, I'm thinking *I* need to find myself a true gentleman.

CHAPTER SIXTEEN

I'm sitting on the edge of my bed, staring at the painting Tim gave me, which has become something of a nightly ritual. I still ache for him, and as far I can tell, this ailment has no cure. The passing weeks haven't helped. Nor has seeing him again, which we've tried. Tim came over to my house once but conversation was stilted. I feel deprived of the language we use. My words make him too uncomfortable. He doesn't want me to ask him complicated questions. Touching is the only way to get through his barriers. I guess I could sing, but my heart isn't in it. So we sat in my room while pretending to watch a movie, when really we were taking turns sneaking glances at each other. The chemistry is still there, but Krista has her thumb on the test tube opening.

I stand, intending to get undressed and into bed, when something hits the window. After it happens again, I know it wasn't simply a suicidal bug. I switch off the lights before returning to the window. In the narrow strip of land between our house and the main street, a shadowy figure raises his arm and waves. The breath catches in my throat. Tim! Who else could it be? I rush to my bedroom door and flick the light switch a few times to let him know I'm on my way. I'm so excited that I almost forget it's impossible for us to be together.

When I round the corner of my house and see him standing against a backdrop of bare branches and a star-swept sky, I stop in my tracks, not trusting myself to take another step toward him. Tim closes the remaining distance between us and reaches for my face. When I feel the warmth of his palm against my cheek, I'm helpless. My face tilts upwards to meet his, and when he kisses me, I give in completely. Forget about morals and integrity. I just want him. I'll lie and cheat and do anything else that's necessary, because going without him is hell and his touch feels like heaven.

"Are you happy?" he asks when leaning away. He doesn't let go. One of his hands is cradling the back of my neck.

"About what?" I ask, straining to reach his lips again.

Tim laughs. "What do you think? I broke up with her."

I stare at him a moment. "Really?"

"Yeah, of course!" His eyes narrow. "Wait, you didn't realize? And you *still* kissed me?"

"I'm only human," I say with a shrug. Then I smile. "Are you serious?"

"Yeah," Tim says, his eyes sparkling. "I'm serious."

I'd kiss him again if I could get myself to stop smiling. I have questions. But they can wait. All except for one. "Do you wanna go up to my room?"

"Hell yeah!" Tim says, taking my hand.

We sprint together to my front door. I can't stop laughing. I guess because I'm so happy. Although I do hush him before we go inside. "My parents are asleep," I warn.

"Let's see if we can wake them up," Tim replies.

Fine by me! I need to reconnect with him. We can talk later. We creep up the stairs. As soon as we're safely in my room, Tim starts kissing me so aggressively that he backs me up against the wall. And I fucking love it. My hands move down his body until I reach his jeans. While getting them unbuttoned, I dodge his lips just long enough to ask, "What do you want to do?"

"I get to choose?" Tim asks after kissing me again.

"Yeah," I say breathlessly. "Anything you want."

He takes a step back to look me over. Then he glances at the bed. I don't know what plan he's concocting, but I'm game. "Let's get naked," Tim says while shrugging off his jacket.

"Okay."

We strip down in front of each other, and I swear I could blow a load just seeing that incredible body again. Once we're both nude, Tim takes my hand and leads me to the bed. His knee hits the mattress as he turns to pull me in after him.

"Come here," Tim says, stretching out on his back.

I figure he wants me to go down on him, but his hands grab my hips to move me higher until our waists are aligned. I'm holding myself up on my elbows so I can search his face, still not understanding what he needs.

"I wanna be close to you," Tim says, his arms tightening.

I stare into silver eyes that are wet with emotion before I finally relax and let my torso press against his. I rest my head on his shoulder, my face turned toward his neck, as I take in the scent of his skin. Our breathing shifts into a complementary rhythm, his chest rising as mine falls. Tim's strong arms remain wrapped around me, constricting on occasion, like he's telling me what I want to hear.

I love you, Benjamin.

We don't need words. Not when we have this.

I don't know how long we lie there. Only that he seems content to hold me. I like it too, although it's not enough. My need for him is insatiable, so I shift and snake my hand between us until I'm able to grab his cock. Tim moans in appreciation and pumps his hips. Then his arms tighten again before he rolls over, taking me with him.

He pushes himself up on one arm, angling himself so he can reach down and touch me too. His fist keeps bumping mine as we stroke each other, so while he's kissing me, I thwap his cock against mine until he takes the hint and wraps his big hand around both of them.

"Damn," he says. "We make one hell of a team."

"Yeah," I whimper as he resumes pumping.

We're kissing when I feel him start to tremble. And not because he's feeling emotional or on the verge. Tim is basically doing a one-armed push-up while the other arm goes to work. "Just a second," he says. "I need to switch."

"I've got this," I tell him, reaching down with my free hand so it can join the other. Out of necessity, because he sure is thick!

Tim holds himself above me and starts thrusting his hips, our cocks rubbing together. His foreskin gives him a natural glide that I don't have, but when he starts leaking precome, the lubrication pushes me toward the edge.

"I think I can finish like this," Tim grunts.

"Don't hold back," I murmur. "I'm right there with you."

"Yeah?" Tim asks, his eyes locked on mine.

"Oh yeah!" I strain my neck to kiss him again, the air shooting out of his nostrils in quicker succession until his entire body tenses. I blow my load at the exact same time, and it's a great big mess, especially when he collapses on top of me. But hey, this is the glue that keeps us together!

The thought makes me laugh, or maybe it's the rush of endorphins, because he joins me, our bodies shaking with mirth and the aftershocks of pleasure. When he finally tumbles off me, I'm content to lie there on my back as I catch my breath. So is he. Although his hand seeks out mine so our fingers can intertwine.

"Welcome back," I say.

I watch him swallow before he says, "I never went anywhere. Not really."

He rolls over onto his side and reaches for me. I mimic this motion so he can cradle me from behind. Then I alternate between wanting to laugh and cry, because this is all I ever wanted. And now that he's broken up with Krista, I've got all I'll ever need.

When I wake up in the morning, I'm buzzing from reuniting with Tim. Until I realize he's still in my bed with an arm wrapped around me. I jerk in shock and roll over to face him. Tim stirs, opens his eyes, and smiles at me.

"Hey," he says casually.

"We're going to get in trouble!" I hiss before scrambling out of bed. "It's a school day!"

Tim shrugs. "I doubt my parents will notice that I'm gone." He sits up, smirking as I sort through the pile of clothes we left by the door.

"Mine will definitely notice you're here," I say. "We've gotta sneak you out."

Tim rolls off the bed and stretches—buck naked—while facing me. When I toss his underwear to him, he hangs them on his boner. "I'm ready to go," he says.

"I can tell!"

As stunning as the view is, it isn't helping. I turn my back to him while throwing on yesterday's clothes. After waking, I usually head straight to the bathroom and use the toilet while letting the shower warm up. I've gotta go now and he probably does too. I can't expect him to hold it all the way home. I check the clock. I woke up a little earlier than usual, so there's still time.

"Let me go first," I say after he's dressed. I open my bedroom door and tiptoe to the stairs. The ground floor is quiet, so I dart to the bathroom, make use of it, and then wave him over. Tim pushes me inside with him instead of letting me go back to my room.

"Wanna hold it for me?" he asks.

"Yes," I admit while shutting the door behind us. "Just not now."

He laughs and whips it out, angling himself in front of the toilet so I can watch, as if I'd be interested. And I do stare, but only until I notice him getting hard again, so I turn my back.

"How'd it go with Krista last night?" I ask, figuring the subject will be a mood-killer for us both. And I *am* curious.

"It was rough," Tim says. "She cried."

"Really?"

"Yeah. But I think it went okay."

After I hear the toilet flush, I switch on the bathroom fan, so we're less likely to be overheard, and turn to face him. "What reason did you give her?"

"For breaking up? I told her that I was still in love with Carla."

"Your ex-girlfriend? The one who…"

Tim grimaces. "Yeah. I made up a story about how—before I moved here—we promised that we'd get back together in college. And that when Krista wanted to take things further, it felt like cheating on Carla, even though we're not together right now. I built up to it over the last couple weeks by getting more and more distant."

"Like you did with me?"

He shakes his head, as if not understanding.

"When you ignored me at school."

"Oh." He squirms. "I was trying to play it safe. So nobody would suspect."

I might have believed that if he'd told me sooner. "Really?"

I can tell that Tim is holding back until he sighs. "And I uh… wanted to see if I could stop doing this. It would have made everything easier. No offense."

"None taken," I murmur, pleased with the result of the experiment. We're in a strong position now. Tim tried to go without, decided that I mattered too much to him, broke up with his girlfriend, and came running back to me. "So it sounds like you're in the clear."

"When it comes to Krista?" he shrugs. "I dunno. She was sad last night, but what if she's pissed at me today?"

I attempt to put myself in her shoes, imagining that Tim and I had dated for a few months before I learned that he still wasn't over some guy from his hometown. Which would suck, but it would be easier than someone new coming along and taking him from me. I'd probably cry myself to sleep. And I might try to get him back. But ultimately… "I think you'll be all right."

"Yeah?" he says with a grin.

I nod while nibbling my bottom lip, transfixed by that smile. And the cocky expression when he tilts his head toward the tub. "Wanna take a shower together?"

"No!" I say, remembering that we could be overheard at any moment. "You've gotta get out of here. Hold on." I leave the bathroom and listen. I can hear the rest of my family in the kitchen, so I wave him over, and together we ease down the stairs to the entryway.

"When do I get to see you again?" he whispers.

"Never, if you get caught," I reply, pushing him out the door.

Tim resists while chuckling, but he finally turns and heads down the walkway.

I exhale in relief until I close the door and spin around. My mom is standing not far away and doesn't look pleased.

"Young man—" she begins.

"I can explain!"

My mom crosses her arms over her chest. "Go right ahead."

Crap! I'm too on the spot to make something up, so I stick close to the truth. "Tim broke up with his girlfriend last night and was really upset. We stayed up late talking and accidentally fell asleep."

"Mm-hm," she replies. "Listen, you're eighteen years old now. That makes you an adult. But while you're living under this roof, I expect you to follow our rules. Your boyfriend isn't allowed over on school nights."

"He's not my boyfriend."

She purses her lips at this. "Honey, I've *heard* you guys."

I don't think she means conversation. My face begins to burn. "Like I said, he just broke up with his girlfriend."

"Oh. *Ooh!*"

"Yeah," I say sheepishly. "It's a work in progress. Him falling asleep here really was an accident."

Her face softens. "Okay. Well… From now on, Friday and Saturday nights are fine, but that's it. Your father and I deserve a solid night's sleep."

"Sorry," I say with an apologetic wince.

"Finish getting ready," she replies. "I'll see you at the table."

I hurry up the stairs to my room to pick out an outfit, wanting to choose something that looks nice, because I fully intend to pass Tim in the hall today. And considering that we've been deprived of being depraved, there's a good chance I'll see him again tonight. I'm excited about our future, although it's almost comical how contented I was last night. I don't feel that way now, because my mom unintentionally put a bug in my ear. Getting to love Tim and sleep with him is great, but now that he's officially single…

I want to be his boyfriend.

I'm strolling through the leaf-strewn woods near my house, occasionally stopping to glance over my shoulder, because Tim is exceedingly handsome, even with so much of his body covered. It's one of those rare December days when the sun is out and the weather is chilly but fresh. I'm layered up in a T-shirt, sweater, and coat. Tim is dressed in a similar outfit, except his coat hangs open and he's not wearing anything beneath the loose V-neck sweater. He could be a model. Everything looks good on him, especially when I get to take it all off. Which has happened a lot lately.

The past couple of weeks have been nice. Allison is no longer grounded and has permission to see Ronnie. Their fathers met over lunch, which sounds so civilized that it gives me hope for her home life. We spend a lot of time comparing notes on the guys we're dating. The emotions are similar, but our experiences are vastly different. Her relationship with Ronnie takes place in public settings, either at school or whenever they go on their dates. My whatever-it-is with Tim remains hidden, a secret nurtured in the precious time that our parents aren't home or awake.

My mom and dad don't have an issue with us being together. Tim does though. He doesn't want them to know, so I've avoided telling him that they already do. He always makes me wait until they go to sleep before he'll get busy with me. And when feeling reckless enough, I sneak into his house late at night. Which makes it especially nice that we're spending the day together. I only had to wait until Tim got home from church. Now we're tromping through the woods that Allison and I used to play in.

"What's up?" Tim asks when I slow to a stop.

I slowly pivot in a circle while pointing, like a witch searching for someone to hex. "Riiiight… there!"

I stab my index finger at a stout tree with branches low to the ground. Then I skip toward it happily, kicking up leaves along the way. "This used to be the mast of our pirate ship," I say, placing a hand on one of the branches affectionately. "You're lucky Anthrax Allison isn't here. She's the meanest captain on the seven seas."

Tim looks amused when joining me. "You guys used to play make-believe here?"

"Yup!" I refrain from mentioning how old we were. Let him imagine two plucky kids instead of nerdy eighth graders.

I'm not surprised when he grabs one of the branches and pulls himself up into the tree. Tim is a very physical guy with a seemingly endless amount of energy. That's why I brought him out here, like you do with a puppy to wear it out. The potential to be alone appealed to me too, because there's something I want to talk to him about.

"What was your sailor name?" he asks.

"Ben Beard the Pirate."

He stops climbing long enough to make a face. "But you don't have a beard."

I slash at him with an imaginary cutlass. "When people called me on it, I always went berserk!"

Tim laughs. He's looking around for the next closest branch when he does a double take. "Hey! Someone carved a heart here."

"Oh right."

He glances back and forth between me and the heart. "It's got your initials. But what about the other letters?" He figures it out without my help and laughs. "Allison?"

"Yeah," I confirm. "I'm pretty sure it was her idea."

"Did you guys ever have a thing for each other?"

"No. I don't think so. And besides, the heart came later. By then I had already figured out what made me different from the guys I had slept with." My pulse picks up. This seems like a good opportunity to broach the subject that I've been dying to discuss. "It takes more than two dudes having sex to make someone gay."

"Oh yeah?" Tim asks, letting himself swing from a branch before dropping to the ground. "What do you mean?"

I try to ignore the hopeful expression he's wearing, like I'm about to provide him with an easy out, when in fact the opposite is true. "It's everything *besides* sex that counts," I explain, "so even if I had insisted on those other guys returning the favor, it wouldn't have meant much. I never caught them looking at me affectionately. They didn't hold my hand during a movie. None of them wanted to spend more and more time with me."

His expression is guarded. I'm not sure if he realizes that I'm describing him, but he must suspect. "I wasn't in love with any of those guys, but I did get crushes on a few. That's the difference: I felt something more meaningful than simply being horny. In the same way that I feel things for you."

He averts his gaze, which makes me feel like I'm suffocating, so I force the words out while bracing for his answer.

"Do you feel anything for me?"

"Yeah." His eyes lock on to mine. "You're my best friend."

"I've already got one of those," I say, nodding at the carved heart. "We'll have to come up with a different title to describe us."

"Like what?"

I swallow and put on my best smile. "I could be your boyfriend."

He looks happy, and I'm overjoyed, until he starts laughing. "That would be weird."

I feel the muscles of my face being dragged down, like gravity just got a whole lot stronger. "Why's that?"

"A straight guy with a boyfriend?" Tim says, as if I'm the one who is being ridiculous.

My temper shoves its way protectively to the front. "How is that any weirder than a straight guy who likes to spoon with his gay best friend?"

That slaps the smile right off his face.

"Then maybe we should stop," Tim grumbles.

"No! I don't want that. And I don't think you do either. But we're more than just friends. Aren't we?"

He shrugs. "Do we have to be?"

I shake my head, but in disbelief more than anything. "For me it isn't a choice."

Tim kicks at a rock. "You must think I'm an asshole."

"No," I reply. "I really don't." He's simply going through the same stage I did, a long time ago, when denying who I was seemed like the easiest path forward, even though it actually took constant effort.

Tim looks around, as if searching for a different subject, his attention lingering on the carved heart. "So you've never felt attracted to a girl? Like… ever?"

I think about it. "Not really. Every once in a while a woman will catch my eye, but it's always a tomboy or a girl who leans toward the masculine. That's what I'm attracted to. Even then, when I think about what parts they do and don't have…" I shake my head.

"Huh," Tim says, seeming relieved. "I don't think we're the same then."

"Not entirely," I reply. "But we have some things in common."

He resumes kicking at the dirt. Then he stares off into the distance. "Wanna keep going?"

"Yeah," I reply, because I do. With him. I'm proud of myself for standing my ground when it came to Krista. But I can't handle another break. This is the kind of issue that we'll need to solve together. Eventually, if I'm lucky, he'll fall in love with me. And then it won't be a choice. For now… "There's a creek up ahead. Allison and I used to dare each other to jump over it. Which is harder than it looks. Wanna try?"

Tim grins. "Yeah!"

As we begin walking, I nudge him with my elbow and smile, wanting to assure him that everything is okay between us. And it is!

For now.

I imagined that my talk with Tim would be a turning point for us. Instead I seem to have shot myself in the foot. By outlining what makes someone gay, I inadvertently gave him a list of things to avoid. He becomes noticeably less affectionate over the following week. Like when we're watching TV in my room and I reach for his hand, he only holds mine briefly before pulling away to scratch at his chest. He doesn't seek it out again afterwards, which is unusual, because he normally seems so obsessed with my hands. He used to toy with my fingers, positioning them in different ways, or stroke my palm with his thumb. He still does on occasion, subconsciously perhaps, because he'll stop suddenly and break off contact.

And for the first time, we have one-sided sex. Which frankly, didn't hurt my feelings too much. Getting to service him was hot. I didn't mind finishing myself off at the same time. Watching him squirm afterwards, as if unsure what to do with himself when usually he'd hold me, was kind of sad. Tim could have made an excuse to leave. But he didn't. Instead he got dressed while looking conflicted, which is what tipped me off that he hadn't intended to simply kick back and enjoy a selfish blowjob. He's experimenting with me in a different way now.

As much as he tries to be aloof, Tim never has much success, and that keeps me going. I'm convinced that we only need some uninterrupted time together, like we had at the beginning, so we can let the cement dry without the outside world tromping all over the progress we've made. So when he mentions that his parents are going out of town for the holidays, my hopes reach an all-time high. I usually count the days until Christmas, and this year is no exception, but I couldn't care less about what presents I might receive.

When the festive day arrives, I wake up early in my excitement. I take pleasure in pounding on my sister's door to wake her up. Then I go downstairs and find my parents sipping coffee. Which isn't usually how these things go.

"This is the second time that we woke up before you on Christmas Day," my mother says with a tinge of sorrow. "You're growing up!"

"Not that we're complaining," my father says with a yawn.

When I was younger, we'd tear through the presents in a frenzy. This year the pace is slower. I intend to savor it all, since I'll be off to college next year and I'm not sure if I'll be home for the holidays. Tim might prefer that we spend Christmas alone together. I might not experience this again until I have a family of my own. I imagine myself cuddled up on the couch with Tim as we watch a gaggle of adopted children squeal with delight over the presents Santa brought them.

After my family finishes exchanging gifts, we revert to our typical morning routines, although I'm more selective when picking out an outfit. I usually opt for comfort on the holidays, but I want to look nice for Tim, so I choose a textured white sweater with a light blue T-shirt beneath, hoping to be his little snowflake. I keep checking the clock, despite knowing that I won't be free until late afternoon. My relatives are coming to our house this year. Once family obligations are out of the way, nothing will stand between me and multiple days spent blissfully alone with my friend who is a boy. I haven't made any progress on that front. Which is a shame, because it's all I want for Christmas.

For now I play the good son, helping my parents in the kitchen and singing carols for the extended family when they arrive. I make sure each relative gets some time with me, but not because I expect to be the highlight of their holiday. I just want to make sure every box is ticked before asking my mother for permission to leave. She probably won't mind. Allison and I usually visit each other to exchange gifts at about this time. This year is different. She already left on a trip with her father, so we celebrated early.

"Can I go over to Tim's house now?" I say when I find myself alone in the kitchen my mom.

"Oh!" She glances around, as if searching for an excuse to keep me there. "I suppose that's fine. When will you be back?"

"In a few days," I say vaguely.

"So many nights?" she asks before shaking her head. "That's too long, honey."

"Mom! We went over this already. Besides, you said that I'm eighteen now and can make my own decisions. I don't have school until after New Year's so…"

"I know, but the holidays are stressful, and it's not fair to expect Tim's family to take care of you all week long. Why don't you alternate? Spend a night there and then a night here."

Is she really trying to change the plan at the last minute? I feel my temper rise before I notice the transparent need in her eyes. This isn't about restraining me. She wants to see her son on the last Christmas we'll have together before I go to college.

"Spend the night there and come home tomorrow," she presses. "You'll have plenty of opportunity to see each other over the holidays."

She doesn't understand. "We need this time together," I explain. "He's still trying to figure everything out, and that's hard to do with other people around. And besides…" I'm hesitant, but I trust my mom, so I let her in on the secret. "His parents are out of town."

"No!" she says in shock. "That can't be right! How long will they be gone?"

She looks distraught. Maybe I made a mistake by confiding in her. Too late now. "Until next week."

"Why? Was there an emergency?"

"No," I say, surprised that I haven't received a scathing

lecture yet. "There's some ski lodge his mom likes going to. It's a tradition."

"They've done this before?" my mother cries. "Your father could surprise me with a once-in-a-lifetime trip to the moon, and I wouldn't go if it meant leaving you children on the holidays!"

"I think it's messed up too," I say, "but not everyone has awesome parents like I do."

The flattery is wasted on my mother, her features crinkling. "Does he have any siblings? Or family in the area? You said they just moved here."

"He's all by himself," I say from around a tight throat. "On Christmas Day."

"Then what are you still doing here?" My mother rushes to a cabinet and starts pulling out Tupperware. "The poor boy is probably starving!" She hands a plastic container to me. "Fill that with roasted potatoes. Does he like green beans?"

Her generosity results in two stacks of Tupperware that I can't possibly carry on my own. "I'll give you a ride," my mother says when I point this out.

That means she'll be able to find me. She knows he lives a couple of blocks over, but not his exact address.

"Hurry up and put on your shoes," she prompts, as if I'm letting her down by still being there. I don't rush from the room though. Instead I hug her. "Thanks, Mom."

She squeezes in return. "You can pay me back by stopping by on occasion. You don't have to stay long. Bring him with you. I just want to see my baby on the holidays." She presses a hand to her chest and shakes her head again. "How could his mother not feel the same way? I simply can't imagine!"

I'm not only grateful for her understanding but for the sympathy she's shown, because it casts Tim's situation in a different light. I usually rejoice when learning that his parents will be out of town. From now on I'll think more about how it makes him feel. I can't wait to get over there. My love for him knows no bounds. I'm certain I can give enough to make up for whatever he's missing.

CHAPTER SEVENTEEN

"Hey," Tim says when answering the door. Then he notices the two large shopping bags I'm carrying—the kind from department stores—and seems taken aback. "Whoa! What's all that?"

"Mostly food from my mom," I say, tilting my head toward the street, where a car is idling.

My mother rolls down the window. "Merry Christmas, Tim!" she shouts.

He smiles and waves before returning the greeting. I bet it's the most festive moment of his day so far, because after taking the bags from me and leading the way inside, I notice just how somber the house is. Most of the curtains are shut. I walk into the murky gloom of the living room, where a Christmas tree hasn't been lit. Beneath it, a dozen gifts remain unopened.

"This won't do at all," I say before rifling through one of the bags Tim holds. I take out the gift I got him. "The rest goes to the kitchen," I instruct.

"Aye-aye, Captain," he replies.

I watch him go before plugging in the tree, taking note of the generic decorations. The branches of ours droop with decades of homemade ornaments. I place my gift with all the others and sniff, noticing an earthy scent. I pluck a needle, impressed that it's real, when we've used the same plastic tree my entire life. I open the curtains before doing the same in other rooms around the house. Then I join Tim in the kitchen, turning on the radio there and bumping him aside with my butt so I can prepare a plate. I don't need to ask if he's hungry. There's nothing but an unwashed cereal bowl in the sink. I sing while working, Tim's expression happier each time I glance over. This feels good. And familiar. I'm taking care of him again!

We sit at the dining room table, although he's the only one eating. I light the candles. Christmas music drifts in from the kitchen while I bore him with the details of my day as he eats. Tim seems to enjoy hearing about it anyway, which prompts me to ask, "So what are the holidays usually like for you? I mean, your parents don't always go out of town. Do they?"

"Nah," Tim says. "When I was growing up, we'd usually go over to my grandpa's place. And boy, if you think my parents are too religious…" He shudders theatrically. "We each had to take turns reading Bible verses. Visiting him was like going to church, but even less fun. Which is probably why everyone went their separate ways after he died."

"They did?"

Tim nods. "My dad's side of the family doesn't get together much anymore." He pushes his plate away and stretches, the maroon sweater he wears bulging with muscle when he relaxes again. He notices me staring and puts on bedroom eyes. "So… What should we do now?"

"I've got something for you to unwrap," I reply flirtatiously, despite having no intention of sleeping with him just yet. I'm too nervous about the present I picked out for him. Because it's heartfelt. And invasive. Just like me!

I take his plate to the kitchen, dodging him when he tries to embrace me so I can take off down the hall. He gives chase, finally catching me in the living room. The sun is on the horizon, the walls awash in a warm orange glow. I turn around for a kiss before gently pushing him away.

"There's something under the tree with your name on it."

"Oh yeah?" he asks.

"Yup." I kneel on the skirt, reaching for the present I brought when I notice another gift tag with his name on it. "Are you waiting until your parents come back to open these?" I ask.

"Nah," Tim says as if disinterested.

"This one is for you too," I say, checking more of the gift tags. "Most of them are!"

"Yeah, I know. My mom was worried about me having a good Christmas on my own."

But not worried enough to actually stay, it would seem. Regardless, having absentee parents would be bad enough without reaping the rewards. "Your mom is going to be sad if she comes home and everything is still wrapped. Or is that the point?"

Tim shakes his head. "I don't want to upset her. It just seemed lame to open stuff by myself."

"Then it's a good thing I'm here," I say, setting the present I got him toward the back. "What's in the big box here?"

"I dunno," Tim says, sitting next to me. "Let's find out. Go for it."

I'm genuinely excited when I unwrap the present and find a new stereo system. After marveling over it, I pass him a gift while unwrapping another. And so it continues. He gets cologne, some new clothes, cash, and the latest video game console. Among other things. Pretty soon we're surrounded by discarded wrapping paper.

"Hey," Tim says, handing me a long flat box. "This one has your name on it."

When I take the gift from him, I can feel something soft shifting around inside. An item of clothing maybe? I can't imagine what he would buy me, but I waste no time in finding out. After tearing off the paper, I open a plain white box, revealing emerald-green fabric. "It's so soft!" I say, running my hands along it. "And I love the color. What is it though?" I stand to unfold the complete length. Then I gasp. "You bought me a coat?"

Tim nods. "Try it on."

I hold it away from me first, admiring the long cut and large black buttons. I've never owned anything so stylish! When I put it on, the coat hugs my hips nicely before ending just above my knees. Tim stands and moves closer to me. He adjusts the collar and smooths down the lapels. I'm naturally drawn to him while he works, leaning forward. Tim notices. He smirks and smooches me before taking a few steps back. "How's it feel?" he asks.

"Like a perfect fit," I say, shaking my head in wonder. "How'd you manage that?"

"I just got lucky," he says with a shrug.

Not a chance. It's all in the way he looks at me, like he's doing now, sizing up proportions and angles in a way that I'm incapable of, because I'm not an artist. I imagine him walking through a department store while thinking of me and the time it must have taken to make a selection.

"I knew it would look good with your hair," he says, moving close again to ruffle it. "What do you think?"

"I'm in love," I say, putting so much emotion into the words that I hope he'll realize I mean more than just the coat.

"Good," he says while doing up the buttons. "Because I lost the receipt. Oh, and there's one more thing."

"No!" I say, already overwhelmed.

"It's nothing big," he says, handing me a small gift bag.

I see a bundle of knitted fabric and pull out a burnt-orange scarf. Tim takes one end and loops it around my neck before folding it over my chest to fill the spot the coat doesn't cover.

"For the really cold days," he says. "Although you look hot now."

I'm not sure if that's a compliment or not, since I really am beginning to sweat.

"Thank you," I say. "Umm… Just a sec. I wanna see for myself!"

I rush from the room to check the bathroom mirror and smile at my reflection. I look so classy! Tim joins me, his eyes half-lidded in the mirror. I turn to face him. He begins unwrapping me, first by untangling the scarf and then by undoing the coat's buttons.

"I'm not your present," I murmur. "You still have to open it."

"But you're all I want," he replies.

I just about give into him, especially when his lips press against mine. But I can't wait any longer. The anticipation is killing me. I take a step back and tie one end of my scarf around his wrist. "Follow me," I say when leaving the room.

I lead him back to the tree, my anxiety increasing. I hope this doesn't upset him. The wrapped gift I hand him is much humbler in size. Tim frees himself from the scarf and sits on the couch. I plop down next to him and hold my breath as the paper is torn away, revealing art supplies. He's silent when sifting through watercolors, pencils, and tubes of paint.

"What am I supposed to do with these?" he asks.

My stomach sinks. It's not the response I'd hoped for.

"I know you have your secrets," I tell him, taking a deep breath. "I don't always understand why. But wouldn't it be nice if there was at least one person you could be completely open with? About everything. I can be that for you, Tim. When you're ready."

He looks over at me and swallows. Then he wraps an arm around me and pulls. I lean over as he cradles me against his chest. I can hear how rapidly his heart is beating. When he releases me, I catch the hint of an apology on his face, like he can't promise anything.

"I love the painting you gave me," I say, deciding that it might help if I go first. "Your art is amazing. I've seen more of it than you realize because um… I've peeked in your sketchbooks before."

"Jesus, Benjamin!" he swears before shaking his head ruefully. "I guess I shouldn't be surprised."

"You really shouldn't," I say, trying a smile. "Just because we've gotten this far, doesn't mean that I've stopped stalking you."

He laughs before his expression becomes more somber. "You really like my art?"

"Yes," I assure him. "You've got real talent."

He looks back down at the art supplies. "These are nice," he says.

"Really?"

"Yeah. Just one question." Tim holds up a clear plastic tube with a brush attached to the end. "What the hell is this?"

I shrug. "I told the guy at the art supply store that you like to draw and paint. He says that thing will let you paint in your sketchbook. The watercolors go with it, but those are weird too, since they look more like little dried cakes."

"No way…" Tim says, mostly to himself as he squeezes the strange brush experimentally. A wild grin breaks out over his face. "No fucking way!"

He leaps to his feet without explanation. When he comes back, he's got the strange brush in one hand and a sketchbook in the other. "I mostly like to paint," he says. "That's my medium. All this sketching and drawing stuff is like, I dunno, jacking off instead of getting laid. I wouldn't want to go without, but it's just to tide me over. Painting makes a big mess. You need lots of space. But this…" He holds up the strange brush and squeezes, water dripping out of the plastic reservoir which has now been filled. "This is a goddamn game changer!"

"Okay," I say, not truly understanding what he's so excited about. I just love that he's talking so openly about his creative side.

"I've gotta try it out," he says. "Uh…" He sets everything down, grabs my hand, and pulls me to my feet. He positions me facing the couch, and after checking the now-dark window, angles me toward the tree. "Stay right there. Okay?"

"Sure!"

I'm grinning from ear to ear as he grabs his sketchbook and

plops down on the couch. He takes one of the pencils I gave him. Then his attention alternates between me and whatever he sees on the page. Tim's expression is open as he works, his thick eyebrows raised as if to take in more of me before he looks down again, his hand moving in a blur. Before long he tosses the pencil aside impatiently. He switches to the weird brush I gave him and starts messing with the water colors. His expression is apprehensive as he works but only at first. When he glances up from the sketchbook, it's with a smile.

"This is so cool," he says.

"Can I see?" I ask, taking a step forward.

"No!" he barks. "Stay right there."

I resume the previous pose, but I make sure my expression is less and less patient each time he glances at me, until my face is twisted up monstrously.

"Okay," he says with a chuckle. "You can come see. This was just a quick experiment."

I join him on the couch, pressing against his side so I can see into his sketchbook. The end result reminds me of a fashion drawing. The form of my body is there, but it's all loose, like a fleeting impression. My new coat is colored in, a striking orange line zigzagging around my neck. Shadows edge in from the right while marigold splatters on the other side represent the sparkling lights of the Christmas tree. My eyes are dark shadows beneath a puddle of brown hair, my smile a crooked white line. And even though form isn't strictly defined, it's perfectly clear what everything is meant to be.

"That's amazing!" I say in awe.

"You have no idea," Tim says, but he's not referring to his art. "This brush is going to set me free. I'll always have a boner for acrylics, but this is really gonna help." He looks over at me, as if self-conscious. "I'm uh... Not used to talking about this stuff."

"Why not?"

"Because it's so personal. When you say you looked through my sketchbooks already—"

"I only peeked, figuring that you didn't want me to snoop, but I wouldn't mind a tour. From the artist himself."

"I'm not an artist," Tim says dismissively.

I point at the open pages of his sketchbook. "You just made art. That makes you an artist."

He chuckles, as if I'm being silly. "This needs to dry," he says, setting the sketchbook aside. "Maybe some other time."

I nearly suggest that we look at one of the sketchbooks in his underwear drawer, but I don't want to test his patience.

"Thank you," Tim says, his expression vulnerable. "For everything."

"My pleasure." I smooch him on the lips. "I love my coat."

"Wanna take it for a spin?" Tim asks.

I glance toward the window. "But it's cold outside!"

"That's sort of the point," Tim says, rising to pull the curtain shut. "Besides, it's a tradition."

"Yeah, okay."

The idea of braving the winter chill is unappealing to me, but I do get excited when bundling myself up in my new coat. Soon we're strolling down the sidewalk together. The moon has risen, a thin layer of snow glowing in response. Tim keeps glancing around with a big grin on his face.

"I've always loved looking at all the lights," he says.

"Does your family usually go for a walk on Christmas?"

"Nah. Just me. I've done this since I was a kid. It's just so beautiful."

That's certainly true. The neighborhood is tranquil. Not a soul is in sight, which makes it feel like the festive decorations are for us alone. Most houses have strings of lights lining the roof or spun around the trunk of a tree. The silence is soothing. But when I imagine a solitary boy walking through the neighborhoods, I can't help but feel a little sad.

"Did you have a lonely childhood?" I ask.

Tim shrugs. "Maybe a little. I always thought it would be cool to have a brother. Sort of like a friend that got to sleep over every night."

"Having a sister didn't feel that way," I reply. "Although it was nice having someone around to conspire with."

"Conspire with?" Tim repeats, sounding confused.

"Yeah! Like at this time of year, we'd try to figure out what we were getting, so we'd shake the presents under the tree or attempt to unstick the tape without tearing the paper to peek inside."

"That's cheating!"

I shrug shamelessly. "Those are the life skills you learn with an older sibling around."

"Sounds nice," Tim says, stopping to look at a warmly lit house with a tree prominently displayed in the front window. "Although I didn't have a bad childhood. I just learned to play on my own." He glances at me with reservation before his features relax. "And I always had my art."

"Yeah?" I ask encouragingly.

"Yeah. I can hardly remember anything about kindergarten, but the day we fingerpainted is crystal clear in my mind. Getting to dip my fingers in raw color and discovering how they blend together… It was a revelation. I felt like I had magic powers. I could create any color I wanted! And you don't have to learn how to use a brush or hold a pencil. It was instant access to art. I was sold."

"I always liked crayons," I say, struggling to relate.

Tim shakes his head. "They were too limiting for me. Paint is more forgiving. You can keep adding layers until you get what you want. I remember going to school the next day and being upset that we weren't going to fingerpaint again. I asked my teacher if we could. She said no, but I kept asking until she let me try again. The other kids went out to play. I stayed inside so I could paint. I still remember how my hands looked when everyone came back inside. My palms were rainbows. When I was told to wash my hands, I refused. The paint had dried by then anyway. After my mom came to pick me up, the teacher explained what happened and sent me home with the leftovers."

Tim is staring down at his open palm before he blinks and glances around. Then he laughs self-consciously. "So anyway, after I ran out of paint, I begged my mom for more. Every birthday and Christmas, that's what I wanted: art supplies. And I usually got them. So in a way, I'm glad I had so much time alone as a kid. I needed it."

He made good use of that time, sure, but I can't help feeling that he needed more from his parents. Even now. But hey, I'm more than happy to pick up the slack. "Let's keep walking," I say, using the excuse to grab his hand and pull on him. "I'm getting cold."

"You're freezing!" Tim says before shaking me off. "I should have bought you some gloves."

"I'm not looking for a sugar daddy," I say as we continue to walk, "but a boyfriend would be nice."

My hopes for a Christmas miracle are shot down when I catch him rolling his eyes.

"Oh come on!" I plead. "Krista got to call you her boyfriend. What can she do for you that I can't?"

"I can think of a few things," Tim murmurs.

"Like what?" I challenge. "Biological children? Unless you were planning to start a family right after high school, who cares?"

"I'm definitely not ready for kids," Tim chuckles. "But trying to make them sure is fun."

"So she's got a vagina," I retort. "Big deal. *Really* big, because entire babies come sliding out of those things. You've got a better option if you're looking for a nice tight hole."

"What if I am?" Tim challenges.

"Then it sounds like you need a boyfriend," I tease.

The prospect has featured in my fantasies more often as of late. I don't have experience with such things, but then, I never felt like trying with any of the other guys. The mere thought of losing my virginity to Tim makes my heart flutter. I want to give that to him and make it a permanent part of my history, like a tattoo that can't be erased. But I don't plan on spelling that out for him.

We continue walking, passing a plastic Santa and a team of reindeer in someone's yard before we circle back around to his house.

"The coat is great," I say while taking it off in the entryway, "but it's too damn cold out there."

Tim engulfs my hands in his before pressing them to his lips. "I've got something that'll warm you up."

"Anything!" I say.

He leads me to his father's den, stopping by the wet bar. "How about some wine?"

"Really?" I ask in excitement.

"Yeah, why not?"

He opens a cabinet and takes out a couple of bottles, setting them on the counter. I'm convinced we're the most sophisticated eighteen-year-olds on the planet until he says, "Red wine is served at room temperature, but I like the yellow kind better, even though it's chilled."

"You mean white wine?" I ask with a snort.

"If it was white, it would look like milk," Tim replies. "What'll be?"

"Yellow wine," I answer, because he's got a point.

I watch him take a bottle out of the mini-fridge and pour two glasses.

"Here's to the best Christmas I ever had," Tim says, holding his up.

I'm taken aback by that, endless festive scenes from my childhood flashing through my mind, but none of them compare with getting to be with him. "Let's make it the first of many," I reply before we clink glasses.

We eye each other while taking sips. I feel a flush of warmth, but it's too soon to be alcohol-induced. Tim continues to watch me. I can't look away either. We both set down our glasses at the same time. Then we kiss, neither of us interested in stopping. I slide my hand beneath his sweater. He flinches, probably because my fingers are still so cold. When I start to pull away, he grabs my hands and places them flat against his body, so I can warm myself. I can feel his skin prickling wherever they slide, but he seems to like it, judging from the way he backs me up against the wet bar as we continue to kiss. I shove one of my hands into his pants. Tim leans back and undoes them before yanking his underwear down, his cock springing out. He wraps my fingers around it with a grin.

"I could melt ice with this thing," he says.

"You aren't kidding," I say, pumping a few times before switching hands.

He's definitely got my blood flowing! I drop to my knees, greedily taking him in my mouth, but he soon pulls me to my feet again. I lean back while he works on my jeans, curious to see what he'll do. As soon as the zipper is down, Tim slides his hands inside and moves them around to my butt. He pulls me close while squeezing my cheeks.

"I wanna do it with you," he grunts.

There's no mistaking his meaning when he spins me around and kisses my neck while grinding against me. I shift so I can pull down my underwear. Tim places his cock between my buns, and I'm so turned on that I want him to shove it inside. Although when he reaches down and angles himself, as if intending to do exactly that, I chicken out.

"Hold on," I say, turning to face him. "I've never done that before."

"I figured," Tim says. "Neither have I."

I know he's slept with girls. And it's true that I can't exactly compete in that department. Not directly. But I like that we've found an area where we're both inexperienced.

"I'll need some sort of lube," I say. And a team of experts to tell me exactly what I'm supposed to do, because glancing down, I'm reminded that he's a big boy.

"I'm sure we can find something," Tim says. "Uhh… In the bathroom maybe?"

I shrug. "Let's go look."

We pull up our pants. I follow him to the downstairs bathroom, where he opens drawers and cabinets until he finds a bottle of lotion. "Think this will work?" he asks when holding it up.

I peer at the label. The lotion is scented, which might be helpful, since I'm a little insecure about him messing around down there. Maybe this isn't such a good idea. Then again, I can see his cock straining against his jeans. He really wants this. I do too but… "Can you give me some privacy?"

"No problem," he says, shutting the door behind him when he goes.

I exchange a look with myself in the mirror before murmuring, "What have you gotten yourself into?"

It's not that I haven't tried. Anal sex is part of being gay, I figure. So every once in a while, I'll experiment by putting a finger inside myself. But none of those attempts actually felt good. Even worse, on the most recent occasion, I could tell that I needed to use the restroom. Talk about a mood killer! I'm petrified of that happening now, so I pull down my pants, squirt some lotion on my index finger, and brace myself when sliding it inside. I poke around, relieved to discover that nobody is in the waiting room. Then I wash in the sink to make myself as presentable as possible.

I'm anything but certain when opening the door to the bathroom. I almost laugh when I see Tim standing there waiting for me.

"Ready?" he asks, his breath sounding short.

"Yeah," I say, despite all my reservations.

He steps forward to kiss me. Then he takes my hand and

leads me back to the living room. We pick up where we left off, slowly undressing each other while continuing to make out. When we're both completely naked, he lays me down on a bed of discarded wrapping paper. I open my legs for him and reach for the bottle of lotion. He grins at me while lubing himself up. I'm petrified when Tim positions himself above me, his aim unnervingly accurate as the head of his cock begins to press against my hole.

"Umm…" I say, wondering if it's too late to reconsider.

Tim's mouth silences me with a kiss. The way he's rubbing against me does feel nice, but when he finally pushes his way inside, I see stars. And not in a good way, because it fucking hurts! "Wait!" I hiss.

Tim pushes himself up to see me better. "Should I pull out?" he asks before starting to.

Which only makes it hurt worse.

"No!" I say. "Don't move."

I pound my fist against the floor while grimacing.

Tim's face is drawn with concern. "I know first times can hurt for girls." he says helpfully.

"I'm not a goddamn girl!" I snarl like I'm in labor. Although the pain is starting to subside.

"We can try some other time," he suggests.

"No," I say, not wanting this moment to end in failure. "I think it's getting better."

"Yeah?" he asks.

When I nod, he moves his hips experimentally, causing more pain, but I try to master it for him, because I want this. Even though it doesn't feel good. "Just go slow," I plead.

He nods before kissing me again, which helps distract from the discomfort. Enough that he manages a steady rhythm.

"Damn, Benjamin," Tim says, pushing himself up on rippling arms. "That feels so good."

I glance up at his handsome face, his eyelids fluttering shut in pleasure. His body glows with the golden light of the Christmas tree as I watch him move with a shallow rocking motion, like a slow seductive dance. I'm so taken by his beauty that I relax, wanting to give all of myself to him. That's when I notice the pain is gone. I reach down and touch myself, the pleasure I usually feel multiplied tenfold, causing me to moan.

Tim notices, his silver eyes locking on to mine. "You all right?" he asks.

I nod eagerly. "Yeah!"

"Can I put it the rest of the way in?"

"You haven't already?" I ask in disbelief.

He smiles and gently thrusts. He was definitely holding back! But to my surprise, it feels even better. Especially when his hips press against my butt and I feel something I never have before. I bite my lower lip to avoid crying out in bliss. Which is a battle I lose, because he starts moving faster, and I'm so into it that I have to hold back. I'm on the verge the entire time, even when I stop touching myself. I cling to him instead, grabbing his butt so he'll go deeper before wrapping my arms around his torso to pull him close. Tim's body writhes against mine, his short breaths matching my gasps.

He pushes himself up, a question in his gaze. I nod and take hold of myself again. With my free hand, I touch his chest, stroke his neck, and pull him in for a kiss that becomes us huffing against each other's mouths. My entire body is overloaded with ecstasy as we come, the pleasure so intense that I feel like I'm going to lose my mind. When my vision clears, Tim's chest continues to heave as he stares down at me with wide eyes, as if he's just as overwhelmed.

"Wow," he manages at last.

"Yeah," I reply with a laugh. "That was…" I shake my head. There are no words.

A smile tugs at his cheek. He looks proud. Or maybe he's just happy. I don't know. But I sure do adore him. When he starts to pull out, I wrap my legs around his waist to draw him back in.

"Not yet," I say demurely.

Tim studies me a moment. "You like that I'm inside you, huh?"

"I love it," the warble in my voice telling him all he needs to know.

Tim settles down on me, resting on his elbows so his hand can brush the hair off my forehead. Then he studies my face. Raw emotion fills his gaze before he kisses me.

"Merry Christmas, Benjamin," he murmurs while nuzzling my ear.

"Merry Christmas," I say, clinging tighter to him.

We hold each other in the glow of the tree, two alchemists who have discovered something better than turning lead into gold. We've figured out how two boys can become one, so they never have to feel lonely again.

CHAPTER EIGHTEEN

I'm sitting naked on Tim's bed while staring at the painting on his wall. In the morning light, a rainbow collides against a drab gray barrier, still trying to break through. If it had some sort of magical Dorian Gray properties, I'd like to think that cracks would have appeared in the painting as we slowly wear down that wall together.

Tim walks into the bedroom while toweling his hair dry. He's not wearing anything except for a grin that gets bigger when he makes his cock bounce. "Wanna do it again?" he asks.

"We just did!" I say in disbelief.

"So?" he says, nodding at my crotch. "You seem up for it."

I cover my swelling erection. "Yeah, but not when you're clean and I'm still dirty."

"I like it dirty," he says with a wicked grin.

"Later," I promise, my eyes darting back to the painting on the wall. "Tell me about that."

Tim follows my gaze. "Oh." He walks to the dresser to take out clothes. "What do you think?"

"I like it. Is that the way you feel inside?"

Tim pulls on a pair of boxer briefs before turning to consider the painting again. "It's a reminder."

"Of what?"

"The way things have to be."

My stomach sinks as he continues to get dressed. I thought the painting represented his spirit trying to break free, but instead, it's his way of walling himself in. And he chose to reinforce that barrier by putting it on display. "Where are the others?" I ask.

I've walked around the house, trying to find more paintings, figuring each would be a clue to his heart. The only other one I can find is of Jesus, nailed to the dining room wall, but I figure he prefers that over a crucifix. I wouldn't have known Tim was the artist had I not asked, since it doesn't feel like either of the paintings in our bedrooms. The style is too reserved, the colors drab.

"Other what?" Tim asks while poking his head through a sweater.

"Your other paintings. There must be more."

He's quiet. I wait patiently, used to these moments, because they happen when he decides just how open he wants to be with me. And considering that I am currently laid bare before him, I'm hoping he doesn't choose to shut me out.

"Do you want to see?" he asks at last.

I perk up. "Are you kidding? Yeah!"

Tim's smile is short-lived before it's replaced by an insecure expression. "Okay."

I hop to my feet. "Show me!"

He laughs. "They aren't here. We'll have to go for a drive."

"I'm ready," I say. "Oh wait!" I grab the T-shirt I was wearing yesterday and put it on. "Okay. Let's go."

I'm still naked from the waist down, of course, which makes him laugh.

"I'll get cleaned up," I say before darting from the room.

I take the quickest shower of my life, although I make sure to be meticulous, because I'm definitely up for a second round later. We haven't gone *all* the way since the night under the Christmas tree, but we both want to again, when the stars align. Not now. I'm too excited to learn more about him. I figure he'll drive us to a storage unit where he keeps all his paintings, so I'm surprised an hour later when we pull up to an office building.

"What is this place?" I ask.

"My dad's business," he says, glancing around the parking lot after we get out of his car. We're the only ones here, judging from all the empty spots.

"Does he sell art?" I ask in confusion.

"No. I wish. That would be awesome." Tim leads the way to a glass door. "He sells medical supplies."

I watch him fish out a key. Once the door is unlocked and we're inside, he taps a code on the alarm system, causing a high-pitched whine to fall silent. I glance around the reception area, expecting to see his paintings on the wall. And while art hangs there, it clearly isn't his, since the style is much too blocky and basic. He leads me deeper into the office. We walk through a large open room filled with rows of cubicles, which in the darkness, remind me of crypts in a graveyard. When we reach the other side, Tim stops before a door with a sign that reads *Conference Room C*. The windows along the wall to either side are covered with paper, making it impossible to see in.

"I used to paint at home," Tim is saying as he unlocks the

door. "Our old house had a basement. After we moved here and I got paint on the guest room carpet, my dad came up with this as a solution. I like it better." He opens the door and gestures for me to enter.

I do so, peering into the gloom until fluorescent lights flicker on above. And it's as if we've been transported somewhere else. The room doesn't feel like an office at all. The toes of my shoes are on one of many drop cloths that cover the floor. Half a dozen easels are set up, each with a canvas in a different state of completion. As for the paintings themselves, they're everywhere. Some are propped up and on display. Most are leaning against the walls in stacks. Tim walks over to windows on the exterior wall and opens the blinds to let in natural light. Then he turns to me with an uncertain expression.

I begin to focus on the art instead of the room, feeling as though I'm romping through the valleys of his imagination. Some things I recognize, like the volcano that is a patchwork of purple and gray stone, the sky behind it having caught fire with orange, red, and magenta. On an easel next to it is a sunbaked woman wearing large tinted glasses, a tower of hair balanced on her head. I'm drawn to it, since most of his paintings lean toward the abstract, but this one is surprisingly lifelike.

"That's my *abuelita*," Tim says, walking over to join me.

"Your grandma?"

"Yeah. She's cool."

One of the woman's eyebrows is raised more than the other. She's wearing a subtle smirk. Her clothes are dark like her hair, the tones restricted to browns and blacks. The empty space around her has been filled with strokes of color. I notice a similar technique on other canvases. Whenever empty space is available, Tim fills it with a variety of hues.

"You must like rainbows," I comment.

"I guess," he says with a shrug. "I'm not really happy with any of these." Tim sweeps an arm around the room. "There's something I'm going for, but I haven't found it yet."

"Are you sure?" I ask, stopping to look at a painting of a solitary farmhouse, tiny against a backdrop of field and sky, making humanity's toils seem small compared to the natural world. "Because these are really good! They're all so evocative."

"Of what?" he asks while following me.

"That depends on the painting. Your grandma's portrait has so much personality that it's like meeting her. The volcano… what was it called again?"

"*Popocatépetl*," he says with a smile.

"I love when you say that. Anyway, the sky hints at the volcano's history, or its potential, even though it's dormant for now. And this one…" We stop before a canvas that is almost completely monotone. Most of the canvas is gray. A solitary figure cast in black stands in the void while peering through a window, represented by a white rectangle. The light shining in is just enough to create an edge of color on the figure's face.

"I know that feeling," I tell him. "Like the world is happening without me, and all I get to do is watch others living in a way that I can't." I turn to him. "It's how I felt before we met."

Tim swallows before shaking his head. "You *are* the light. Most of us are standing at the window watching you while wishing we could be that brave. That's what I was thinking about when painting it."

I consider the canvas again, amazed how he managed to flip the story. I was already free but didn't realize it. Not until we found the window—this connection—that allows us to see each other. If only I could convince Tim to climb through it. We could finally leave the darkness behind. I'm so moved by the thought, and his art, that I have to wipe at my eyes.

Tim takes my hand and toys with my fingers, lingering on a spot made wet from my tears. Then he glances up at me. "Do you want to see something really personal?"

"Yeah, of course!"

I follow him to one of the stacks leaning against the wall. He takes a canvas from the very back and holds it up. I'm presented with a guy our age. Black hair frames an angular face. His eyes are brown and mischievous. What stands out most is that the canvas has been repeatedly slashed, like a serial killer took out his frustration on it.

"Who's that?" I ask.

"Cole. My ex's little brother."

"He's hot," I say, feeling intimidated.

"He didn't look exactly like this," Tim says. "I aged him up. This is how I…" He hesitates. "I guess this is how I wanted him to look."

Which already proves that I'm not the exception to the rule. "So what happened?" I ask, poking a finger through one of the holes.

"I got mad at myself for painting it," Tim says, already returning the painting to the back of the stack.

"But not mad enough to throw it away," I point out.

He seems surprised by this observation. Then he shrugs. "I guess not."

Tim leads me to another stack, where he shows me some of his earliest work, like a frog floating down a river in a teacup. "That's cute," I say. "I'm surprised your mom doesn't haven't it hanging up at home. My mom kept the first poem I wrote taped to the refrigerator for years and years, until I begged her to take it down. Now it's in my baby book."

Tim is peering at me like I'm speaking a foreign language. "My parents don't really get it," he replies. "They aren't into art. Like at all. They never went into the basement at our old house, and they never come in here."

"Ever?" I ask in disbelief. "You don't think your dad peeks every once in a while? I mean, you're his son. And this is part of his office."

"I know he doesn't," Tim replies. "My dad doesn't have a key. He might *think* he does, but I made sure to match it to the one I have before I took his copy. Nobody comes in here but me."

"Do you wanna change that?" I ask flirtatiously.

"Sure," he says, moving toward me. "Just don't get any ideas about how we could use this place."

"Is it too sacred?"

He laughs. "There's usually a security guard. He knows who I am. But if he hears you moaning…"

"Hey, you're just as loud," I counter before dodging a kiss. "So you've really never shown this to anyone else?"

He shakes his head.

"Not even Krista?"

"Nope," he replies, his lips nearing mine again. "This is the sort of thing I'd only show to my boyfriend."

I pull back, already wounded, because that's not a joke. It's important to me. Then again, he's not laughing. Those silver eyes of his are filled with affection.

"Are you serious?" I ask.

He nods. "Yeah. You're my boyfriend."

I continued to search his eyes. "Are you mine?"

Tim laughs, but not cruelly. "Yes, Benjamin. I'm definitely yours."

When he kisses me, I wrap my arms around him, a sob escaping my throat, but I can't help it. I'm just so happy! His expression is gentle when he leans back to smudge the moisture on my cheek.

"Can I paint you?" he asks. "I almost never have a live model."

"Sure!" I say, taking a few steps back to strike a pose. "What do you think?"

"Take off your coat," he suggests. "And your sweater," he adds soon after.

"Okay," I say while complying.

He moves to an easel and sets up a fresh canvas. Then he leans to the side to look at me again.

"Get rid of your shirt too," he says.

I laugh. "Is this going to be a nude painting?"

"Are you cool with that?"

I blink a few times. Then I shrug. "I guess so."

I'm undoing my pants when he walks around the easel, already pulling the sweater over his head.

"Do you usually paint shirtless?" I ask in confusion.

"No," he says, unbuttoning his pants. "I'm not in the mood anymore. Because I'm *in* the mood."

"What if someone hears us?"

"It's the holidays. Nobody is here. And besides, I'll make sure your mouth is full."

I laugh again, and after kicking off my underwear and jeans, open my arms which are soon filled to capacity... with my boyfriend.

I love being in Allison's room. Posters of her favorite singers cover the walls. She'll be a pop star someday, I'm sure of it. A busy quilt of mismatched patches covers her bed. We found it at a vintage shop, where she often buys decorations, like the ornate lamp next to her bed with beads woven into the shade. Small planted pots soak up sun on her window sill. Music plays from an old turntable. I love it here, although I don't usually feel this comfortable. Not with her dad around, but he's returned to work while we're still on winter break.

"Guess what?" I cry when leaping onto her bed. I've only just arrived, and even though I promised myself I'd be polite enough to ask how her trip was, I can't help it.

Allison laughs from where she sits at a small desk. She closes her journal and steeples her fingers. "Does it have something to do with love, by chance?"

"It does," I say, settling into the pile of pillows that nestle against the headboard. "I have a boyfriend now!"

"Really?" Allison looks confused. "Did you meet someone new?"

"No, you big dummy! I'm talking about Tim!" My scowl dissipates. "Although I don't blame you. I was starting to think it would never happen."

"This is major!" Allison leaps up to join me on the bed.

"I know!" I grab her hand in excitement. "We both have boyfriends! At the same time!"

"I sure hope so," she replies. "A week is a long time to be away."

"I bet Ronnie never stopped thinking about you," I assure her. "Not even for a second. Hey, tell me about your trip! Is your aunt cool?"

"She's okay," Allison says without much enthusiasm. "But nothing like my mom. I can see why they weren't very close."

"Oh. That's a bummer." She had wanted to reconnect with her mother through her aunt. I can't imagine how that must feel. Like if my dad had died when I was a kid and I had to visit my deadbeat uncle hoping to see a glimmer of the man I missed.

"It's fine," Allison says. "She's nice… But you know my mom. She was all heart. My aunt is surprisingly analytical. She got along great with my dad."

I snort at this. "I bet!"

"Listening to them talk to each other was fun. They both have different memories of my mom, so I got to hear a bunch of new stories about her. And it was nice to celebrate Christmas with a big family again. Even if my cousins *are* a bunch of weirdos. As for my dad…" She shakes her head and smiles. "That was the best part."

"How come?"

"He didn't drink as much, so it was more like how things

used to be. We talked and laughed on the drive there and back. We spent a lot of time together. I mean, it's always just us these days, so that's not unusual. But he didn't seem as sad." Allison inhales sharply, as if overwhelmed with emotion. She smiles again, despite her eyes filling with tears. "I went on the trip hoping to find a piece of my mother, but I found him instead. The dad that I've missed and needed."

"Aww!" I say, leaning forward to hug her. "I'm so happy for you."

"Thanks." Allison wipes at her cheeks after I pull away. "I'm hoping we can do it again next year."

"Hey, what about your dad's side of the family? You could visit them instead. How come they're never around?"

Allison shrugs. "He had a bad childhood. I don't know much about it. Only that he broke off contact when he was old enough to move out."

"Let's promise to do the same," I joke, even though we both love our families.

She snorts. "At this rate, you'll have started your own family with Tim before we even graduate. What changed?"

"Nothing," I say. Then I grin. "Actually, I do have some exciting news."

"Even more exciting than netting your first boyfriend?"

I nod while biting my lower lip, releasing it to declare, "I lost my virginity!"

"Look who just took the lead!" Allison says, before tilting her head. "So how does that work when it's two guys? Are you saying that he… Which of you…"

"I'll need to take a pregnancy test," I say helpfully.

Allison laughs. "Oh my god! What was it like? Did it hurt?"

"At first, yeah. But then it felt really good."

She places a hand over her heart. "Please tell me it was romantic."

"It really was!" I confirm before launching into details.

"I'm so jealous," Allison says at the end of my story. "Although, I've always wondered…" She shakes her head, as if it would be too much, which is a joke because—

"When have we ever held back?" I ask.

She laughs. "I don't know if you'll want to get *this* personal, but okay. Was it messy?"

"I was so nervous about that! Luckily the timing was right.

We've done it again since then, but I made sure to wait until I *knew* the coast was clear. Girls are so much luckier in that regard. You can just let a guy stick it in whenever he wants."

"Um, no, it's not that simple. Are you forgetting that we bleed? Imagine if you had a nasty bout of diarrhea every month that could last up to a week. How much of a mood killer would that be?"

I grimace. "Sounds rough. I'll stick with what I've got."

Allison laughs. "I'm not trading mine either. Boy parts are weird. You've got all that extra stuff dangling around down there that you can't even control."

"Does that mean Ronnie is in for a long wait?" I tease.

"Maybe," Allison says before reconsidering. "Or maybe not. I *am* curious."

"Just make sure he's the right one," I advise. "I'm glad Tim was my first. Nobody can ever take that away. Actually, if we do get married, he might also be my last!"

"Wow. Things have really turned the corner for you guys. So now that you're his boyfriend, does that mean no more secret relationship?"

"No," I say with a sigh. "He still doesn't want anyone to find out. We won't get to spend New Year's Eve together because he's going to some big party with his dumb friends."

"Good!" Allison says, grabbing a pillow and thwacking me with it. "I don't want him to get *all* your time. You still have to be my best friend, and there's no way that my dad will let me stay out with Ronnie until midnight. So you better pucker up, because it's going to be me and you as usual!"

"I don't mind," I tell her.

And it's true, because if my boyfriend doesn't have time for me, I can always rely on my best friend. What more could a guy ask for? Although I am a little nervous about going back to school. Everything was perfect when Tim was stuck at home with a sprained ankle. Everything has been perfect during the winter break, especially when his parents were out of town. I'm not sure what the future will bring, but whether I like it or not, I'm about to find out.

CHAPTER NINETEEN

The year gets off to a good start, despite my concerns. The first few weeks of the semester follow a familiar routine. I sneak over to Tim's house on random nights, so we can mess around, and he sleeps over at my place on the rare weekend nights when he's able to ditch his friends. Tim still jogs, despite the cold, but I don't try to find him when he does. I save my hunting for the school hallways, feeling a thrill each time his eyes meet mine, like a secret kiss. That's what I'm craving today. I know his entire schedule and can choose to find him between any two classes. I know I won't see him tonight, since he'll be in his studio. I'm tempted to surprise him there, but I understand that he needs privacy to work. I can be a distraction. He never did paint me after we had sex there, although he still talks about wanting to. I keep thinking how romantic it would be if—

My train of thought is broken when I spot Tim's friends in the hallway ahead of me, and I'm puzzled, because they're hanging out with my physics partner Danny. Or so it first appears, since the popular kids are clustered around him. Danny even seems to turn and wave a gangly arm in my direction. That's when I see something red sail above his ginger hair that bounces off the tips of his reaching fingers. Bryce snatches it out of the air, Danny's expression becoming even more distraught. My pulse picks up along with my pace.

I watch as Bryce tosses a red ball cap over Danny's head. Darryl leaps up to grab it. He waves the hat around, taunting Danny with it until he tries again. As soon as he's close to grabbing it, Darryl flings the hat to another guy, who is overcome with laughter.

"Give it back!" Danny cries.

"Hey!" I call out, about to break into a sprint.

I hesitate when I notice Tim. He's standing with his back to me. The hat is tossed to him. I feel a surge of relief, certain in my heart that he'll put a stop to this. Danny turns to Tim, his face just as red as the ball cap. He looks like he's on the verge of tears. I can't see my boyfriend's expression, but he better be pissed off at the behavior of his stupid friends!

"Over here," Bryce says, getting behind Danny and cupping his hands, like he wants Tim to toss a football to him.

Tim tosses the hat over Danny's head, my stomach sinking with its descent. I can't believe he's going along with this! Bryce catches the hat. I grit my teeth and march right into the middle of their group. By the time I do, Bryce is holding Danny at bay with an outstretched arm while waving the hat around with his free hand.

"Give it back!" I yell, pushing on the crook of Bryce's elbow to force his arm to bend. That frees Danny, but I'm not relieved, because I've spent a lot of time feeling Tim's muscles. Bryce's bicep and forearm are even thicker.

"Get the fuck off, faggot!" Bryce growls before shoving me.

I stumble backward into Tim. I feel his hands on my shoulders, stabilizing me. I'm yanked out of his grip when Bryce grabs me by the shirt and swings me around, slamming my back against the row of lockers.

"Hey!" I hear Tim say. "Take it easy!"

"What the fuck is your problem?" Bryce yells, his breath hot in my face.

I look past him and see Danny picking up his hat. His eyes are wavering with fear, like he wants to bolt.

"Try picking on someone your own size," I yell back.

Bryce's face twists up. "You're half my size, pipsqueak!"

"Exactly," I snarl. "That's what makes you a bully!"

His massive fists clench around my shirt. Then he releases me, but only with one hand, the other balling up. I'm about to get punched.

"Let him go!"

The hero who comes to my rescue isn't Tim. Danny barrels into Bryce from the side and bounces off his bulk before losing his balance and falling to the floor. The guys around us laugh. I see pure terror in Danny's eyes as he stares up at me.

"I'll go get a teacher!" he says before scrambling away.

"It'll be too late by then," Bryce says, returning his attention to me.

"You really are pathetic," I reply. "Are you sure you don't need reinforcements? I mean, it took four of you to pick on Danny."

I look past him and see Tim's chest heaving. His expression is twisted up with concern, which counts for something, I suppose, but it's not going to make me feel better when my eyes are swollen shut.

"What's going on here?" Stacy pushes past Tim and scoffs at the scene. "Let him go," she says casually. Bryce only spares her a glance before sneering at me and shoving me against the lockers again.

"Hey!" I hear Tim shout.

"*Now*," Stacy adds, her tone firm.

Bryce finally releases me.

I brush myself off, but I don't flee. I glare at each of them. "You're all cowards," I growl. My gaze settles on Tim. "You especially!"

He swallows, as if wounded. I don't care. He's not the man I thought he was. I'm still surrounded, so I march toward him. Tim steps aside. So does Stacy, who is looking between us in a way that would have worried me this morning, but not anymore.

I'm halfway down the hall when I see Danny hurrying toward me with a teacher in tow.

"Are you okay?" he asks.

"Where is this fight?" the teacher demands.

"Everything is fine," I reply. "It was just a misunderstanding."

I keep walking. Danny can tattle on them if he wants. I wouldn't hold it against him. I'm too angry to stick around. My next class passes in a blur of barely contained rage. I can't believe Tim just stood there while Bryce manhandled me! Which bothers me half as much as what I caught him doing. Danny had looked so small and helpless when trying to get his hat back. What kind of sick mind finds that entertaining? Bryce and his friends are a bunch of savages. Tim included. I hate him!

If only that was true. My anger slowly abandons me, replaced by sorrow. I trudge to my final class, feeling as though I'm about to lose everything that made me happy. How can I be with someone like that?

"Hey!" Danny says, already seated at the table we share. His posture is rigid, his eyes wide. "Are you okay?"

"Yeah," I say, sitting next to him with a grimace. "What happened?"

I only mean the aftermath, but Danny launches into a play-by-play. "Darryl has been making fun of my hat." Which is sitting on the table between us. The ball cap is mostly red with a mesh back. Only the front is white, where black letters spell out: *Keep on truckin'!* "My dad gave it to me for Christmas," Danny continues. "I don't get to see him much." He pauses to swallow against whatever he's feeling. "I know we're not allowed to wear hats in class, but I figured there was no harm in wearing it in the halls. I guess I should just leave it at home."

"Don't," I say, clenching my jaw. "You keep doing whatever you want. People like Bryce—" (and my boyfriend, I add mentally) "—are just jealous because they're too afraid to be who they really are. Don't let them make you into one of them."

"Like zombies do?" Danny asks.

"Yeah, exactly. I guess that's why they went after your hat, so they could get at your brains easier, because they sure as hell don't have any of their own."

Danny laughs before his expression grows somber. "Thanks for saving me."

"Hey, you came to my rescue too," I say easily.

I'm relieved when class starts. Keeping up the cheerful act is too much right now. The bell rings an hour later. I pretend there's someone I'm supposed to meet and leave in a hurry. Although it makes me feel a little better when I see Danny put on the hat again.

I meet my best friend in the parking lot. Allison takes one look at me and can tell something is wrong. We drive around while I rant and rave about how fucked up the whole mess is. I refuse to go home. I don't want Tim to be able to find me. When I'm in my bedroom later that night, I turn my phone's ringer off and toss it into the closet, so I won't be tempted to call, even if it's just to yell at him for being such a jerk.

I should probably throw the painting he gave me in there too. I'm looking at it when I hear something hit my bedroom window. I scowl and roll into bed despite still being fully dressed. Even covering my head with a pillow doesn't help. I can still hear him pelting my window, trying to get my attention. I clench my jaw a few times before my anger gets the best of me. I shove the pillow away and march outside.

"What do you want?" I demand when turning the corner of my house.

Tim winces at the volume of my voice. "Can we go up to your room or something?" he whispers.

"No!" I shout. "Are you kidding me?"

"Are your parents awake?" he asks, glancing at the house with apprehension.

I huff at his concerned expression. He sure does care… about himself. But he's right. I'm angry at him, not my parents, who don't deserve to get woken up. "Fine," I say before returning to the front of the house, where they're less likely to hear us. I don't bother checking to see if he follows me. I couldn't care less. But he's there when I spin around again, so I cross my arms over my chest. "Well?"

"I'm sorry," Tim says.

"For what?" I demand. "Getting caught? Letting me see your true colors?"

"That's *not* who I am," Tim says, sounding defensive.

"Then why'd you do it?" I spit. "How come you felt the need to gang up on someone who has never done anything to you?"

"I didn't want to."

"And yet you did."

"It's not like we were pushing him around or anything," Tim grumbles.

"That's true," I say sarcastically. "Danny was obviously having a blast. Did you know that his estranged father gave him that hat? Which seems like a pretty hokey gift to me, but it obviously means something to him, or he wouldn't take it to school just so he can wear it between classes. But hey, that's not okay with you and your friends, so it's a good thing you made him feel like shit."

"I sure as hell didn't feel good about it!" Tim snarls.

"Then why didn't you do something?"

"Because I don't need my fucking friends turning on me!"

I pinch the bridge of my nose. "You can't blame everything on the lies your ex-girlfriend spread about you. And it *definitely* doesn't give you the right to torment other people!"

"You don't get it," Tim says, rolling his eyes. "Why do you think we moved here?"

I shake my head, not understanding.

Tim takes a deep breath. "My dad was talking about hiring someone to sort out the office down here. My parents didn't say a damn thing about us moving. Not until Carla went around telling people that I raped her. That's when the plan changed. All of a sudden we were moving. When I asked my dad why…" Tim scowls off into the distance. Then he swallows. "He just said, 'Why do you think?' You should have seen the look he gave me, like it was all my fault."

"Okay," I say, wrapping my arms around myself to stay

warm. "But you refusing to pick on someone is completely different than getting falsely accused of rape."

Tim notices me shivering. "How come you're not wearing the coat I gave you?"

"Why do you think?" I say snidely.

Tim glowers at me, but his anger doesn't last long. "You should put something on." He reaches for my hands. "You look cold."

"I'm fine." I pull away from him with a glare. "I'm about to go back inside. Without you."

"Wait!" Tim takes a step toward me. "Have you ever heard of that popular kid who used to go to our school? Fuck! What's his name? It was something old-fashioned, like Theodore."

I snort. "The guy who had to go to the hospital because he stuck a frozen hotdog up his butt?"

"Yeah," Tim says. "Whatever happened to him?"

I shrug. "Didn't he switch schools? How do you know about that? It was last year."

"I know because Darryl told me. They made up the story after Theodore pissed them off."

I stare in disbelief. "Are you serious?"

"Yeah," Tim says.

"This is exactly what I don't understand. Why are you friends with people like that?"

"They're not so bad," Tim says with a shrug. "Darryl is actually pretty funny. Stacy is cooler than you realize, and Krista has been really nice about the breakup. Bryce is a dick though, I'll give you that."

"They're *all* assholes," I say dismissively. Then I glower at him. "So that's your big excuse? You picked on Danny so they wouldn't make up a mean story about you? Who cares! That just proves they aren't the kind of friends worth having."

"You've gotta put it all together," Tim says. "If I ditch them, what happens?"

"You get to hang out with me and my friends."

He shakes his head. "People will notice. And when they do, what conclusion do you think they'll reach? It doesn't matter how careful we are. You know what they're going to assume."

"That we're together," I say with a shrug. "Would that be so bad?"

"Yeah! It would be really fucking bad when they start stirring up shit and it gets back to my parents. My dad already wants to send me to the same stupid Catholic school he went to for college, and it's nowhere near here. What's going to happen to us then? Think about it!" His face becomes drawn with pain before he manages to hide it.

"We're eighteen now," I tell him. "After we graduate, we can do whatever we want."

"With what? The sports scholarships I keep sabotaging?"

"We'll figure something out. I promise."

He takes this as an invitation to move toward me again. There's so much need in his eyes that I don't pull away when his hands envelop mine.

"Jesus!" Tim hisses. "You're freezing!"

Only when he tries to wrap his arms around me do I finally resist and squirm free.

"I can't do this," I splutter. "I don't care how hot you are, or how much I—" My voice strangles to a halt, and I'm glad, because now isn't the time to tell him. At this point, I don't know if I ever will. "I can't be with a bully," I force myself to continue. "I won't!"

"I fucked up," Tim murmurs. "I'm sorry."

"Tell Danny that!"

"I will," he replies, staring into my eyes as if to prove his sincerity. "And I won't do anything like that again."

"That's not enough," I say, my voice trembling. "Stop them from picking on *anyone*. I mean it! If you see them messing with someone, I expect you to do more than just stand there."

"I'll try," Tim says.

He looks ashamed as he takes a step back. He can't even meet my gaze. "It's cold. You better get inside."

I should walk away—leave him there to stew on it all. And I start to. But when I look back and see him watching me with longing, it matches what I feel in my heart. "Wanna come up to my room?" I ask.

Tim nods. "Yeah. More than anything."

I lead him inside, eager to mend the rift between us. But I also can't help wondering if I deserve the same amount of judgment. Tim had abandoned his ideals when deciding not to give Danny his hat back. Isn't that what I'm doing now? Compromising what I really believe so that I can keep doing what I want? I'm not sure, but I remain troubled, even after he takes me into his arms.

— — —

I'm shoveling snow on a Sunday morning when a sports car pulls up, the black exterior a stark contrast to a world freshly draped in a sparkling white gown. I watch as the car parks directly in front of my house instead of continuing halfway around the block like it used to. The breath catches in my throat when Tim steps out. He's even more beautiful in the snow, his silver eyes like ice but with none of the chill. I feel my blood rushing when he fixes his gaze on me. He's wearing a gray jacket with wool lining. I'm not surprised that it's hanging open. I swear he never gets cold. I'm tempted to throw off my gloves so I can slide my bare hands beneath his sweater to feel the warmth of his skin.

"Hey," Tim says with an upward nod. He's grinning in a way that I've come to recognize.

"Hey yourself," I reply. "Did church get you in the mood again?"

"It's all the talk of sinning," Tim says. "Wanna mess around?"

"I'm a little busy here," I say, wiggling the snow shovel.

"Oh right." Tim surveys what little progress I've made. Then he reaches for the shovel. "I'll take care of it."

"Really?"

"Yeah! Why not?"

I hand him the shovel and retreat to the front stoop. I watch him as he works, surprised by how much has changed. Not only is his car parked right outside my house. Now he's in my driveway, making short work of the snow. Anyone could pass by and recognize that he's here. Which is exceedingly unlikely, so I'm not worried about it personally. That he's not either gives me hope.

We've found our way back to a good place. Tim kept his promise. He showed up in my physics class before it began the next day and apologized to Danny right in front of everyone. And went a step further. *"If my friends ever mess with you when I'm not there, just let me know. I'll take care of it."* I wish he would have stuck around to see Danny's reaction. After looking confused, a big goofy grin had filled his face.

I'm not completely over what happened. It definitely shook my faith in Tim. The gesture would have been more meaningful had he apologized on his own, without me insisting that he do so. But at the very least, it's proof that he cares enough about me to stick his neck out. And he's continued to do so, up to this moment. I watch him clear the sidewalk and stick the shovel in a snow drift with a satisfied smirk. Then he saunters over to me.

"Are you busy now?" he asks.

"I'm about to be," I say, leading him inside and upstairs to my room.

"That was a good workout," Tim says while shrugging off his jacket.

"Oh yeah?" I ask innocently.

"Uh-huh," Tim says. "Got my muscles all pumped up."

The words alone make my cock swell, but when he takes off his sweater and flexes a bicep, I'm rock hard.

"Wanna feel?"

"It's a start," I reply before running my palm over the steaming hot curve of his arm.

He's searching my eyes, but there's something more than lust in his gaze. "Valentine's Day is coming up," he says.

"Isn't that my line?" I tease, since I keep asking him what we're going to do.

"Not anymore," he says with a grin. "My parents are going out of town."

"Really?" I'm unable to hide my excitement. As much as I want him to have a nice supportive family, our relationship is at its best when we're on our own.

"Yup!" he says, matching my happy expression. "I thought we'd make a night of it. I wanna paint you. For real this time. What do you think?"

"Sounds romantic," I say, batting my eyelashes at him, "I love the idea."

"Cool." His eyes move over me. "I also want to paint you now, Jackson Pollock style."

I shake my head, not understanding.

"He's the paint splatter guy," Tim says helpfully.

"Oh." I squint at him. "Huh?"

"I want you to be my canvas."

"*Ooh!*" I say, getting it at last. "Okay!"

I'm pulling my arms out of my sweater when we hear the doorbell.

"My mom will get it," I say when he stops undoing his pants. I glance at the clock with a jolt. "Oh shit! I bet it's Allison. We're supposed to go shopping."

We both stop to listen, and sure enough, we can hear her talking to my mom.

"Think she'll be willing to wait downstairs?" Tim asks.

"While we do it?" I ask incredulously.

"Yeah! I'm insanely horny. I've been saving it up for you."

Damn, that's hot! I don't want his sacrifice to be in vain. Or to miss out on that great big load. "Umm. We'll be done shopping in the afternoon. Come back then."

"Can't," Tim says, shaking his head. "I've got plans."

Which has become code for hanging out with his friends. He avoids mentioning them around me, since I still get my back up about it all. I don't even try to find him in the school halls anymore. I'd rather not witness that side of him. But there is plenty that I *am* eager to see.

"I could sneak over tonight," I suggest. "If you can wait that long."

"I'll try," he says, leaning in for a kiss.

My bedroom door swings open.

"Oh my god!" Allison says when she sees us. She starts to close the door, but hesitates as she takes in Tim's bare torso. "Oh my god," she repeats, breathlessly this time.

"Hey," Tim says to her while puffing up his chest.

He's such a show-off.

"Should I come back later?" Allison asks while continuing to stare.

"It's okay," I assure her. I grab Tim's sweater and toss it to him, accidentally hitting him in the side of his head. He slings it over a shoulder instead of putting it on. "He was just leaving."

"I'd rather be coming," Tim murmurs under his breath when kissing me goodbye.

I laugh and push him away. "See you later."

"Yeah," he says, grabbing his jacket. "See ya."

Allison steps aside to make room for Tim, her head pivoting to follow him on the way out. "He's not really going to drive home like that," she asks when entering my room, "is he?"

I shrug. "Is it wrong that I hope he does?"

"Not at all," she says, fanning herself theatrically. "I can see why you've given the boy so many chances."

"I am nothing if not superficial," I reply shamelessly.

"Did I tell you that I saw Ronnie naked the other day?" Allison asks.

I rush over to shut my bedroom door before pressing my back to it. "I need details!"

We have fun catching up and also when out shopping. Enough that I'm glad I don't have to rush home in the afternoon. Although once we do say goodbye, the evening drags on until it's finally time to sneak out. I bundle up and hustle down snow-lined sidewalks, slipping on ice at one point, but I'm certain the peril will be worth it. I just hope he hasn't given into temptation yet. I know he'd be up for another round, but I really want to expose myself to the arts.

My hands are shaking from cold by the time I slide his key into the lock. I try to stomp the excess snow off my boots before opening the door. After pulling it shut behind me, I turn around and am about to ascend the stairs when I hear a woman's voice.

"Tim? Is that you?"

I freeze. It's his mom! Her voice came from upstairs. Opening the door again and fleeing would definitely alert her, so I creep into the living room, and just in time, because a light flicks on.

"Tim?" she repeats.

"What's going on?" I hear my boyfriend say.

"I think someone is in the house!"

"I didn't hear anything," Tim replies.

"Maybe I should wake your father."

"Nah, let him sleep. I'll go look."

I'm momentarily relieved until I hear his mother say, "Not alone you won't!"

Shit! I glance around the living room but can't find a convenient hiding place. I'll be trapped in here if I don't hurry. I see two pairs of feet coming down the stairs as I sneak across the entryway. I'm moving slowly, so I won't make a sound, but they don't share this concern and are coming down the stairs much faster. I can hear his mother whispering a prayer in Spanish. I finally reach the threshold of carpet, but they're bound to see me at any second, so I dart into the guest bathroom. My options here aren't any better. There's only a toilet and a sink.

"The front door is unlocked!" I hear his mother hiss. "And the floor is wet!"

"That was me," Tim says. "I went for a run not too long ago."

"Maybe someone followed you home!"

"Well there's nobody in the living room."

I squeeze behind the bathroom door, press my back against

the wall, and listen to footsteps approach. Which sound noisier than they need to be, I guess to warn me, but I can't leave my hiding spot now without being seen. The bathroom light turns on. I glance in the mirror and see Tim staring back at me.

"All clear," he says with wide eyes before shutting off the light. "Hey, you know what this reminds me of? When I used to make you guys check for monsters. *Under my bed.*" He speaks the last line with added emphasis. I guess that could work. I'm certain that the front door will be locked and too noisy to open.

"Let's check the back of the house," Tim says.

His mother says something in Spanish. *The saints are pregnant?* No idea. I really should pay more attention in class. Tim responds to her in turn as their voices fade away. I hold my breath and leave the bathroom, my legs stiff and unwilling. I creep along until I reach the stairs and place a sweaty palm on the handrail. I've done this enough times to avoid the squeakier steps, but my heart thuds anyway as I climb, because I'm worried his father is going to wake up and come investigate. My worst fear fails to manifest. I make it into the safety of Tim's room, forcing myself to proceed cautiously, when really I want to run and dive beneath his bed. I leave his bedroom door open, just like I found it, since his mother could give Sherlock Holmes a run for his money. I kneel, stretch myself out on the floor, and scoot horizontally to hide myself.

An eternity later, I hear Tim and his mom upstairs again. She makes him check the guest room and home office before they return to the hall.

"Don't worry about it," Tim says. "I'll still be up for another hour. Any bad guys will get scared off when they see these babies." I can imagine him flexing.

His mother laughs quietly. *"Dulces sueños, Gordito."*

Candy dreams, fatty? My translation can't be right, but there's no mistaking the affection in her voice. His mom sounds nice. I want to meet her. Just not like this. I watch Tim's bare feet pad into the room. He shuts the door and locks it. I scoot out from under his bed. Tim raises a finger to his lips. When I open my mouth to whisper, he shakes his head. Too risky, it would seem.

He helps me out of my coat. Then he pushes on me so I'll sit on his bed. Tim grabs one of my legs, lifting it so he can take off the boot before doing the same for the other. When he starts to undress, I do the same. Once we're both naked, he gets into bed and pulls me on top of him, like a blanket. I shift and reach down to touch him, but he shakes his head and murmurs in my ear, "Not yet."

His arms constrict around me, pressing our bodies together, and I relax onto him. I can feel his heart beating against my chest. I breathe in the scent of his skin, goosebumps racing across my own when he traces a finger down my back. I'm not sure how long we hold each other. I only know that it's heaven.

I'm horny, of course, but the longer we've been together, the more my physical urges intermingle with my feelings for him, sex and love becoming almost indistinguishable. Not that I would abandon one for the other. Tim's fingers slip between our hips. I lift my rump, giving him more room to work as he takes us both into his hand and begins to pump. He doesn't seem in a hurry. He shakes his head when a moan escapes my lips. This isn't going to be easy! When he tries to switch arms, I get my hand in there instead, studying his face until I see his eyes glaze over.

Tim rolls over, so he's on top of me. He pushes himself upright, straddling my hips with his knees. I watch, enraptured, as he jacks off in front of me. I barely touch myself, already on the verge, but I really want him to go first. Tim's chest swells, his arms bulging as he pumps faster. And then…

A white rope of come strikes my cheek. The next splatters across my chest. Then he starts soaking my stomach, and it doesn't seem like he's ever going to stop. My cock is wet with his come when I touch myself again, using it as lube, but it only takes a few strokes before I add to the mess. When I begin to whimper, Tim silences me with a kiss, holding himself above me. He pushes himself upright again once I've gotten myself under control and looks down at me with a smug expression.

"You look like five dudes just unloaded on you," he whispers.

I laugh quietly. "Can I get a towel?"

Tim shrugs. "Can I take a photo first?"

"No!"

He chuckles before looking to his door with concern, but the house remains silent. Tim crawls off and goes to his dresser, tossing a T-shirt to me. Then he sizes me up before throwing another. Once I'm cleaned up, he crawls on top of me again, pinning me down with his weight.

"That was a close call," I say.

"Yeah. I don't think you'll ever be able to leave. I'll have to keep you under my bed."

"You'll use up a lot of T-shirts that way," I murmur. "Won't your mother get suspicious?"

"I'll buy more," he says, nuzzling my nose before he kisses me again. "Can you stay the night? I wanna sleep with you. It's been a while."

My throat feels tight with barely contained emotion. I nod happily before he shifts off me. I roll onto my side and press my back to his chest, not needing a blanket as he wraps himself around me possessively. I notice his plush rabbit, Captain Bunbun, looking jealous from a nearby pillow, so I cradle him close as we drift off, like a secret family slumbering in the suburbs.

CHAPTER TWENTY

I'm hanging out in Leon's basement, which is filled with old couches, chairs, and rugs that were probably moved down here when his family bought new furniture. All of it has been arranged in a U-shape to face a tangle of microphones, guitars, and amps. This isn't my first visit. After much cajoling from Ebony and Ivory, as Ronnie and Leon have dubbed their band, I stopped by a week ago to sing with my best friend. And it was so much fun that I agreed to do it again. Although this time I brought a plus-one.

Tim seems comfortable enough as the guys set up their instruments. He's done well up to this point, easily making conversation with them. He flipped through the crates of vinyl records that Leon keeps down here, commenting on the album art more than the music. And he was eager to help when we rearranged some of the furniture. Tim seems to get along with most people, no matter how intolerable they are, considering the company he keeps. That's part of the reason I invited him. I figure if he gets to know my friends better, the prospect of trading one social circle for another won't be so daunting. Especially since mine have already proven that they don't judge people for simply being who they are.

That, and it's fun to see Ronnie and Allison together outside of school, where they are free to be affectionate without teachers or parents around. They were curled up on the couch just moments ago. I even caught Ronnie smelling her hair before he kissed her on the temple. He's crazy about her and it shows. Such as now, in the way he fusses over her microphone stand, wanting it to be just right.

"I haven't grown any since I was last here," Allison teases.

"Yeah, but were you happy with the height then?" Ronnie asks.

Allison smiles demurely. "I suppose I wouldn't mind if it was a *little* shorter."

Ronnie grins, eager to please. I take my mic out of the stand, already knowing that I'll be dancing around too much to use it.

"What about you, Tim?" Leon asks while plugging his guitar into an amp. "Do you play anything?"

"Nah," Tim says. "Music isn't really my thing."

"What is?" Leon asks in interest.

I watch Tim struggle with the question. *Just be real*, I want to tell him. *These are good people. We're safe here.*

"Baseball," he answers.

My heart breaks for him. Because as much as Tim seems to like other people, I'm not sure that he likes himself, and that worries me. A lot.

His gaze is guarded when meeting mine. I offer a supportive smile, not wanting to feed into his fears by judging him, no matter how depressing it is to watch Tim censor himself. Although it does lift my spirits when he adds…

"And running. I freaking love running!"

"You're making my lungs jealous," Leon says with a stoner's croak. "They're sick of my abuse. Anyway, you've gotta play something. The drum machine we use kind of sucks, so you're on bongos."

"No way!" Tim says, already shaking his head.

"*Anyone* can play the bongos." Leon takes an attached set over to the couch. "Just hit them in the middle for a deeper sound, or toward the edge for a sharper tone."

"Uh…" Tim says before rapping on them with his knuckles.

"More like this," Ronnie says, walking over to show him how. "It's all about maintaining the rhythm. Just like when you keep a steady pace when running. It's the same kind of thing."

Tim tries again, and when he produces a short beat, grins in surprise.

"Now we're talking!" Leon croons before strumming a few chords. "Everybody ready?"

"Yup!" Ronnie says, adjusting the strap of his bass.

They launch into one of the songs I practiced with them last week, an Ebony and Ivory original. I move close to Allison and read from a music stand where lyrics have been scrawled across the page of a notebook in Leon's handwriting. Ebony and Ivory's songs are politically driven, which doesn't mesh with my personal taste, but the chorus is fun to sing.

"Inequality is paltry compared to all the gold you can hold!" I shout into the mic while springing around.

Tim grins at me while banging on the bongos. He does great, even on the next two songs when he's given slightly more complex beats. There's no way he has this much fun with his friends. Sure, they might party more, but Leon *did* offer to get him high. Tim turned him down. So did I. The bliss I'm feeling now is all natural. And mutual, as it turns out.

"I like that one!" Tim says at the end of the song.

"Does anyone else see what's happening here?" Leon asks while glancing around. "We've got a real band!"

"I'm in!" Allison says before turning a pleading expression on me.

"Yeah, okay," I say, even though joining a band has never been one of my aspirations.

"That just leaves the drums," Ronnie says, grinning at Tim.

"Uh…" My boyfriend looks to me for help. He doesn't get any. "I mean, this is fun, but I can't see myself performing in public."

Allison smiles. "It's not so different than baseball. That's just as public."

Tim squirms. "True, but there are a lot more people on the field than on a stage." He sets the bongos aside to underscore his decision.

"We'll keep working on him," Leon says easily. "For now, it's back to the drum machine. Should we try the love song? I rewrote the lyrics."

Allison flips through the notebook on the music stand. I move closer to see. Once we nod that we're ready, Leon cues the drum machine and starts playing a moody riff. Ronnie joins him. I let my mic hang limp at my side so I can share Allison's, although we keep turning our faces away to check the lyrics again. The chorus is still the same, so I use the opportunity to sing to Tim, even though the words aren't powerful enough to capture what's in my heart. I try to put those feelings into my voice. Tim's eyes lock on to mine and remain there, even though witnesses are around. I walk away from Allison, who has the better voice, but his head turns to follow me. As much as I enjoyed making music together, if he was our drummer, I'd probably keep my back to the audience just so I could sing to him.

"What do you think?" Leon asks when the song ends. His expression says that he's not satisfied, which makes it easier to be honest with him.

"We have to rush the second line of the chorus," I say. "There isn't enough time to get it out."

"Some of the verses rhyme and the rest don't," Allison adds.

"Yeah, it's a mess," Leon admits.

"Are you sure it's a love song?" I ask. Like his other compositions, the music has an edge of anger to it, which is more suited to activism.

"Pretty damn sure." Leon sounds frustrated. "If we can get this one figured out, we'll have four songs. That's enough to do an EP. Then we'll really be set."

"We still need a bitchin' band logo," Ronnie says. "All the greats have them."

I look to Tim with raised eyebrows. He gives a barely perceptible shake of his head.

"The music comes first," Leon says. "Without our own songs, we'll just be a cover band."

"Ben can write," Allison supplies.

"Oh yeah?" Leon asks in interest.

"Just because I've tried before," I say dismissively, "doesn't mean I actually know how."

"That makes two of us." Leon tears a page out of the notebook and hands it to me. "See what you can do with this."

"Speaking of cover songs…" Allison says leadingly.

Yes! That was the best part of practicing last week. Allison and I have been singing other people's songs together since we first met. It's one of our favorite pastimes, so we both eagerly lose ourselves in the next batch of songs. We coax Tim into playing the bongos again for a few tunes, but I swear he starts messing up on purpose, just like those sports scholarships he keeps tanking.

My face hurts from smiling so much when he's driving me home.

"Are you disappointed in me?" he asks out of the blue.

I snort. "Do I look like your dad?"

"Ouch," Tim replies with a grimace.

"I only meant that it sounds like something our parents would say. You know… 'I'm not angry, son, just disappointed.'"

"Oh right."

I continue to study him. "You really think your dad is disappointed in you? How could he be when you do everything he wants?"

Tim merely shrugs.

I can't imagine how that must feel. My parents have always

been loving and supportive, which has empowered me to be who I really am. My sister is that way too. She's unapologetically true to herself, abrasive opinions and all. I wonder what his family passed on to him. Maybe that's the missing piece. I won't get a complete picture of Tim until I meet his parents.

"Wait," I say after mentally replaying the conversation. "What were you trying to ask me?"

"Oh." Tim shifts in his seat. "I figured it would bug you that I don't want to draw their band logo. Although I *do* have a few ideas. It's just that once they start asking about my art, it'll get personal. And complicated."

"Only because you make it that way," I say, nudging him affectionately. "And no, I'm not upset."

"Good." He glances over at me and grins. "I'm all booked up anyway. When we get back to your place, I wanna sketch you again. More studies for the painting I want to do."

"Okay!"

"While you read me some of the stuff you've written," Tim adds.

"Huh? No way!"

"What's the matter?" he teases. "Worried it'll get too complicated and personal?"

I think about it and laugh. "Not really. That's kind of our whole vibe."

So far, Valentine's Day hasn't gone as expected. Not that I had anything particular in mind. I kept trying to imagine how this day would go. Gifts, for instance. What's a gay guy supposed to get his straight boyfriend? They don't make greeting cards for that sort of thing. I can't imagine Tim wanting flowers. A box of chocolates might have worked, but I thought it would be more meaningful to bake something for him. When I tried last night, the brownies came out as hard as stone and stuck to the ceramic baking dish, which I ended up breaking. My mom banished me from the kitchen after that.

Probably for the best, because he didn't shower me with gifts either. My eyes dart across Tim's studio to where a box of takeout pizza rests on an old crate that he uses for a table. We sat on the adjacent couch while eating and passed a two-liter bottle of cola back and forth when thirsty. Not exactly fine dining.

"Ronnie took Allison to a Vietnamese restaurant," I say from where I'm perched on a stool.

I listen to the sound of paint being slathered on canvas before Tim leans to the side so he can see me. "That's a long way to go just for dinner," he replies.

"Have you ever had Vietnamese food?"

"Nah." Tim disappears behind the easel again. "I bet it's weird."

"Sounds exciting to me."

A silver eye peeks around the canvas. "I thought this is what you wanted to do."

"It is!" I assure him. I simply didn't think it would dominate so much of the evening. "How come I can't sit on the couch while you paint?"

"Because you would move around too much," Tim replies.

I'm intrigued by his process. He often stops to clean a brush or to mix a new color on his palette. Which is already way more involved than what I do. If I want to sing, I simply take a sip of water if need be and open my mouth. Likewise with writing, all I need is pen and paper. Or even better, a laptop.

"How come you're not in an art elective?" I ask, intimately familiar with his schedule.

"Because my parents don't let me," Tim replies.

I roll my eyes, thankful he can't see me. "So how did you learn?"

"We all had art classes when growing up."

"You mean back in grade school?"

"Yup."

I glance around his studio, which is filled with paintings both abstract and realistic. The art classes we had as kids didn't impart such skills. It was mostly stuff like rolling clay into the shape of a snake or covering a balloon with newspaper strips dipped in glue.

"So you're self-taught?" I ask in disbelief.

"I wouldn't go that far," he replies. "I've watched my share of Bob Ross."

Well sure, but Tim is doing *way* more than painting happy little trees. "Do you *want* to take classes? Like in college?"

"Sort of. I'm going to study architecture."

That surprises me.

"Are you into buildings and things?"

"Yeah."

I glance around his studio again. While there are a few paintings of buildings, he seems to favor living subjects and the natural world. "Wouldn't you rather just sell your paintings and earn money that way?"

Tim is quiet. For a long time. "My great-grandpa was an architect," he says at last. "It's the only visual art that my father has any respect for."

I've never even met the man, but sometimes I wish he'd get run over by a car. Or maybe Tim just needs someone to advocate on his behalf, because if he can accomplish this much on his own, he has the potential to become one of the greatest artists of the era. But not without support.

"I'd like to meet your parents," I say casually.

Tim scoffs. "Very funny."

"I mean it!"

An incredulous expression appears from around the canvas. "Why?"

I have a list of reasons, but only one that could sway him. "Because your mom came *this close* to catching us. What would I have said to her? If you introduce me to them, then at least we can have a few excuses prepared."

"Like what?"

"We could hide a backpack in your room and put some of my old stuff in it. I'd pretend I left it there on accident and called you so I could run by and pick it up."

"In the middle of the night?"

"I have an assignment due in the morning!" I say, making myself sound distraught. "I'm so sorry for disturbing you, ma'am. I didn't want to wake anyone up. That's why I didn't knock or ring the bell."

"I told him he could come right in," Tim says, getting into the act. "Sorry, Mom! We didn't mean to spook you." He nods, as if it could work. "We'll start with that actually. You can come over when my parents are home and say you forgot something. I'll introduce you to them then."

He seems happy before ducking behind the canvas again. I am not. "I want them to actually get to know me," I press. "Think how panicked your mom would have been if she'd seen me for real the other night. A brief impression might not be enough for her to remember me. Not under those circumstances."

"I'll make sure they get a good look at you."

"*And* it would help if they had a sense of who I am. Like if I make a good impression, they'll be more likely to believe me if I get caught."

"I'll be sure to tell them what a great guy you are."

He sure is good at parrying! "Or you could invite me over for dinner. That way they can really get to know me."

I hear the wooden sound of a paintbrush being set down. Tim physically lifts the easel and sets it aside so I'm no longer obscured, his gaze even. "That's a terrible idea."

"It's not," I say, shaking my head.

"You don't understand."

"I want to though." I hop off the stool and walk to him. "Your family is part of who you are. It's important."

Tim meets me halfway. He places his hands on my shoulders, stoops to look me right in the eye, and says, "No."

"Oh come on!" I plead. "I'm not going to blab about everything we've been doing together. You've had friends over before, right?"

"For sleepovers or to hang out with me. I've never asked my parents if Bryce can join us for a three-course meal and some polite conversation."

"We'll find a way to make it seem natural."

Tim laughs and shakes his head. Then he guides me back to the stool. "I want my Valentine's Day present. You promised to pose for me."

"Okay." I hop back on my perch and wait until he's behind the easel again before saying, "Maybe that's what *I* want as a present. Dinner with your parents."

"Oh, I'm going to give you something," Tim threatens in a way that makes me eager to serve. "Now let me work. Put on some music if you're bored. You can sing for me."

"I'm not your caged bird," I grumble.

But of course I hop off the stool, turn on the radio, and do exactly what he wants… but only because it's what I want too.

He resumes working. I wait for each glorious moment that he checks on me to capture some other detail and revel in being the focus of his attention, especially on the occasions when his gaze locks on to mine and lingers there. I don't think he needs to be reminded of my eye color. When he looks at me like that, I'm convinced of his feelings for me. Other times I'm not so sure. I certainly wouldn't mind if he spelled it out.

I tried, over the past week. Tim was encouraging when listening to some of what I'd written previously. I thought a poem would make a nice Valentine's Day present, but I couldn't find the right words. Actually, that wasn't the issue. I know exactly what I want to say to him. A poem is too long and cumbersome when it's really quite simple.

"Hey," I say before licking my lips.

"Yeah?"

I wait until Tim leans over to look at me, the breath short in my lungs, but it's enough to speak three little words that have never felt so huge. "I love you."

Tim stares, a battle playing out across his face. Surprise precedes a hint of panic before his chin quivers. Just when I think he's about to burst into tears, Tim smiles, his eyes glistening as he walks over and takes my face in his paint-stained hands so he can kiss me. I practically melt into him, but I'm jarred out of my bliss when he grabs my hand and begins to pull.

"Come here," he says, leading me toward the canvas. "It's not done, but I still want to show you."

My heart is thudding in excitement. I've dreaded confessing my feelings to him, no matter how obvious they must be. I didn't know how he would react. It could have been too much for him, or worse, unrequited. Which might still be the case, because he didn't say it back. I want him to. I'd give up all my worldly possessions just to hear him speak those words. Why didn't he? That's the social contract. If someone declares their love, the recipient is obligated to respond with words of their own. The kiss was nice—incredible actually—but I need more.

"Look." Tim picks up the easel and sets it down again so it's facing me. He remains at its side, studying my reaction.

My eyes dart to the canvas. The breath catches in my throat. The painting is of a handsome young man with waves of brown hair that tumble over his ears. His eyes are expressive and full of emotion, sensual lips curling in a subtle smile. He's beautiful. As in, *way* too beautiful. "That's not me," I say. "Maybe he could be my brother but… I'm not *that* hot!"

"Yeah you are," Tim says, looking between me and the canvas. "I got it just right."

"Surely not!" I say, considering it again. "I mean, it's a great painting. You did an amazing job. I only wished I looked that good."

"That's how I see you," Tim says. Then he swallows. "Do you get it?"

Streaks of rainbow light cut across the canvas, as if cast by an unseen prism. The effect is so believable that I nearly glance around for the source. Tim has the skill to paint anything he wants. Convincingly. That includes me. And I *have* seen the man in the painting before, but only in the mirror when the lighting was especially kind, or in a photo with a particularly good angle.

"That's my Benjamin," Tim says, his voice raw with emotion. *"You're* my Benjamin."

He pulls me into his arms, and while they aren't the words I wanted to hear, it is the answer I need.

"You really like it?" he asks after kissing me.

"Yeah, of course!" I turn toward the canvas again. "It's so flattering."

"It's really not," Tim says with a chuckle.

"My lips aren't so luscious."

He rolls his eyes. "Fine. Let me make a quick adjustment."

Tim picks up the paintbrush and palette. He turns to me with a critical eye, as if wanting to get the details just right. Before I know it, the wet end of a paintbrush collides with my lips.

"What's the hell?" I splutter.

"Much better!" Tim cackles, spreading his arms wide to protect the canvas. "Now you match the painting."

I touch my lips experimentally and see globs of green paint on the tips of my fingers. "It's not even the right color!"

Tim raises his palette. "Want me to try again?"

"I have a better idea," I say, taking a step forward. "You've really got me in the mood. Pucker up!"

"No way!" Tim says while retreating.

I chase him around the studio, refusing to give up until I've got him backed into a corner of the couch.

"Just one kiss," I negotiate. "Then I'll stop."

"Fine!" he says, squinching his eyes shut in anticipation.

I grab his head in my hands and rapid-fire kiss his lips,

cheeks, forehead… anywhere I can manage until he pushes me away.

"You cheated!" he growls.

"All's fair in love and war," I retort, plopping down next to him. "You look ridiculous, by the way."

"I think you're hotter than ever," Tim says, grinning at me. "I want to paint you."

"You already did."

"No, I want to paint *you*."

I shake my head. "What is this, the county fair?"

"I'm thinking more than just your face," Tim says, pulling on the T-shirt I'm wearing.

I laugh and resist him. We wrestle on the couch, which is hot, but he's determined.

"Please," Tim says.

"Fine."

"Cool. Take off your shirt."

I comply and feel ridiculous sitting there on the couch while he grabs his art supplies. Tim makes it interesting for me. He teases my nipples with an unladen paintbrush, which starts to turn me on, until he glances at my face and gets distracted. Watching him work this close up is intense! I notice how he sometimes holds his breath when being especially careful. Or he'll often lean back, his eyes narrowing critically before he tries again. Tim makes me sit up and puts his legs to either side of mine, facing me as he begins to paint on my chest. When he settles into my lap, I grind my boner against his butt.

Tim laughs. "Not a chance in hell."

"Fine by me," I admit, preferring our usual dynamic.

I can tell he's hard too, although not fully, since he keeps losing himself in his creative impulses. One of my favorite songs comes on the radio, so I sing while he works, his brush moving across my chest as it rises and falls. This has to be one of the most unusual art collaborations. Somebody find us a willing gallery. We'll be the talk of the town!

"Done," Tim leans back. "Now you really are my butterfly."

"Show me!"

Tim leads me out of the studio, but only after checking to make sure the coast is clear. When he flicks on the light in an office restroom, I see myself in the mirror. Green leaves and brown branches cover my face and most of my chest, making me resemble some sort of nature god. Right in the middle, over my heart, is a butterfly with rainbow wings.

"That's incredibly beautiful," I breathe before seeking him out in the mirror. "Do I get to paint you?"

"No!" Tim says. "In fact, we probably shouldn't leave that on for long. It's only acrylic paint, so it's water-based, but it's probably not great for your skin."

I imagine myself covered in acne and reach for the sink.

Tim grabs my wrist. "Not here! It'll make a mess. My dad will flip. Let's go back to my place. I'll hose you off in the backyard."

He's such a bastard! I know he's kidding though. The days are getting longer, but it's still way too cold for running through sprinklers. I get some strange looks on the drive home. Especially at stop lights. I almost joke that we should do this more often, so he doesn't have to worry about anyone recognizing me, but that's an idea he'd probably like, so I don't.

Once back at his place, we go upstairs to the bathroom. Tim turns on the shower. Then he strips off his shirt. I stare, as always. I'm glad he didn't let me paint him. He's already perfect.

"Are you getting in with me?" I ask.

"Yeah," he says. "You're going to need help."

I don't see why, but it's an offer I can't refuse. I scramble out of my clothes. We're both hard when stepping into the tub.

"Sword fight!" Tim cries, thwapping his wiener against mine.

I laugh and do the same until I get water in my eyes. And it stings a little.

"Shit," he says. "Hold up."

I see him grab a washcloth before I'm forced to shut my eyes.

"Keep them closed," I hear Tim say.

One of his hands is on my chin while he dabs at me with the washcloth. He's gentle when doing so, occasionally guiding my face back to the water for a rinse.

"Ouch!" I complain when the washcloth rips at the paint stuck in my eyebrows.

"I've got this," he murmurs.

I hear the washcloth hit the bottom of the tub before he carefully uses his fingers to massage the paint out of my eyebrows. His lips press against mine suddenly. I kiss him back, eager to be close to him.

"Just a sec," he says, guiding me toward the warm spray of water again. "Rinse off."

I tilt my head toward it and then turn around, wiping my eyes so I can look at him again.

"That did it," Tim says, nodding in approval while lathering up a bar of soap. Then he gestures for me to step forward.

After I do so, he begins washing the paint off my chest, but he doesn't stop there. He bathes my entire body. Every nook and cranny. And while it's erotic, the gesture is also unmistakably affectionate.

"I love you," I say, pressing my sudsy body against his.

The words don't take him by surprise this time. Tim smiles and kisses me, and while he doesn't say it back, I'm certain now that it's true.

He loves me.

CHAPTER TWENTY-ONE

I'm standing on the front stoop of Tim's house, wearing a button-up shirt and the coat he bought me. It's finally happening. I'm about to meet his parents! I'm more excited than apprehensive. I usually do well at this sort of thing, having won over my fair share of mothers over the years. Dads can be trickier. Especially when you're gay. The door swings open after I knock. Tim's expression is grim, like we're on the front lines and about to rush into battle.

"Are you ready?" he asks.

"Yeah!" I say, grinning broadly.

"Okay." Tim hesitates. I can tell he wants to say more, but he doesn't. Instead he ushers me inside.

"Hey, Mom!" he calls. "Benjamin is here!"

His mother meets us in the entryway. The fleeting impressions I've had of her previously are reinforced. She's beautiful! Her long black hair has a healthy sheen, her body slim and graceful. She's wearing a yellow dress that complements brown skin a shade darker than her son's. His mother smiles warmly and extends a delicate hand.

"Welcome!" she says with the slightest hint of an accent. "It's so nice to meet you."

"Thanks for having me over for dinner," I reply, gently gripping her hand before letting go. "To be honest, this entire thing is just a set-up."

"In what way?" she asks, cocking her head in confusion.

"I invented an excuse to be here."

Tim is standing a step behind her, his eyes already wide like I'm about to blow the whole thing up.

"Your son is always bragging about how good your cooking is, so when my Spanish teacher told us we needed to choose a subject to write about, I saw my chance and took it. But I really am interested in Mexico City and its culture. And especially your cooking."

His mother's eyes sparkle as she turns toward her son. "Such a charmer. You should have invited him sooner!"

"Yeah," Tim says, managing a half-hearted laugh. "We'll be upstairs. Just holler when dinner is ready."

"Unless you need any help," I offer. "I'm the worst guy for the job, but I'd try my best anyway."

"I'll keep that in mind," his mother says with a smile.

Tim ushers me up to his room and shuts the door behind us. "Did you watch the game last night?" he asks, sounding concerned.

"I put it on," I say vaguely.

"Oh yeah? Who won?"

"The good guys?" I venture.

"Benjamin!" Tim scolds. "It's important. My dad will want to talk about it!"

"I'll manage," I assure him.

We each contributed something to this plan. I came up with the idea of needing to write a paper and created a list of related questions to make it convincing. Tim ran with this, writing his own list of things I'll need to know if I'm going to get along with his dad. Which are mostly sports-related facts that I just can't seem to wrap my head around.

"Let's study," Tim says, grabbing a notebook.

"I don't *actually* have an essay to write," I remind him.

"Shut up!" Tim hisses, like we'll be overheard. "Sorry," he adds when seeing my reaction. "But c'mon… If we're gonna do this, we have to do it right."

I agree on the first part, although we disagree about what "right" entails. Regardless, I can tell how nervous he is, so I sit on the bed with him and dutifully repeat athlete names and statistics. Eventually I start sniffing. "What smells so good?" I ask.

"My mom's chiles rellenos," he says with a grin. "They're my favorite, so I asked her to make them for you."

"Aww!" I say, leaning toward him for a kiss. "That's so sweet!"

Tim pushes me away before our lips can meet. "Don't say things like that!"

I scrunch up my face. "Even in here?"

"Just… No gay stuff. All right?"

"No gay stuff," I repeat, before slugging him on the arm playfully. "Buddy."

Tim looks even more distraught. "This is going to be a disaster."

"It won't!" I promise him. "I'll be on my best behavior."

"Good," he says, consulting the notebook again. "So who's your favorite player and why?"

"That's easy," I say to buy time. And it works, because we hear his mother shout from downstairs.

"Gordito!"

"Is that your dad's name?" I ask in confusion.

"Jesus Christ, no! Don't call him that." Tim gets up and eyes me with transparent concern. "I can tell them there's so much work to do that we need to eat in my room."

"Stay here if you want," I say, getting up and going to the door. "I'm having dinner with your parents."

I'm the first one down the stairs, but I fall back when nearing the dining room, because I really do want this to go well. I'm not here to upset anyone. The opposite, in fact.

"Hey, Dad," Tim says when pushing past me. His tone is more reserved than usual. "This is my friend, Benjamin."

A man stands up from the table. I've seen photos of him, so the short white hair and silver eyes are expected. His build is much more intimidating in person. He's even bigger than Tim. Not as toned, I would guess from the brief impressions I get when my eyes dart down to his body, but the dress shirt sleeves are rolled up over thick forearms and his grip is strong when he wraps a hand around mine in a formal handshake.

"Nice to meet you, sir," I say.

"Welcome," comes his terse response before he nods to an empty chair.

Tim and I sit across from each other on the long sides of the table, his parents at each end. A spread of steaming food is laid out before us. I don't have to fake my enthusiasm, because it looks and smells incredible. I'm trying not to drool when the others fold their hands and bow their heads. I stare for a moment before doing the same, grateful that Tim prepared me for this. The voice I hear is rougher than my boyfriend's.

"Bless us, oh Lord, and these, thy gifts, which we are about to receive from thy bounty. Through Christ, our Lord. Amen."

"Amen," I add a little later than the others, but I'm pretty sure I scored points anyway.

"Tim insisted that I make his favorite," his mother says while serving helpings onto each of our plates, "but if I was going to represent Mexico City, I would have made *tacos al pastor*."

"I bet you'd like those," Tim says. "It's pork and pineapple. Sort of like the pizzas we order."

"I can come back tomorrow," I say to his mother with a hopeful expression.

"I don't cook like this every day!" she says with a laugh. "Besides, the Mexican rice is my mother's recipe. You can't get more authentic than that."

We talk about food during the beginning of the meal. The main course, *chiles rellenos*, consists of battered and fried peppers stuffed with cheese that are served in a tomato sauce. When I take a bite, the suspicions of my nose are confirmed by my mouth. It's delicious! While we eat, his mother shares memories of cooking as a child, which is interesting, but I'm eager to get to the really personal stuff.

"So how did you two meet?" I ask, looking to Tim's father.

"I was a Catholic missionary," he replies.

"Even though eighty percent of Mexico is Catholic?" I ask. "Or was it way lower before you got there?"

His father smirks. "If only I was that effective. No, we were both missionaries overseas when we met."

"In a foreign country? Wow, that's romantic!" His father raises an eyebrow at this until I add, "My parents met in a bowling alley. And neither of them bowl."

The others laugh, which helps me feel more at ease, so I follow up with another question.

"When you decided to get married, how did you agree on where to live? Why aren't we having this meal in Mexico City?"

"I love it there," his mother says. "I still consider it my home. But I got the travel bug while evangelizing and was eager to discover life here."

"Is it very different?"

She thinks about it and nods. "I feel like people here visit a city to work, or to have fun on the weekend. Mexico City is *alive* with a diverse community. Like visiting your relatives, the city won't allow you any peace and quiet, but it also reminds you of where you belong. That's too easy to forget here. Otherwise people wouldn't move around so often."

She's already my favorite. I keep asking her questions, almost forgetting that I don't really need to write a paper. The information she shares with me is valuable anyway, because it's part of Tim's heritage. His father interjects on occasion but is mostly quiet. I'm not sure how to engage with him. I can see why Tim wanted me to talk sports, but there's something penetrating about the older man's gaze that makes the prospect too intimidating. I feel like he'd detect my insincerity. Still, I do have a few burning questions for him.

I glance around the dining room as Tim and his mother rise to clear away the plates, settling on the painting of Jesus, who is gazing down at the table serenely, seemingly without appetite. "Hey, is that one of Tim's?" I ask.

His mother follows my stare and smiles. "It certainly is. My favorite of all his paintings."

"It's really good! If I had that kind of skill, my parents would make me churn out art to cover the walls. Where are the others?" I ask, making a show of looking around.

"I wish I could show you more," his mother says pointedly. "Tim has gotten so shy about such things."

That strikes me as significant, because his art is hardly controversial. The slashed-up canvas of Carla's younger brother might raise a few eyebrows, if his parents chose to read into it, but the rest is harmless. Like the nice painting of his grandmother. Why isn't that hanging up here? I can't think of any reason for Tim to feel so vulnerable about his art. Unless…

I turn my attention to his father. We're alone in the dining room now. "Does the artistic stuff come from your side of the family? Tim mentioned a grandfather who was an architect."

"My grandfather actually," he corrects. "But no, we aren't an artistic family."

"You might be now. Tim has real talent."

"Painting is a hobby," his father says dismissively, "not an occupation. I told Tim the same thing when he wanted to take art courses."

"But he *could* make a living off it. Picasso was rich and famous."

His father doesn't seem offended by my persistence, but he does have a certain air, as if I'm being naïve. "Have you met many people who paint for a living? Aside from Picasso."

I smile in response. "No, but I also haven't met any professional baseball players or architects."

"And yet, there are architectural firms Tim could apply to.

The same with baseball teams. Such jobs already exist with established organizations. Where can an artist apply for work?"

He's got a point. Except… "He could take his work to a gallery. That would be the equivalent."

His father eyes me for a moment. "It would seem that Tim has something of a fan in you."

I'm not sure I like what he's implying. Actually, I *love* what he's implying, but I don't want to rouse his suspicions, so I shrug casually. "I just envy what he can do. I walk past our school's art department all the time. They have assignments hanging up in the hallways, and none of it can compare to that." I nod at Jesus. "Tim has a rare gift."

His father breathes in through his nose before exhaling just as slowly. "He's welcome to try selling his paintings if he wants. Preferably on the weekend, when he's not busy working a job that pays the bills."

Which would be decent advice if Tim was allowed to choose an occupation that actually appealed to him. Not that I don't get it. Most parents probably want their children to follow in their footsteps. As my mom once said, *I must be the only interior designer to give birth to a gay son who doesn't like to decorate.* The difference is that she doesn't force me to take classes about altering curtains. And it's not like he wants Tim to join the family business. Becoming a baseball player is probably his own discarded dream.

"And you?" His father prompts. "Where do your aspirations lie?"

"Hey," Tim says when reentering the room with his mother. "What are you guys talking about?"

"Career goals," I say, smiling to show him that everything is okay. "I was just about to explain that I like to sing, and that I enjoy writing, but I haven't figured out what to do with either yet."

"Find a practical occupation," his father suggests. "When raising a family, a reliable paycheck will matter more to you than what you dreamed of when young."

That sums up his stance. He's not the overbearing monster I expected, but he is strong-willed. And annoyingly enough, I'm not sure that he's entirely wrong. But when I look at the painting of Jesus again, I'm reminded that some parents are willing to hang their kids out to dry, just to further their own ambitions.

"When I was a little girl," his mother says, placing a plate in front of me, "I wanted to be a baker."

I look down at a square of sponge cake covered in whipped cream and topped with a strawberry. All of which is sitting in a puddle of some sort. I look up at Tim, who is seated across from me again while rubbing his hands together gleefully. "You're so freakin' lucky!" he says with a grin. "And so am I. This is my absolute favorite. It's even better than *chiles rellenos!*"

His mother smiles as she takes a seat. "You always did have a sweet tooth, Gordito."

"Sorry," I say, shaking my head. "My Spanish isn't great. *Gordo* means fat, doesn't it?"

"He was a very large baby," his mother explains. "My chunky little monkey!"

"Mom!" Tim moans.

"Perhaps you don't want any cake," she replies. "If you're so concerned about such things."

Tim hunches over his plate and surrounds it protectively with his arms. "Call me whatever you want. I'm eating this."

His father chuckles at his antics. Tim's mom pats his arm lovingly, so he'll stop pouting. His family isn't so bad. Not at all! And when I pick up a fork to take a bite… "Okay," I say, sitting back after swallowing. "I'm moving in. You can't say no. Look how skinny I am. I *need* this food. Adopt me, please!"

His mother laughs. "You're welcome anytime. It's nice to finally meet one of Tim's new friends. He's been so private since moving here. We haven't even met his girlfriend yet."

I look up at him in confusion. "I thought you guys broke up?"

Tim's mouth is full, so he kicks me under the table while struggling to swallow. "We did," he manages to say. "Now we're back together."

"When did that happen?" I reply, kicking him back.

"Just the other day," Tim says before looking to his mom. "It was only a misunderstanding. Krista caught me talking to a girl she doesn't like and got the wrong idea."

His mother eyes him a moment longer before seeming to relax. "You'll have to invite her over soon. Prom will be here before you know it. I want to meet the girl you are going with."

"She's really busy with cheerleading," Tim grumbles, avoiding my gaze.

"I'd still like to meet her," his mother insists before turning shining eyes on me. "What about you? Do you have a girlfriend?"

"No," I reply. "But I am seeing someone."

Tim's head swivels toward me, and now I'm the one who avoids making eye contact, because this wasn't part of the plan. Then again, neither was Krista.

"A guy, actually," I continue sheepishly. "Kind of weird, I know, but it's just who I am."

The table is silent.

"I'm sorry," his mother says at last, shaking her head. "I'm not sure I understood you correctly."

"You did," I say, keeping my tone upbeat. "I'm gay." I smile at them both. "Have you ever met someone like me before? Because it's not so different really. I'm just like anyone else except for one little detail. I fall in love with guys instead of girls."

"Oh," his mother says.

Tim's father remains silent.

As for my boyfriend, when I look at him again, his eyes are pleading with me to take it all back. But I won't, even for him. He might not like it now, but I'm paving the way, because I don't think his parents will make a big deal out of one of his friends being gay, especially if I don't.

"*Tres leches* means three types of milk, doesn't it?" I ask. "Is the whipped cream one of them?"

"Actually, no," his mother says, before launching into an explanation of how three types of milk are combined and poured over the baked cake.

"Whipped cream is number four then," I reply. "I think we should start a campaign to rename it *cuatro leches* cake instead."

She laughs at this. His father snorts. They aren't fuming with anger or dousing me with holy water. But just to make sure that everything stays smoothed over, I talk sports with Tim's father, who does all of the heavy lifting. I mostly just need to nod along while he expresses his opinions. By the end of the meal, it's like I never confessed anything at all.

Wanting to stick the landing, I thank them for dinner and insist on doing the dishes. Tim helps me in the kitchen. He's quiet, occasionally looking at me like I've lost my mind.

"They seemed to roll with it well enough," I tell him when this keeps happening. "Don't you think?"

Tim slots a few plates into the dishwasher before nodding. "Actually… Yeah!"

He loosens up, especially when I turn on the radio and start to sing. His mother joins us in the kitchen, applauding me for my efforts. If she hated me, she'd be upstairs counting rosary beads or whatever Catholics do after encountering evil incarnate. But hey, it's a modern world and I'm a modern kind of girl. Maybe his mom and dad are too.

"Wanna walk me to my car?" I ask when we're standing outside his house later.

"You don't have one."

"Sure I do," nodding down the street. "It's parked in that shadowy spot over there where no one will see us."

Tim laughs. "I don't think anyone's looking now."

He kisses me, even though we're standing on his front stoop and the light is on. When it comes to who delivered the biggest shock of the night, I think he just took the prize. "You aren't *really* dating Krista again. Are you?"

"Of course not, you idiot!" Tim says, rolling his eyes. "Way to almost blow my cover."

"How about some warning next time?" I retort.

"I didn't think it would come up."

"On that same token," I say, touching his hand briefly. "I wasn't planning on telling your parents about the whole gay thing. But when someone asks me about that, I can't lie."

"Maybe it's for the best," Tim says. "They didn't react at all like I thought they would."

"If they have any questions, let them know that I'd be happy to stop by and talk about it."

"Oh no," Tim says, already shaking his head. "You're not going *anywhere* near my family again! Not unless there's a script that you stick to."

I laugh, and when he glances around before kissing me again, I smile against his lips, knowing that this will be a turning point in our relationship.

I've got a backpack slung over my shoulder as I stand by the front window, waiting for Allison to pick me up for school. My eyes widen when a black sports car roars down the street and screeches to a halt in my driveway. Tim doesn't usually give me a ride, but I love the idea. Last night's dinner is paying off already! I'm grinning on my way outside, but the smile slides off my face when I see Tim standing next to his car with a scowl, his chest rising and falling in angry huffs.

"Are you okay?" I ask, rushing over to him.

"No, I'm not okay!" Tim's face twists up. "My parents don't want me to see you again."

I stare in disbelief. "But everything went so well! They were nice to me!"

"Just because they were polite, doesn't mean they actually like you," Tim grumbles. He seems to regret these words when seeing the hurt on my face. "They *did* like you. My mom especially. But they're Catholic, Benjamin. Cozying up to them isn't going to change their beliefs. To them you're a sinner." He clenches his jaw. "They made me pray for you."

"What?" I ask, shaking my head in confusion.

"Yeah," Tim spits. "While you were having cereal this morning, I was praying with my parents for your immortal soul."

I try to imagine them, clustered together with bowed heads while muttering some ancient incantation, like something out of a cult. I can't help but snort.

"It's not funny!" Tim snarls, his voice cracking. "You should have seen the way my dad kept looking at me. And no fucking wonder! I invited a gay guy over for dinner, and they've never even met my girlfriend. What the hell was I thinking?"

"You don't have a girlfriend," I say evenly.

"*That's* what you're worried about right now?" Tim splutters incredulously. "You should be asking yourself if you've got a boyfriend!"

My throat constricts. "What are you saying?"

"What do you think?" he shoots back.

"Are you breaking up with me?"

Tim glowers, like he hates my guts, but I refuse to believe it. Not for one second.

"Is that what you came over here to do?" I ask softly. "Do you really want this to end? Because I don't. I love you too much."

His eyes fill with affection before his face crumbles.

"Hey!" I say, reaching for him.

The strength seems to drain from Tim as I pull him close. He clings to me with so much desperation that I ache for him.

"We fucked up," he croaks. "It's all ruined."

"It's not!" I pull back to look him in the eye. "We can make this work."

Tim is shaking his head. I place my hand on his cheek to stop the motion.

"It'll be all right. I promise. We'll go back to the way things were. Okay?"

Tim swallows and nods. Then he wraps his arms tighter around me, like he's holding on for dear life, and I wish I could protect him from the world. But that's not possible. I need him to find his courage, because no matter how strong I try to be for him, this is a battle that can only be fought from the inside. If he succeeds in overcoming his fear, we'll be unstoppable. Otherwise, this might be the beginning of the end.

CHAPTER TWENTY-TWO

"Put your head in my lap."

The words sound romantic. At one time I would have been thrilled to hear them. But not now, so I turn my attention to the passenger-side window and don't respond.

"Seriously," Tim says. "Someone might see you."

I roll my eyes and maintain my silence. Things have gotten so much worse since the dinner with his parents. His paranoia has reached an all-time high. Tim doesn't want me to sneak over anymore. Staying the night at my place is deemed—by him—as too risky, which has left precious little opportunity to see each other. I talked him into going with me to an art museum downtown, hoping that would capture his attention, but he spent most of the day looking over his shoulder. Now he's driving us home. Or was. The car slows and begins to pull over.

"You've gotta hide," he says. "Krista's house is—"

"I know where she fucking lives!" I snap before leaning my seat all the way back.

I glare at the fabric that lines the roof of his car, counting the turns until I know we're on my street. Then I sit upright and watch my house go by as Tim drives around the block to park.

"Sorry," he says. "But you know why."

I try to set my frustration aside. I don't want to be angry with him. "Are you going to come in?"

Tim licks his lips nervously, like I've just invited him to go swimming with sharks. "Is anyone home?"

"I'm not sure." Need rises up in me, even though I try swallowing against it. "But we could go up to my room."

Tim looks me over, taking a few deep breaths. "Okay. I'll uh…" He glances around the neighborhood. "I'll meet you there. All right?"

I don't answer. I just get out and start walking. I hate this. And I love him. I'm not sure how to reconcile the two, but there has to be a way.

"Mom?" I shout when entering my house. "Dad?"

No response.

"Hey, Karen!" I yell. "Something really embarrassing just happened to me!"

I know she's not home, or intentionally ignoring me, because there's no way she could resist that bait.

"It's all ours," I say when opening the front door to let Tim inside.

"No shit?" he asks.

"We're alone," I assure him.

"For how long?"

"I don't know."

He glances at the stairs that lead to my room and then looks to me with transparent longing.

I feel the same way. "Let's go!"

We race up the stairs. I slam my bedroom door and lock it. He's already stripping off his clothes when I turn around. We've been starved of each other. At least in the past, we could sleep together to reconnect. Now we're playing a game on the most difficult setting. I fall to my knees to take him in my mouth. He's anything but gentle, but that's fine with me. Tim rams the back of my throat until he loses patience and pulls me to my feet, both of us working to get each other undressed the rest of the way. He tosses me on the bed and climbs in after, kissing a foot and biting the inside of my thigh before he goes down on me. His hair slides between my fingers as I buck and moan.

I'm getting close when he crawls higher up to kiss me. "Is it a good time?" he asks.

"No idea," I admit before opening my legs to him.

"I'll try not to go too deep," Tim says before spitting into his hand.

I'm thinking there's no way that'll be enough, but we make it work. I'm willing to risk embarrassment and pain to feel closer to him. We need this. I whimper as he pushes inside. When he pulls back to check my face in concern, I wrap my legs around his waist and beg him not to stop. Our eyes glaze over while locked. We're whole again. I could nearly cry. Neither one of us lasts long after that. Tim collapses onto me as we pant. When he pulls out and rolls over, I hold my breath as he looks down to check himself.

"We're good."

I exhale in relief. Then I roll onto my side, cuddling up to him before resting my head on his meaty shoulder. I trace a finger over the contours of his body as the endorphins slowly fade. I wish we could remain like this, safe in our little bubble. Although when I glance up and see his troubled expression, I realize that the outside world has managed to intrude, even here.

"What are you thinking about?" I ask him.

Tim swallows. "God."

"Oh."

"You don't believe in any of it,do you?"

I choose my words carefully. "I mean, it's a nice idea. For the most part." He's quiet. I push myself up on an elbow so I can study his face. "Do you think you're going to Hell?"

Tim presses his lips together. Then he nods. "If we keep doing this. Yeah."

My stomach sinks. "Why would God forbid this? I can understand him not wanting us to kill people or steal from them, but what's wrong with love?"

"The Bible says—"

"I don't care," I interrupt. "I want the reason, not the rhetoric. We're not hurting anyone. So what's the problem with us being together?"

Tim thinks about it before responding. "Because this isn't how God intended for things to work. It's supposed to be a man and a woman. So he's not happy when people go against his plan."

"And he responds by throwing anyone with their own inclination into a pit of fire for all eternity? Isn't that a little reactionary? Talk about being thin-skinned."

Tim shrugs, my head wobbling with the motion. "I mean, he did give us life."

"And he gets to decide what we do with it?"

"Well, no, because we have free will."

"But only under duress."

"I don't make the rules. It's in the Bible. That's the word of God."

I raise my head and scoff. "Every religion on this planet claims to have the exclusive scoop on what God wants, but they can't all be right. And he sure as hell hasn't weighed in on it recently. Doesn't he have any more kids to play messenger? It's a shame Jesus was an only child. I bet his sister would've been a stone-cold bitch. She'd cut right through all the melodramatic bullshit and lay it out straight. 'Don't be a dick, people of Earth! That is all.'"

Tim laughs. "You are *definitely* going to Hell!"

"Wanna meet me there?" I ask with a toothy grin.

His handsome features are marred by concern again. I remind myself that, for him, this isn't merely a mental exercise. He actually believes reality works that way.

"If there is a god," I tell him, "he knows what's in our hearts. I'm not afraid of being judged by that." I think of who raised me. "The only creator I can be one hundred percent sure of, my parents, don't have a problem with what we're doing. And neither should yours."

Tim still seems troubled. Which I suppose makes sense. It would take more than a little pillow talk to undo my entire upbringing. "Do you want kids?" I ask.

"Yeah!" Tim says. "Someday."

"Imagine you had a son, just like you, who met a boy just like me, and they fell in love. What would you do if, one day, he told you about their relationship?"

Tim is silent for a moment. "I'd probably hug him. Yeah. I'd hug him and tell him that I—" His voice strangles to a halt before he shakes his head.

"Does your mom ever say that she loves you?"

Tim nods.

"What about your dad?"

He sits up. "What is this, a therapy session?"

"No," I say, pushing him back down so I can rest my head on his chest. "I'm just trying to understand. That's all."

"I'm not sure I want to," he grumbles.

"Well you aren't going to Hell," I assure him. "No matter what."

"How do you know?"

"Because they say God is love. And I love you. So if anything, my feelings for you are a manifestation of his will. How's that for a new religion?"

Tim thinks about it and smiles. "Sounds like heaven."

Allison and I are sitting cross-legged on her bed while facing each other. Six envelopes rest on the comforter between us. We regard them with nervous excitement, since each has the power to decide our future.

"What do you think?" she asks. "Should we save the best for last?"

I shake my head. "The anticipation is killing me!"

"Okay." Allison fondles an envelope from a university that specializes in the arts. She could pursue her singing career there while I figure out what exactly I want to do with myself. "I can't!" she gasps. "You go first!"

I pick up my envelope from the same school. We've dreamt about how amazing it would be to move across the country and begin the next phase of our lives together in one of the nation's biggest cities. I tear into the envelope and pull out the letter contained within, my eyes darting around the page even as it unfolds, trying to find a hint. *–pleased to inform you that your application has been accepted and approved–* "I got in!" I cry. "Open yours!"

Allison hurries to do so, her eyes wide with excitement. I watch them move back and forth before the muscles of her face go slack with disappointment. "They don't want me."

"What?" I cry in disbelief, snatching the letter from her to scan it. Sure enough: *–regret to inform you that after careful review of your application–* "Did we get them mixed up?" I check to see who the letter is addressed to and still can't believe it. Our grades are roughly the same. Allison's voice is better than mine. She should have the edge! "This has to be a mistake."

"Par for the course," Allison replies, not sharing my confusion.

I can't think of any reason they would reject her and accept me unless… Oh. We each included a performance video with our application. "Is it because you're black?"

"Or because you're a boy. Who knows. You should still go."

"Fuck these racist sexist bastards!" I say, tossing both letters away.

"Ben! It's a good school!"

"They just proved otherwise," I say, her feelings my only concern. "Are you okay?"

"Yeah," Allison says. "I didn't have my heart set on going there anyway. Okay, I did, but it would be hard to move so far away from Dad. He'd be all alone. And I'd miss him."

"Well you aren't going to miss either of us, because I'm not going. Let's try our luck again."

We both pick up letters from the next school, which is just a few hours away. We're enthusiastic about it too, even though it doesn't specialize in the arts.

"At the same time?" Allison asks.

"Yeah," I say with a nod.

We mirror each other's movements while watching each other remove and unfold the letter. Allison gives into curiosity first. I study her face until it lights up with a smile. I quickly check my letter before grinning.

"You got in?" Allison asks.

"Yeah! Did you?"

"Yes!"

We both squeal with delight before hugging each other. Then we go through the acceptance letters more carefully, taking turns reading important details aloud. We don't bother with the third school. Neither of us were passionate about going there.

"Tuition will be a lot cheaper," Allison says. "That'll make my dad happy. Ronnie is going to cry though."

"Why's that?"

"The school he got accepted into wasn't far from *those* people." She glares with disdain at the rejection letter. "He was hoping we could keep seeing each other."

"You could try a long-distance relationship."

"During our first year of college? I don't think either of us wants to be tied down. Not when we can't really be together. Which is a shame, because I do love him." Allison sighs. Then she shrugs. "Oh well. I'll make sure we go out with a bang. I won't be waiting until prom now."

"Really?" I ask. "You're finally going to do it with him?"

"Yes," Allison replies. "Although it'll be sad that my first time will also be one of the last times. With him, anyway."

"That is sad," I say while contemplating it. "But also really *really* romantic!"

"Right?" Allison says, fanning herself with the acceptance letter. "What about Tim?"

I grimace. "He's not sure yet. His parents are pressuring him to go to some Catholic school, which would suck, because it's either a three-hour flight or a twenty-hour drive from here."

"You could always try a long-distance relationship," Allison says innocently.

"I might."

"No!" She thwaps me. "That would be so boring! Make him apply to our school. It's a liberal city. I doubt any of his friends will be there. His parents certainly won't."

"It's kind of last minute."

"He's kind of charming. And he's got a couple different talents to use as a lure. If it's not baseball, they might like his paintings."

My mind starts to race with the idea. I've been so focused on keeping us together in the present that I haven't spent much time contemplating our future. This could fix everything!

"I love you so much," I tell my best friend.

"I love you too," she says, turning around and resting her head in my lap, the acceptance letter held above her. "Now let's read through this one more time."

I listen to her narrate, but my mind soon begins to wander as I imagine moving to a new town with both my best friend and my boyfriend. We could share an apartment. Meet on campus for lunch. Go to parties and make terrible mistakes. It would be a beautiful mess, sharing our lives together like that. Now I just need to make it happen.

I'm on a double-date! Allison and I have been dreaming of this since junior high. And now it's actually happening! Persuading my closeted boyfriend to go along with the idea had taken some doing. An hour-long blowjob to be specific, and yes, Tim actually timed it. Even without the bribery, I think he's genuinely enjoying himself on this date. Although an outsider might mistake him for a hired bodyguard, considering the way he keeps scanning the mall for anyone he might know.

"What do you think?" I ask him, holding a shirt with a busy pattern to my chest.

"Looks good," Tim says distractedly, his gaze elsewhere in the department store.

I grab the summer dress that Allison has been carrying around and drape it over my chest. "What about this one?"

Tim's eyes flick toward me and away again. "I like yellow."

My face twists up. Yellow has never looked good on me! And I doubt a sleeveless dress would either.

"I wanna see you both try it on," Ronnie says. "Grab another. Let's have a beauty pageant."

"Do it, Ben!" Allison says. "It would be so fun!"

"I don't want to give him any ideas," I say, tilting my head toward my boyfriend, "or he'll have me dressing up as a girl each time we go out."

"Huh?" Tim says, looking at everyone in our little group while catching up with the conversation. His attention settles on me. "Hey, that *is* a good idea! We'll get you a wig. It'll be hot!"

"I'm getting a little turned on just thinking about it," Ronnie murmurs.

"For real," Tim replies with a grin.

"Okay, never mind," Allison says, snatching the dress from me. "I do *not* need extra competition."

Just as well. I tried on my sister's clothes once, when I was still figuring everything out, and didn't feel anything but awkward. "You know what *would* be cute," I say innocently. "If we put our men in matching outfits."

"You're a genius!" Allison says, turning toward a rack of clothes.

Ronnie recoils at the suggestion. "That would be so lame!" He nudges Tim. "Nothing personal. I've just got my own style."

"Hey, I'm right there with you," Tim replies.

"Doesn't matter," Allison says, considering a leather jacket before returning it to the rack. "It's gonna happen."

Our boyfriends are good sports as we walk around the department store, assembling an outfit that includes a pink button up shirt, a white bow tie, and soft gray slacks.

"This relationship just became abusive," Ronnie says, shaking his head as we corral them toward the dressing rooms.

"You're going to look hot," Allison assures him.

"I don't know how to put on a bow tie," Ronnie says while peering at it.

"I'll help." Allison winks at me before dragging him into one of the private booths.

"She always has been my inspiration," I say, taking Tim's hand to pull him into another.

He tenses at the public display of affection, but when we're safe in the dressing room, he finally seems to relax.

"Better get out of all those clothes," I say, leaning against the wall to watch.

Tim smirks and strips off his T-shirt. He looks good. That's no shock, although I do wish he hadn't cut his silky black hair, which had gotten longer than my own. Now it's back to the short gelled spikes he had when we first met. If that's his preference, then so be it, but I worry that he only cut it to appease his father.

"Stop staring," Tim says with his jeans bunched up around his ankles.

"How come?" I ask. "It's not like I haven't seen it all before."

"Because you're giving me a boner," Tim says before flashing me proof. Then he turns around. "Actually, you better change the subject."

"Hey, I might have got it up, but you *brought* it up."

"Seriously," Tim says. "It'll be embarrassing."

"Okay. Um…" I watch him shrug on the pink dress shirt. "Oh! I know! Have you ever worn a tuxedo?"

"No. How come?"

"I was trying to imagine what you'd wear if we went to prom together."

"Oh. You know we can't."

That's what I figured, but I like the dream despite the reality. Ronnie recently asked Allison to go with him. I've been hinting ever since, although this is the first time Tim has said outright that it's not going to happen. Which is fine, I guess. "Did you go to prom during your junior year?"

"No," he says, pulling up the slacks. "Everything had fallen apart by then. Carla went with my former best friend."

"Ouch."

"Yup."

Tim turns around and holds up the bow tie with a confused expression. I've never worn one either, but I'm eager to be close to him, so I wrap my arms around his neck and try to figure it out blindly. I don't make much progress, maybe because I keep nuzzling my nose against his and kissing him.

"Would you stop!" Tim says with a laugh.

"Another boner?" I whisper with exaggerated concern.

"Nah. I just want to look good."

"Oh, so we *are* having a beauty pageant," I say. "In that case, you better turn around."

When he does, the bow tie is much easier to clip together and adjust.

"Are we tucking in their shirts?" I call after taking a step back.

"Yes!" comes Allison's muted response. "Don't let him roll up the sleeves!"

Tim is in the middle of doing just that. He sighs and holds out his arm, so I can undo it all.

"You guys sure have fun with your life-sized dolls," he murmurs. "Is this what you were like as kids?"

"More or less," I admit, before smoothing down the front of his shirt, mostly as an excuse to feel the firmness of his chest. "You look really good dressed up."

"Oh yeah?" Tim asks, turning toward the mirror.

"Yeah." I nibble my bottom lip and feel a pang of sorrow. "If we did go to prom, in some crazy alternate reality, what would you wear?"

Tim shrugs. "Something in black."

Which is almost a shame, considering how well the pink shirt complements his brown skin.

"A classic tux then," I reply.

"Yeah, I guess. What would you wear?"

"If you're in black?" I think of the wedding I've so often dreamt of. "I'd go white."

"I'd bet you'd look nice," Tim says, turning toward me again.

I catch a hint of longing, like he wouldn't mind taking me to prom. Or maybe it's just wishful thinking on my part.

"We're ready!" Allison calls. "Are you?"

"Yeah!" I holler. In a quieter voice, I say, "You've got this. Get out there and take first prize!"

Tim puffs up his chest and struts out of the dressing room. Ronnie, by comparison, slinks out of his booth with a hangdog expression.

"Oh my god, I love it!" Allison cries.

"Me too!" I declare while surveying them both.

The shirt pops against Ronnie's dark skin. When his girlfriend starts clapping, causing him to smile, he does indeed look dashing. But not many guys have killer silver eyes or such impressive pecs. Although we both start fanning ourselves when our boyfriends strike different poses. My favorite is when they lean against each other. Ronnie puts a hand on his chin, looking both thoughtful and cool. Tim tilts his head and raises an eyebrow, as if in invitation. They'd make a smoking-hot couple. Especially with me in the middle. I file that fantasy away for later.

"All right," Ronnie says at last. "Have you two had your fill?"

"You should both buy that shirt," I say.

"But not those slacks," Allison adds.

"I was thinking the same thing," I say in surprise. "Black would have been a better choice."

Allison nods. "But still the same style. Actually, if you guys wait, we can grab a pair for you to try."

Ronnie arches an eyebrow at Tim. "Oh hell no!"

"Yeah, we're done here," my boyfriend agrees.

They wordlessly return to their dressing rooms, shutting us out.

"Let's buy the shirts," I whisper.

Allison nods. "Agreed."

We're waiting in line not long after, the two cashiers clearly overwhelmed. I suspect some stores do that on purpose, so we're forced to stare at the displays of impulse items that wall us in.

"How come you're still carrying that shirt around?" Ronnie asks, noticing at last.

"So my boyfriend can wear it on our next date," she replies.

"It's not really my style," he retorts.

"I didn't say *you*," Allison teases. "I said my boyfriend. We'll see who that is by then."

Ronnie laughs. "You really thought I looked good in it?"

"Some guys are so insecure," I stage-whisper to Tim.

Although he doesn't seem to hear me. He's gone rigid as he stares at something behind him. Then he quickly turns around and glares at my puzzlement. He shakes his head rapidly when I begin leaning to see past him. "Stop looking at me," he says like a ventriloquist, his lips barely moving. He snatches a pair of socks from the display closest to us. "Seriously!" he hisses. "Turn around!"

I do as he commands, shrugging at Allison and Ronnie, who have noticed his behavior. Tim must have spotted someone from our school. "I'm glad you're getting that dress," I say to Allison. "Although it would be fun to figure out a matching outfit we could both wear for our next double date."

"Or that all four of us could wear," she says with a laugh. "That would be the height of cheesiness!"

We're hashing out ideas when I hear a woman's voice behind us.

"Tim?"

I glance over my shoulder—I can't help it—and see Stacy. And she definitely notices me! Her brow creases slightly before I turn toward the front again.

"Oh hey!" Tim says, as if surprised. "What are you doing here?"

"Entertaining myself while the others eat at the food court," she replies. "What are *you* doing here?"

"Just buying some clothes."

"Wow, a whole pair of socks. You must be exhausted!"

Tim laughs. "I didn't find anything else that I like."

"I thought you had some sort of family thing tonight," Stacy says pointedly.

"I did. It got canceled."

"You should have called us!"

"I thought you guys were going to that party downtown."

"We were. It got canceled."

"Oh."

I listen to Tim laugh nervously. "So uh… What are you up to?"

"We decided to catch a movie. Wanna come with? Krista will be there."

"You know that it's over," Tim says, perhaps for my benefit.

"Well sure, but I'd rather see her with you than Darryl."

"What?" He sounds concerned. "When did that happen?"

"It hasn't. Yet. Even if you don't want to get back with her, your presence will at least remind her that she has better options. Oh my gosh… Is that Alli-gator?"

I turn around to glare at Stacy. She came up with the mean-spirited nickname in eighth grade after Allison broke out in a rash. Which should be ancient history, but bullies never let you forget.

"Oh my gosh," Allison says, mimicking her tones. "Is that someone who thinks she's still in junior high? I'm sure your name-calling skills will be appreciated by whatever horrible sorority you join next year. I've had my fill though, so leave me and my friends alone."

Ronnie puts an arm around her protectively.

My own boyfriend doesn't say or do a damn thing.

"I always liked you," Stacy says, not seeming the least bit offended. "Anyway," she says, turning to Tim again, although her gaze does linger on me along the way. "The others should be done eating by now. Let's go find them."

"Oh." Tim says, lifting the socks up for her to see. "Uh…"

"Are they really worth standing in line for?" Stacy says. "Especially when some people don't understand which way they're supposed to face."

That means us, I guess. I roll my eyes and turn around. Allison and Ronnie do too.

"Let's go," Stacy insists.

"Yeah, okay."

Such simple harmless words, but they feel like the ultimate betrayal.

I glance over my shoulder in shock, but it's Stacy's gaze that I meet. She smiles sweetly at me. I turn my back to her and don't look again, even when my friends do.

"Is he coming back?" Ronnie asks in confusion.

I finally release the breath I've been holding and spin around. A pair of middle-aged women are standing behind us now. I can see Tim and Stacy, a raven-headed pair, walking toward the mall corridor.

"Because he's our ride," Ronnie adds.

Allison is watching me with concern. And the hint of a question.

"I don't think he's coming back," I say with burning cheeks.

Ronnie makes a face. "That's messed up!"

Allison nudges him. "Shh!"

They both glance at me. This is so awkward. And painful.

"It's cool!" Ronnie says, sounding upbeat. "I'll call Leon and ask if he'll pick us up. Or uh… I guess I could walk home and get the car while you guys are watching a movie."

"What do you think, Ben?" Allison asks.

I contemplate the whole stupid mess and swallow. "Can you have Leon come get us? I don't want to be here anymore."

"Yeah, sure!" Ronnie says easily. "I'll call him."

"Thanks." I put on a brave smile that Allison sees right through.

The line shuffles forward. I wait until the others are distracted before I set aside the pink shirt that I'm carrying. No matter how good Tim looks in it, I'll always be reminded of this moment, which I'd already like to scrub from my mind. And besides, after today, I'm not sure I'll have a boyfriend to give it to, or that I want one anymore.

CHAPTER TWENTY-THREE

I'm sitting on the front step of my house, alternating between anger and sorrow. The evening wasn't a complete disaster. Leon came to pick us up. We ate dinner on the other side of town and went to a different movie theater than originally planned. He was my date, I guess, not that there's any chemistry between us. I almost wish there was. A white guy with dreads doesn't give a shit what anyone thinks about him. It would be so refreshing to have a boyfriend who was fearless. And loving.

I think about what it's like to be alone with Tim. He's affectionate, always touching me and wanting to be close. I adore his artistic side. His body drives me wild. I love the sound of his voice and all the things we talk about. He makes me laugh. And feel beautiful. But then all of that gets bottled up and hidden away when other people are around. Which I thought I could deal with, until tonight, because him ditching me… no, him ditching *my friends* really pisses me off. I might have signed up for this sort of thing, but they didn't. And what happened to his promise to not let his friends pick on people? Stacy dredging up her old nickname for Allison was so uncool. I regret holding my tongue. I guess I'm just as bad, but I did it for him. I should have pounced on Stacy! And then broken up with him. Which might still happen. That's why I'm out here. When he shows up—and I know he will—we're going to have a serious talk.

I continue to be buffeted by my turbulent emotions until Tim's car drives by my house and keeps going. Maybe he didn't notice me. Doesn't matter. I'm already on my feet and walking to the place where he usually parks. We meet each other halfway, Tim breaking into a jog when he sees me.

"Benjamin!" he says when nearing. "I'm really sorry!"

"Bullshit!" I snap, taking a step back when he reaches for me. "If you actually cared, you wouldn't have ditched me and my friends."

"I *had* to," Tim says. "You saw what happened."

"Oh that's right," I reply in mock sympathy. "Stacy sure twisted your arm. You couldn't possibly have made an excuse like, oh I don't know, 'I have some more errands to run but I'll catch up with you guys some other time.' That would have really blown your cover!"

"She knows," Tim says, his chest heaving.

I blink in surprise. "What?"

"Stacy thinks she saw you at that party I threw."

I know for a fact she did. "She brought that up?"

"Yeah. Stacy straight up asked if I was hanging out with you guys. Someone else saw us together too. Except that time, it was just me and you."

"When?"

"I don't know. She didn't say who, but there's more: Stacy said it's obvious that you have a thing for me. Then she asked if we're sneaking around together. I just laughed it off, but she's smart. I'm not sure she believed me."

"Good." I cross my arms over my chest. "Then there's no reason to keep it a secret."

"Are you kidding me?" Tim says in disbelief.

"No! What's the point of playing this game anymore? You're gay! Or bi, at the very least." He's already shaking his head, but I press on, because I'm so tired of dancing around the subject. "Can we please face reality? I mean, how many times have you sucked my dick?"

"Would you shut up?" Tim hisses while glowering at the dark and silent houses that surround us.

"No! How can you still pretend that you're straight? I don't get it!"

"I can't be gay!" Tim snarls. "It'll make everything worse."

"Yeah, well, I don't have that luxury." I start walking back to my house.

Tim sprints in front of me to block my path. "Wait!" he says. "You don't understand."

"Oh really? Let me take a wild guess: You can't deal with anyone not liking you. Because you're not sure if your dad does, and that makes you needy, so you look to everyone else to give you the love that he doesn't. Am I right?"

Tim looks wounded. "It's not that simple."

"Of course. There are also religious reasons. Which is ridiculous because it's all made up. You aren't going to Hell, Tim."

"My mom thinks I will."

I look skyward and groan. "I've heard all of this before!"

"But you don't get it," he growls. "It's going to break her

fucking heart! Until her dying day, she'll be convinced that I'm gonna burn in Hell."

"Or maybe, when learning that her own child is gay, she'll be forced to reevaluate her beliefs and recognize that what she's been taught doesn't add up."

Tim scoffs. "This is exactly what I mean. You don't get it! They aren't going to change their beliefs for you or anyone else. Including me." He shakes his head in disgust. "I never should have let you lure me into this."

"Are you kidding me?" I splutter. "I didn't lure you into anything! This is who we are, Tim! If you want to talk about things that can't be changed, take a long hard look in the mirror. The only choice you have is if you're going to let superstition and fear rule the rest of your life."

"You're wrong about that," he grumbles. "I do have a choice. I can be with a woman."

The fight goes out of me. I shouldn't have to convince someone to love me. Not the right guy anyway. "So choose," I tell him, jutting out my jaw. "Right now. What's it going be?"

Tim's scowl disappears. His face becomes drawn, like he's contemplating losing me, but I'm honestly not sure if that'll be enough to make him stay. "I need you," he says at last, taking my hand. He stares down at it and toys with my fingers, seemingly lost in thought. Then he looks up. "And you need me. Isn't that enough?"

I search his eyes, my own desperation mirrored there. "I want it to be," I croak. "But you're not making it easy."

"I know," Tim says. "I'm sorry."

"Just not enough for anything to actually change."

"I don't know what to do," he says, sounding genuinely lost. "I think about it all the time, but I can't figure out a move that doesn't… I love my mom."

"What about me?" I ask, my voice wavering.

"You know." Tim says. He places his hands on my cheeks, his earnest expression promising so much.

But he still can't say it.

I gently wrap my hands around his wrists and hesitate, knowing that it might be the last time I touch him. Then I pull down, moving his hands off my face.

"I don't know if I can do this anymore," I tell him.

Tim swallows. "I can't walk the same path that you did. We're not the same. Our families are too different. But there's got to be some other way." He takes my hand and brings it to his lips, silver eyes wavering at me from over it until a couple of tears break free. He's crying. For me! "Please, Benjamin," he says after lowering it again. "I don't want to lose you."

The thought alone is enough to make my heart ache. Even more than it has been already. "If you really want to have a future together, we need to start planning."

"Okay," he says. "Tell me what to do."

"The town that Allison and I are moving to for college, if you apply there and get in—"

"Isn't it a little late for that?" he interrupts. "I've already been accepted by three other schools."

I clench my jaw, which he must notice, because he raises his palms in surrender.

"I'll look into it," Tim says.

That doesn't sound like much of a commitment.

"Let's go on a road trip," I say. "As soon as we can. I want to show you what our future could be."

"Okay," Tim says, studying me with unease. "So you're not mad at me anymore?"

"I didn't say that!"

"But you're still my boyfriend?" he asks, squeezing my hand.

As if I have a choice in the matter. Two wet trails left by tears remain on his face. I've never felt so weak in my life.

"Yeah," I tell him. "I'm still yours."

When I step out of Tim's car, I'm conscious of the moment my shoe touches the pavement, because I'm literally setting foot in my new home. This isn't the first time, but on the previous visits, I didn't know for sure that I'd be going to school here. We're in the downtown area, which is full of cool shops and quirky restaurants. That's not what I want to show Tim. It's part of the whole package, but there are three specific things I need him to see while we're here that are much more important.

For now, I go easy on him. We stretch our legs while exploring the area, which feels good after the three-hour drive. When we get hungry, we stop at a café that has outdoor seating near the street. We're exposed while we eat. Countless witnesses see us together. I'm not sure if Tim realizes the implications of that just yet. He has a funny glint in his eyes, the one he gets when he locks on to something that he'd like to draw or paint. And it doesn't go away during the meal, because we are *surrounded* by life. In the town we left, people get in their car from doorstop to destination. Here there are throngs of pedestrians, rushing around or stopping to talk to each other. We see people jogging, biking, panhandling, and so much more. I can tell that he's inspired. But just to be sure…

"I don't know about you," I say with a theatrical yawn, "but I'm already bored."

"What?" Tim looks at me in disbelief. "This place is awesome!"

I crack a smile. "Yeah, it is pretty cool. Are you ready to keep going?"

"Sure. Want me to run for the car?"

"Nope. Let's leave it and walk."

The day is sunny, the temperature mild. Spring is here again, which means my boyfriend is back to wearing T-shirts and shorts. But even the allure of his bare skin can't hold my full attention as we wind our way through tree-lined streets, stopping frequently when Tim notices murals or unusual architecture. When we finally reach the campus of my university, I feel like I've been granted redemption for surviving the soul-crushing insanity of high school. We traverse paved paths that wind through green lawns and between imposing buildings, seeing people our age with wild hair colors, prominent piercings, or extravagant tattoos. None of whom are being hounded by bullies for standing out. In fact, judging from some of the unorthodox fashion choices, people here seem to take pride in their individualism.

"This is cool," Tim says, stopping to look at where a webbed line has been tied between two trees so a group of shirtless guys can practice walking along it.

"Sure is!" I say, staring at all the glistening muscles on display.

Tim tries to cover my eyes. "All right, that's enough!"

I duck and dodge so I can keep staring. He gets his revenge when a pair of girls in tight-fitting T-shirts jog by.

"I can see why you chose this school," he says with a shit-eating grin.

"Hilarious!" I reply. "If it's big boobs you're after, I'll start binge-eating. Just wait until I have great big man-tits."

"I'd fuck 'em," Tim says shamelessly.

Our humor is low-brow but our spirits are high as we continue exploring the campus. I lead him to the building dedicated to the arts. As soon as we walk in the doors, he gets quiet. The walls are covered in charcoal etchings, custom-made textiles, mixed-media concepts, and plenty more outside my scope of expertise. Which is fine, because Tim soon begins raving about each piece before he notices something else and goes rushing off, like a dog who has been set loose at a convention for squirrels.

This is the first thing that I wanted him to see. "In high school, art is an elective," I tell him. "Here it can be your major."

"I want this," Tim says, slowly panning to take it all in. Then he swallows. "Really bad. But I can't imagine getting accepted into an art program. I haven't taken a single class. What do I have to show?"

"Uh, nearly a dozen sketchbooks and an entire studio full of work? I can help you put together a portfolio. I know absolutely nothing about that kind of thing, but I'm sure we can figure it out together. As long as we get someone to look at what you've done, they'll recognize what you're capable of."

Tim turns to me, his expression insecure. "You really think so?"

"Yeah," I assure him. "And it's not just because I love you. You've got real talent."

"Thanks, Benjamin."

We leave the arts building and hang out at one of the dining halls while guzzling caffeine. Then we set out again, taking a different route back to the downtown area. I guide us to a street where most of the businesses are flying a rainbow flag.

"What's this?" Tim asks.

"The gay district."

"Gay district?" he repeats.

"Or bisexual, or trans, or lesbian. If you're queer, you belong here. Even straight boyfriends are welcome."

Tim laughs. "For real? This is all gay?"

"Yup. Even the fire hydrants." I nod at one that has been painted pink.

"Wow," he says in awe, even though it's literally just one street on this particular block. But compared to the scarce representation we grew up with, it feels massive. This is the second thing I needed him to see. "Homophobes exist everywhere," I say, "but at least here, people like us can pool our strength and form a community. This is a liberal city. Even in the other areas, there are plenty of allies."

We stroll down the street until we reach a bookstore with a number of alluring displays in the window. One focuses on queer history, another features erotic art. Tim is staring at the cover of a Tom of Finland collection when I ask if he wants to go inside.

"Right now?" he says, before glancing around with the sort of paranoia I haven't seen since we left my hometown.

"If you want," I say patiently. "Or you could kiss me, right here, because nobody knows who we are. Not a single person in this entire city has ever seen you before today or knows your name. We're hundreds of miles away from your friends. And your parents. It's just you and me, like when we're alone, but this time we're not."

This is the third and most important thing I wanted to show him while here. Not a tourist attraction or any sort of destination. It's a promise of what could be. I watch Tim's face as the potential sinks in. He grins suddenly. I smile back, only bringing my lips together again when he leans forward to kiss me.

Tim starts laughing against my mouth before he leans away. "This is so awesome!"

He intertwines his fingers in mine. A woman is walking down the sidewalk, but he doesn't shake me off. "How ya doin'?" Tim says to her as she passes. "It's a beautiful day!"

"It certainly is," she replies with a smile.

After that, I'm practically dragged along the street. He's swinging our hands between us gleefully, which only draws more attention to the fact that we're together. And yet it doesn't seem to be enough for him, because when we approach a pair of guys walking in our direction, he says, "Hey! I'm Tim. This is my boyfriend, Benjamin. We hope you have a good one!"

The guys laugh, their eyes lingering on Tim. What have I unleashed upon the world? Even when we leave the gay district, Tim doesn't let go of me. When we stop to look at something, he often kisses me right there in the daylight. Which is almost enough to make me weep tears of joy.

"So what do you think?" I ask him once we're sitting in his car again.

"I love it here," he replies. "But admission deadlines were months ago. My parents are already freaking out that I haven't committed to one of the schools that accepted me."

"Why haven't you?" I ask.

He shifts uncomfortably. "Because the first one is Catholic. That's their favorite. The other two only want me based on my athletic achievements."

"Oh." I refuse to give in to despair. "It doesn't hurt to try. I bet you'll get a fast answer, since they've probably gone through most of the applications already. I'll do anything I can to help."

Tim glances around, but for once, he does so with hope instead of fear.

"Yeah," he says at last. "Let's try."

CHAPTER TWENTY-FOUR

I'm singing my heart out while rinsing off dishes in the sink. My dad joins me on the chorus, his voice dry and toneless, as he sticks a fistful of cutlery in the dishwasher. I love the oldies. In fact, I don't think there's a single genre of music that I don't appreciate on some level. I'm holding out the dish brush to my dad so he can sing into it like a microphone when the doorbell rings.

"This is your big breakthrough moment!" I say, passing the dish brush to him. "It's all you!"

My dad takes the mic and keeps singing, but only another line or so before he notices that I'm retreating from the room. "Hey! What about the rest of these dishes?"

"Just think of all the exposure you'll get!" I call over my shoulder. "It'll be so worth it!"

I hurry to the front door, hoping Tim has come to share news of the application he submitted. Everything rides on him getting accepted. Otherwise we'll end up in different cities. Although, unlike my best friend, I would be willing to try a long-distance relationship.

I open the front door to find the very person I was just thinking of. And for some reason, Allison is wearing sunglasses, even though it's already dark out.

"You look so mysterious!" I say with a chuckle. "Are you practicing how you'll avoid reporters when you're famous?"

"Has my dad been here?" Allison replies.

"No." Concern drags my smile back down. Something is wrong. "What's going on?"

"Can we get out of here?" Allison asks, her voice sounding shaky.

"Yeah, of course! Let me just grab some shoes."

"I'll wait outside." She walks away without an explanation.

My heart begins to race nervously as I slide into a pair of sandals. If not for her opening line, I'd assume that Allison and Ronnie had gotten into some sort of argument. When I step outside and she hands me the car keys, I'm even more worried, because neither one of us is a great driver, but she's definitely better.

"Where are we going?" I ask once behind the wheel.

"Anywhere," Allison says. "Just don't stop."

I wait until we're a block away before asking her what happened.

"My dad," she says, her voice strained. "He came home early and caught me and Ronnie messing around."

"Oh shit!" I glance over at her in concern. "Wait, why are you wearing sunglasses?"

"Don't freak out," Allison says.

I pull over and park under a streetlight. "Take them off."

She does so with reluctance, revealing a nasty swollen welt on one cheek, just beneath her eye.

"My dad hit me," she croaks.

"With what?" I say, the blood pounding in my ears. I already want to kill him! "Never mind," I say, shaking my head. "We're going to the police."

"No!" Allison cries.

"Why not?"

"Because I love him."

"That doesn't matter! This isn't okay!"

"I don't need a lecture right now," Allison snaps. "I need you to listen!"

I take a deep breath and exhale, trying to calm myself. "Were you and Ronnie *doing it* doing it?" I ask. "Why would your dad attack you like that?"

"We weren't dressed," Allison says glumly. "And I think he was already drunk when he got home. It's my mom's birthday." Her face crumples before she buries it in her palms and begins to sob.

"I'm sorry," I say while rubbing her back. "This is so messed up. You don't deserve any of it."

"We took a stupid risk," Allison says, wiping her eyes. "I should have known better, but you know how my dad is. He's usually like clockwork. I didn't hear him arrive. I wasn't even listening for him yet. When the door to my room flew open…" She shakes her head. "It went so fast. My dad started yelling. Ronnie put on his underwear while trying to reason with him. He apologized and… It got ugly. Ronnie did fine. I think he was mostly shocked, but my dad threw the rest of his clothes at him and started knocking things over. As soon as Ronnie got his shirt on, my dad grabbed him by it and dragged him to the front door."

"Like, down the stairs?" I ask in disbelief.

Allison nods rapidly. "It was horrible! I tried to get my dad to stop. I started pulling on his arm, so he'd let go of Ronnie. I was scared they'd both fall down the stairs and get hurt. That's when it happened. Everything was so confusing but…" Her chin trembles. "My dad backhanded me."

I study the red welt on her cheek, wincing in sympathy. The swelling has already spread. She's going to have a black eye.

"You can't go home," I say.

"I know." Allison sighs wearily. "Not tonight anyway."

"Not ever again!" I growl, my temper rising.

"I'll be fine," Allison says. "This has never happened before. At least, not this bad. I just need to make it to summer, when we move."

I'm not okay with that. What if he pushes her down the stairs the next time he goes on a drunken rampage? "You can stay at my house," I tell her. "For as long as you need to. I'm sure my parents will be fine with it."

Allison shakes her head. "I don't want them to get mixed up in this."

"Why not?"

"Because of what they might do," she says, her voice strained. "My dad isn't abusive. He's just lost."

I flip down the visor on her side, so she can see herself in the mirror. "That sure looks like abuse to me!"

Allison barely glances at herself before flipping the visor up again. "It's not that simple."

I press my lips together before putting the car back in drive. "I'll sneak you up to my room. How about that?"

"Your house is the first place my dad is going to look. I'm surprised he hasn't already."

And when he does, my parents will come knocking on my bedroom door. Even if I manage to hide her, if they hear us talking afterwards, they'll get involved.

"This is why we need more friends," I say. "You can't stay with Ronnie. That would only throw fuel on the fire. What about Leon?"

"His parents will have questions too."

"Right."

We both think in silence. All she needs is a couch to crash on.

"I might have an idea."

Allison perks up. "Really?"

"Yeah. We'll need Tim's help."

I can practically feel the temperature dropping in the car. She hasn't been fond of him since the ditching incident at the mall. Allison keeps questioning if he's good for me, when really, I suspect she's projecting her own opinion of him. She's already shaking her head.

"I don't want him to know about this."

"I won't tell him the details. But it would be a place to stay for the night. Without any adults around. And trust me, your dad will never think to look for you there."

After more coaxing, I manage to talk her into the idea. Then I jump through every hoop necessary to get Tim to meet me at the end of his block. We drive over to his house, Allison remaining in the car when I step outside to talk to him.

"What's going on?" Tim asks.

"Allison had a bad argument with her father. Like... *really* bad. She needs somewhere to stay until he calms down."

He seems puzzled. "My parents are in town. She can't stay with me."

"I was thinking of your studio."

Tim recoils at the idea.

"I know, I know," I say, raising my hands to ward off any protest. "It's your fortress of solitude. I wouldn't ask if it wasn't important."

"Does she know about my art?" Tim asks guardedly.

I tilt my head. "She's my best friend. Allison knows everything."

"All of it?"

"Yes! Pretty much."

I know it's asking a lot of him. Letting someone see his paintings is tantamount to him ripping open his chest and exposing his heart.

"Please," I say. "Do it for me."

Tim shakes his head. "How am I supposed to argue with that?"

"Can we drive there now?"

He shrugs. "I guess so. Anything else?"

"Can you grab some blankets and a pillow for her?"

Tim salutes. "I'll meet you guys there. How's that sound?"

"Heroic," I say, giving him a quick kiss. "See you soon."

Half an hour later, we're walking through an office so dark that it forces Allison to take off her sunglasses. When we reach the conference room used as his studio, Tim flicks on the light. He glances at Allison with insecurity before doing a doubletake.

"Holy shit!" he exclaims, no doubt noticing the welt on her cheek. "What happened?"

"I don't want to talk about it," Allison says stiffly.

"That's cool," he replies. "Hell, it's practically my motto! Uh… Let's see."

Tim carries the bedding he brought to the couch and starts spreading one of the blankets out. "You should be fine for the night," he says while working. "Tomorrow is Saturday, so nobody will be here."

"What about the security guard?" I ask.

"If he sees a light on, he'll assume it's me," Tim replies. "Although I can go tell him that I'll be working late tonight. And that I might crash on the couch. If you think it's a good idea."

"Do you mind?" I ask, grabbing the blankets so I can take over.

"No problem! Be right back."

Once the bed is made, I turn around and find Allison perusing Tim's art. She's found the painting of me from Valentine's Day, which turned out great.

"He did all this?" she asks, sounding surprised.

I nod. "That's what's so hard to explain. I know he can be…"

"An ass?" she suggests.

"Yeah. But this is the real Tim. I love the artist, not the jock."

She considers the painting of me again. "Looks like he loves you back. How come this isn't hanging up in your room with the other?"

"A painting of myself?"

"Oh. That would be weird. So how come it's not hanging up in *his* room?"

I shrug. "I don't know, but if you ask nicely, maybe he'll give it to you."

Allison laughs, the happy sound welcome after seeing her

in so much pain. "I'm not sure I want a painting of anyone in my room, even my boyfriend. But I feel like Ronnie should have one of me."

"You could always have Tim paint your portrait!"

I'm not sure she hears me. Allison seems distracted, which is understandable. Cracking a few jokes and letting her crash here overnight isn't going to solve her problems. I'm only buying her time so we can figure out how to deal with everything. She sits on the makeshift bed. I join her.

"We'll get through this," I promise. "I'm not sure how, but we will."

Allison nods and leans against me. "I miss her so much," she murmurs. "Everything stopped making sense after my mom died."

"I'm sorry," I say, taking her hand. "I wish I could protect you."

"It was an accident, Ben. I don't think my dad wanted to hit me. It just sort of happened in all the commotion."

He was on a raging bender and his daughter got caught in the crossfire. I clench my jaw and hold my tongue, knowing that my anger won't make her feel better.

"I found Vince," Tim says when returning. "The security guard, I mean. You're all set." He holds up a pair of soda cans in one hand and a bag of chips in the other. "There's a breakroom down the hall with vending machines." He sets the food on the table in front of us and pulls candy bars out of his pockets. "Emergency rations."

"Thank you," Allison says.

"It's all good," Tim says easily. "Anything else I can do?"

"Yeah." Allison jerks a thumb at me. "Don't break his heart."

Tim nods. "I'll try my best."

We hang out a little longer. I promise Allison that I'll meet her here in the morning. Tim goes over some details, like how the alarm system works. Then he walks around his studio, turning certain cavasses around and covering a work-in-progress. As if that would stop my best friend from snooping.

When we part ways, I want to tell her that everything will be okay. But I don't, because I'm not sure it's true. I'm worried about her. If you can't feel safe in your own home, then something is very wrong.

"You should probably leave your car here," I tell Tim when we're standing outside in the parking lot. "I figure the security guard will recognize it, unlike Allison's. I can give you a ride home in hers."

Tim eyes his car with longing before he sighs. "Yeah, that makes sense. When will I get to see her again?"

"Allison?" I ask in confusion.

"No, my car!"

I roll my eyes. "Tomorrow morning. I'll need your help to get inside. Does that work for you?"

"Yeah," Tim says. "Is she going to be okay? Allison, I mean."

I shake my head. "I'm not sure. But thank you for doing this."

"Yeah, of course," Tim says.

I drive him back to his house. He asks if I want to sneak inside with him. I turn him down, because I have a feeling that I'm needed at home. And sure enough, the second I walk in the front door, my mother comes to meet me.

"Honey?" she says, sounding concerned. "Where were you? Out with Allison?"

"With Tim," I reply. "How come?"

"Because her father stopped by."

I put on a puzzled expression. "Weird. How come?"

"He was trying to find Allison." The worry deepens on her face. "He smelled a little drunk."

"It's her mom's birthday," I explain.

"Oh!" My mom presses a hand to her heart. "The poor girl! And that poor man!"

"Yeah," I say, not feeling any sympathy for him. "I think Allison wanted some alone time to deal with everything."

"That's understandable," my mom says before wrapping her arms around me. "I'm so grateful that our family hasn't gone through anything like that. Count your blessings."

I hug her back, reminded more than ever of how lucky I am.

I figure Allison will want a change of clothes, so early the next morning, I drive over to her house. She gave me her entire keychain. I won't have any trouble getting in. I could knock, but I'd rather avoid her father. And besides, I've practically become a master at stealthily unlocking front doors. The house is silent when I stand in the entryway while listening. I creep upstairs to her bedroom and push open the door, a rectangle of light moving across her darkened room to the bed… which is occupied.

Allison's father raises his head, shielding his eyes against the light. "Alli?"

I'm frozen with indecision, but only at first. I wordlessly move to her dresser and begin gathering clothes.

"What are you doing here?" her father growls.

"Your daughter will need something fresh to wear today. Especially if we go talk to the police." It's an empty threat, but I hope it'll make him hesitate the next time he loses his temper.

I hear shuffling behind me before the light flicks on. "Where is she?"

"Somewhere safe."

"Safe from what?" he demands.

"You!" I snarl, spinning around to face him. My anger has found a target, and it's the right one. "You're lucky I don't tell my parents everything! If I had my way, you'd never see her again!"

Allison's father is standing not far away from me, wearing a rumpled dress shirt and slacks that he no doubt passed out in. He raises a finger at me. "You better start making sense! Is she with that boy?"

"Is that really all you can think about?" I demand. "That she found someone who actually loves her and treats her right? Ronnie should have given *you* a black eye instead!"

Allison's father scrunches up his face in indignation. "All I did was throw him out!"

"I'm not talking about Ronnie."

I watch as his expression goes from confused to horrified. "What are you sayin'?"

"You don't remember what happened?"

"Tell me!" her father demands.

"Or what? You're going to hit me like you hit her?" I almost hope he does, because I won't hesitate to report him. Not one second.

"You're making it up," her father says, shaking his head.

"She has a cut on her cheek. You'll see for yourself."

"A cut?" His fingers seek out the wedding ring on his left hand before realization dawns. "Oh lord!" He sits on the edge of her bed, shaking his head while fingering the wedding ring in agitation. "What you must think of me," he whimpers to himself.

"If you're watching down on us, you must be so ashamed."

I don't know if he's talking to his god or his dead wife, but it's a pitiful sight, especially when he looks up at me with tears in his eyes. "What happened?"

"You really don't remember?"

"Bits and pieces," he admits.

"You were dragging Ronnie down the stairs. Allison was trying to stop you. That's when you backhanded her."

A moan escapes his lips, making him sound like a wounded animal. His pain is so tangible that I swallow against tears of my own. I don't want to feel sorry for him. He hit my best friend!

"What do you have against Ronnie anyway?" I demand.

"Nothin'," he says, shaking his head. "I'm trying to protect her."

"From what?"

"Getting knocked up and ruining her life before she has a chance to get the hell out of here." He massages his temples. "This is no home. I've tried to keep it together, but Alli needs to find her own way."

"She needs her father," I reply. "Just stop drinking so much."

He laughs without humor. "What do you know? Huh? They don't tell you what it's like, when you lose the person you love most in the world. You die *with* them. If you ever experience that—and god forbid you do—then you can come back here and give me a damn lecture!"

"Is it really that bad?" I ask without judgment.

Allison's father looks up at me. Then he swallows and nods. "Yeah. It's a living hell."

"I'm sorry," I say, sitting down on the bed, making sure to leave space between us. "That sounds horrible. Does the drinking really help though? I mean, you're obviously still in pain. Maybe it gives you a break or something but… You're hurting her."

"How bad is it?" he asks, his face strained in anticipation of my answer.

"It'll heal," I say. "I'm more worried about the emotional wounds."

"She must hate me."

"Nope. I wanted to go straight to the cops. Allison wouldn't let me. Because she loves you. That's exactly what she said."

He covers his face, his shoulders shaking as he weeps. I let him get it out of his system, no longer thinking about my own indignation. I'd rather find a solution that actually helps.

"We both love her," I tell him. "Right?"

"More than anything," he assures me.

"Then prove it. I'm sorry that you lost your wife, but she lost her mom. If Allison can get through it without drinking, so can you."

"That's what her mother would want," he says.

His hand is trembling when he brings it to his mouth, so he can press his lips to the wedding ring. Which must remind him of the damage it had done, because he lets out a sob. I reach over to pat him on the back, half-expecting him to rip my arm off. Instead he topples over, his head landing in my lap as he continues to weep. I start crying too. I can't help it. My tears are mostly for her, but I'm not cold-hearted. Her father isn't a monster. He didn't want to hurt his daughter. But he did, and now he has to live with it.

Eventually he sits up again. We awkwardly wipe at our noses while avoiding eye contact. Then he stands.

"Come on downstairs. I want you to see this, so you can tell her."

I follow him to the kitchen, where he opens a cabinet and removes a cluster of liquor bottles. Her father unscrews the top of each before pouring the contents down the drain. He'll need to do more than that, from what I gather, like attending a support group. But for now, it's a hopeful first step. With the final bottle drained, he turns to face me.

"Take care of her until she's ready to come home," he says. "Tell her that I love her, and that I'm sorry. I'll say that and more when she gets back. It's high time that we talk about it all."

"Okay," I say, swallowing against another wave of emotion. "I better go. She's expecting me."

He thrusts out his hand, which I readily accept.

"I'm glad she has a friend like you," he says. "You're all right."

I can only hope that she will be too.

CHAPTER TWENTY-FIVE

Prom fever is sweeping through our school. The upper classes anyway. I feel like a lowly freshman who doesn't stand a chance of being asked and can't attend on his own. No matter how bad I might want to, because I'd love to end high school by strolling into the ballroom with Tim on my arm. I can already imagine the look on everyone's faces. The haters especially. But I wouldn't do it for them. I simply want to go to the dance with the guy I love. If I was his girlfriend, there would be no question. It would be a given that we'd attend together.

I'm reminded of how easy such things are for straight people when I'm sitting in my economics class. Krista walks into the room carrying a single red rose, a folded note dangling from it, attached by a shiny blue ribbon. The stem is clutched close to her chest, the bloom near her nose like she's on a smelling marathon. A girl in the row of desks next to mine notices.

"Did you get asked to prom?"

"Yes!" Krista cries with delight. "I didn't think he would, but I kept waiting and hoping."

"That's wonderful!" the other girl says.

They aren't friends, so the conversation ends there, sparing me from having to hear about another happy heterosexual couple. But I can't help wondering who she ended up with, because Krista continues to glow throughout class. I watch her doodling in her notebook, occasionally covering her mouth with a dainty hand, as if to stop unadulterated joy from bubbling out. When the bell rings, I hop to my feet and walk past her desk. Before she closes her notebook to put it away, I see a sketched heart surrounding two sets of initials, the lines bold from being traced over and over again.

KN

TW

My stomach sinks. The bottom pair of initials belong to Tim. Or maybe it's just a coincidence. I rack my brain, trying to remember what I overheard at the mall when Stacy and Tim were talking. She mentioned who Krista's latest suitor was. Darryl, if I'm not mistaken. So it can't be him. I need a yearbook, *right now*, to check for other suspects. Or I could just ask my boyfriend. That makes the most sense. I try to put the issue out of mind until given the chance.

Which comes sooner than I expect. Tim shows up at my front door shortly after I get home from school. That's unusual, now that baseball is in season. He's often busy after school. I've been sneaking into his house at night again, just so we can have some time together. Catching up is difficult when we have to worry about his parents overhearing us, so I do more pillow biting than pillow talking.

"Are your parents home yet?" Tim asks with a grin.

"You know they're not," I reply.

His grin gets bigger. So does my cock. We race up to my bedroom, kissing while undressing each other. We'll talk afterwards, when it won't matter if my parents are home. And yet, I can't stop thinking about Krista's rose. And the initials in her notebook.

Tim slips between my legs before shoving his tongue in my mouth. I try to lose myself in him. Which should be easy, especially when he presses his dick against my hole. It's been a while since we've done that. I keep fantasizing about it, loving how close it makes me feel to him.

"I wanna fuck you," Tim pulls back to say.

I nod and kiss him while casting around for the bottle of lotion. When I find it and squirt some into my palm, the flowery scent reminds me of the rose again.

"Better open up," Tim says, thrusting against me with a playful grin. "Or this battering ram is going to break down the gates!"

"Maybe we should use something else," I say, rubbing my hands together to soak in the lotion.

"Why?" Tim asks. "Does it burn like the other kind did?"

"No," I reply. We learned the hard way not to use anything that contains mint. "The smell is bothering me."

"How about good old-fashioned spit?"

My hands reek of roses. I'm not even hard anymore.

He's searching my eyes for an answer. I stare back, wishing I could read his mind, because even after all this time together, he continues to elude me. I'll have to ask. In my own way. I watch his face carefully when saying, "Krista got asked to prom today."

I see a flash of panic before Tim sighs and rolls off. "That was fast," he grumbles. "Who told you?"

"You just did!" I sit up so I can glare down at him. "What the hell? Why would you ask her?"

Tim rubs his eyes while groaning. "You know why!"

"I really don't!"

He moves his hands away, his expression weary. "My mom expects me to go with her."

"Why's that?" The answer comes to me before he can reply. "She still thinks you're dating Krista. Doesn't she?"

"Yeah, but I'm not, so why make a big deal out of it?"

"Because you're my boyfriend!" I shake my head. "I can't believe I need to explain this to you!"

"It's just a stupid dance."

"It's not to me! And besides, what happens before then? Does she think you're back together? Wait, *are* you?"

Tim squirms under my stare. "No. Not really."

"Not really?" I repeat incredulously. "What the hell does that mean? And what happens if she tries to kiss you? It's going to seem weird if you don't want to. You're her freaking prom date!"

Tim swallows.

I rock back on my butt and pull my legs up to shield myself. "*Are* you going to kiss her?"

"If I do, it'll only be for show."

My jaw drops. "You're *my* boyfriend! You don't get to kiss anyone but me! How would you feel if I took some other guy to prom and made out with him, just so my parents wouldn't think that I'm dating an inconsiderate asshole?"

Tim sits up and grabs a pillow to cover himself. "I know it sucks," he says. "But there's no way around it."

"I can think of one," I growl. "Don't go! It's that simple."

"It's too late," Tim murmurs.

"Why? Because you don't want to hurt her feelings?"

He shrugs. "Yeah. It would be messed up if I ditched her now."

"*This* is messed up!" I say gesturing between us. "What about my feelings?"

Tim reaches for me. I knock his hand away and roll out of bed to get dressed. "When were you going to tell me?"

"I was hoping you wouldn't find out."

"That's great." I grab his clothes and fling them at him. "So I was supposed to sit all alone at home on prom night, waiting for you to finish so I could get some sloppy seconds?"

Tim presses his lips together while pulling up his underwear. "I know it sucks..." he starts to say.

I turn to face him and cross my arms over my chest. "But what?"

He's silent when putting on his shirt. "This is the way it has to be."

"Wrong," I say, turning my back to him while getting dressed. "This is the way you want it to be. Otherwise you would man up and tell your friends and family about the guy you've been with for seven months now. Seven fucking months, Tim! And I'm still a dirty little secret while Krista gets to go with you to—" My voice cracks. I turn to face him again. He's standing behind me, wearing a glum expression. "I wanted you to ask me," I croak.

His shoulders slump. "I'm sorry."

"Just not enough to do anything about it. Am I right?"

Tim looks exasperated. "What am I supposed to do?"

"You really need me to tell you?" I shake my head. "Get out."

"Benjamin…"

I point at the bedroom door. "Get out! Go home or go screw your stupid fake girlfriend. I don't care anymore!"

"Fine!" he snaps. "Maybe I will!"

"Great! Have fun! You deserve each other." He's already halfway out the door. "Just don't ever come back!"

"I won't!" he snarls in response.

I slam the door. Then I pace my room, seething while resisting the urge to cry. I won't let him make me. That would be even worse. Eventually, when the adrenaline begins to ebb, I flop onto my bed and stare up at the ceiling, feeling like I did get fucked by him. Just not in the way that I wanted.

"What are we doing here, Ben?"

"Enjoying the beautiful weather?" I reply, even though I know Allison won't be convinced.

We're sitting on the bleachers that overlook our school's baseball diamond. Which is a first for us both, because we've never cared about sports. I just want to see him again. Tim and I haven't talked for a week. That was easy the first few days, with anger fueling my determination to avoid him. But now it's slowly starting to sink in that our relationship might not recover.

"Most of the weather is up there," Allison says, lifting my chin skyward.

As soon as she lets go, I return my attention to centerfield, where Tim is keeping a vigil on—I don't know—wherever the ball goes, I guess. I haven't been tracking it myself. I keep waiting for the brim of his ball cap to turn in my direction so two silver eyes can glimmer at me from the shadows. He seems completely unaware of my presence. Just like it used to be.

"I thought it was over," Allison presses.

"I'm not sure," I admit.

She arches an eyebrow at me. "He's dating someone else, and you're not sure?"

"Everyone deserves a second chance. You know that better than anyone."

Her other eyebrow raises, completing the set. "Are you talking about my dad? Because that is *not* a fair comparison. He lost his wife. The only thing Tim lost is his backbone."

I swallow, knowing that she's right. "How did the support group go last night?"

"Just fine. We both listened more than we talked, but I really like the woman who runs the group. She reminds me of a wise old owl. And boy can she bake! You might want to fake losing someone, just to get access to those brownies."

"Smuggle some out for me. So this was the survivors' group?"

Allison nods. "Dad is going to the Alcoholics Anonymous meetings by himself. I thought about driving him there and waiting in the car, just to be sure, but he came back with enough pamphlets that I know he's taking it seriously. He hasn't touched a drop." She hesitates. "Except for the six-pack of beer the other night."

"You said he drank two and poured the rest out, right?"

She nods. "He thought it wouldn't be as bad as the whiskey, so I sat there and made sad eyes at him until he changed his mind." Allison shakes her head. "I know how this is going to sound, but I'm almost glad it happened." The welt on her cheek has faded to a flat pink line. "As the woman who runs the support group put it, 'Nobody wants their toilet bowl to be filled to the brim with shit, but at least it gives you the opportunity to flush.'"

"Wow, she does sound wise!"

"Uh-huh. And so am I, so don't think that change of subject threw me off."

The crowd around us erupts in excited roars for reasons that are beyond me. Allison doesn't even look at the field. She keeps her gaze trained on me until the applause has died down. "We could be jamming with our band right now. Especially with the talent show coming up. We should be practicing! Besides, it looks to me like Tim already has his own cheerleader."

She nods across the heads of spectators to where Krista is sitting with her step-brothers. I can already picture Tim meeting them after the game to autograph a ball or ruffle their hair affectionately. I bet he'd be a great father. He could play catch with any of our kids who are into sports and teach the rest to paint. I imagine him going for a run with our daughter, who is in track and field, while I stay home and sing with our son, who loves to play guitar. What would their names be though? And how many kids would we have?

"Ben!" Allison says, pulling me back to the present. I was staring at him again. She points at Krista this time, who is standing and waving as Tim's team jogs toward the dugout, clearing the field. He notices her and waves back.

"Okay, I hate him again."

"Me too," Allison says, before standing and waving.

"What are you doing?"

"Come on," she says. "Let's see what he does."

Why the hell not? I launch to my feet. Soon we're both waving, which attracts the attention of multiple players. Including him. Tim is close enough that I can see his puzzlement, and the way his face becomes an impassive mask when he recognizes us. He doesn't wave back. It really is over. So why can't I get myself to accept that and leave a game I care nothing about?

I sit down with a lump in my throat.

Allison joins me and winces at my expression. "I'm sorry," she says. "I didn't mean to hurt you."

I shake my head. "You're right. He'll never change."

That's not entirely true, because we did make progress together. Or so it seemed. Would it have killed him to flash a smile? Or give an upward nod? Especially after a week of us not talking. He should have been happy to see me waving at him! But no. And I can guess why.

I turn my head to the left, to a couple of rows in front of us where his parents are sitting. They haven't noticed me and aren't likely to. But maybe his mother would have turned around to see who Tim was waving to, and god forbid that it be a gay person. She'd be forced to call the Vatican's emergency hotline. I can imagine the Popemobile tearing onto the field with sirens blaring before a fire hose blasts me with holy water.

"You'll find someone new," Allison says, taking my hand. "A sweet guy who treats you right."

"Tell me about him," I say as the visiting team takes the field.

"Let me look into my crystal ball." Allison lets go of my hand to wiggle her fingers through the air. "Ah! I see him now. He has red hair and freckles. His name is Billy Bob."

"Hmm," I reply, not yet enamored.

"Did I mention that he was raised on a farm and is built like an ox?"

"Oh yeah?" I ask, perking up.

"Yes. He's a giant beefcake of a man who is soppy and sentimental. He always cries during sad movies."

"I love him! Wait… Does he have an artistic side?"

"Indeed he does! He plays the musical saw."

"Really? That's one of the most heartbreakingly beautiful instruments in the world!"

"I thought you would find it funny, but that works too. Now can we please get out of here?"

"Yeah, okay."

I'm starting to stand when the commentator announces the next player up to bat. And it's Tim. I turn a pleading expression on my friend, who sighs and sits back down. Tim is wearing a dark blue helmet now. I've already decided that if he turns around and points at me, all will be forgiven. Although I think that's only done when a player is showing where they intend to hit the ball, so maybe it's a dumb idea.

"Go, Tim, go!" cries a voice from somewhere behind us. "You've got this! Hit a home run!"

I glance over my shoulder in confusion that doesn't abate, because I recognize the speaker. Danny is wearing the red trucker hat. He's on his feet while clapping and grinning, rivaling even Krista's enthusiasm. Especially when I hear a crack. Danny begins jumping up and down. I return my attention to the field and see a blur racing toward second base. And he makes it! I almost forget that I'm supposed to be angry at him. But when I see Krista and Tim's parents applauding this result, my curiosity gets the better of me, because I don't understand why Danny has joined their fan club.

"Just a second," I say to Allison. "I'll be right back."

I make my way down the row and up the aisle to where he's sitting.

Danny's face lights up when he sees me. "Ben! What are you doing here?"

"I was about to ask you the same thing," I reply. "Are you into sports?

"Not usually," Danny admits. "But there are some aspects I find interesting. Like the statistics." He starts talking about RBIs and ERAs, leaving me totally lost. Another crack interrupts his lecture. "He made it!" Danny cries in delight.

I glance at the field. Tim is on third base now. "Is he your favorite player?" I ask casually.

"Yeah," Danny replies with a sheepish expression. "He's really good."

"That's the guy who was picking on you, right?"

"Well sure," Danny says dismissively, "but he doesn't anymore. Tim is actually really nice. He always smiles at me in the hall."

I feel the stirrings of jealousy. And a growing concern that my situation isn't as unique as I'd thought. "Are you guys friends?"

"Huh? No. We don't talk or anything. Not since that day in class. I just think he's…" Danny's pale skin turns pink. "That he's nice. And talented." So much that remains unspoken is shining in his eyes.

Another cracking sound. The audience erupts in excitement. I watch as Tim runs back and forth between third and home base, a ball being passed back and forth between players on the opposing team. Everyone is freaking out. I am too, but not because of the game. I glance at Danny, who is almost manic in his adoration of Tim, and feel like I've gone back in time to witness myself at the beginning of it all.

"Yes!" Danny cries before leaping around. "Way to go!"

I don't bother looking. Tim got a home run. Of course he did.

"Wow!" Danny breathes. "Didn't I tell you? He's amazing!"

"He's something all right," I murmur.

Danny looks a little self-conscious, even though the smile keeps returning to his face. "Do you want to watch the game together?" he asks.

"I can't." I nod to where Allison is looking at me with a

pointed expression. "I'm with my friend and she doesn't want to stay."

"You could though," Danny suggests.

"We have band practice. The garage kind, I mean."

"You're in a band?" Danny asks. "That's really neat! What do you play?"

"I sing."

"Oh. Funny how we don't really know much about each other." This doesn't seem to be a guilt trip, judging from the lingering joy on his face. "I guess there's not much time to talk during class. But maybe after school sometime? I think we have…" He hesitates before nodding to himself. "We have a few things in common."

More than either of us realized. "Yeah," I say. "I'm up for that."

"Great!" Danny says, beaming at me. "We could go to a movie or something."

Is he asking me on a date? I'm honestly not sure. "We'll figure it out some other time. I've really got to go."

"Okay," Danny says. "It was nice seeing you."

"Yeah! You too."

I feel troubled when walking away, which is strange, because this is what I always wanted. Another gay guy at my school. Probably. I should be thrilled, and maybe I would be, if it wasn't like looking in the mirror. Danny clearly has a thing for Tim, whether it's platonic or otherwise. But he doesn't really know him. The sad thing is, I'm not so different. Oh sure, I know more details about Tim's life, and that he likes to paint. I know the scent of his hair and the taste of his skin. He's literally been inside of me. But what is any of that worth? If someone had predicted a month ago that Tim would ditch me to take Krista to prom, I would have arrogantly proclaimed their ignorance. How ironic, coming from the king of fools.

That's me.

I'm a royal idiot.

CHAPTER TWENTY-SIX

I keep thinking of the last time we slept together. Or tried to. Neither one of us knew that it was the end. If we had, I like to think that we would have made it special. Nearly two weeks have gone by now. Prom is a few days away. On the weekend. I've given up hope that Tim will show up last minute at my house with a corsage and an apology. He wouldn't do that to Krista. Or his mother. Me? I'm fair game. The least of his priorities. Maybe because he knows that I love him. Ugh! I never should have said that out loud.

And yet, I want to again. One final time. So when the house has fallen silent, I slip on my shoes and walk to his place. I'm still wearing the necklace he gave me. Sometimes the metal of the key will touch my chest, shocking me with its cold. At others, if I press the key against my skin, it'll grow warm. Not so different than the person who gave it to me. I'm not sure how he'll react when I show up unannounced, but it can't be worse than how we parted.

Tim is already in bed when I pad into his room. I carefully close the door. When I turn around, he's propped up on an elbow, watching me. There's so much I want to say, but words have never been reliable. Not with us. We've always had to depend on another language. I approach the bed. Tim moves the blankets aside in invitation.

I undress in front of him. As soon as my knee hits the mattress, he reaches for me. I tumble into his arms and sob against his lips, because it's such a relief to be close to him again. I don't care what he did or how much it hurt. Not right now. His touch is all that matters. I lower myself onto his naked body, craving the emotional closeness that always accompanies these moments. Tim brushes the hair from my forehead. He must see my tears, but he doesn't try to wipe them away. His eyes are full of sympathy or maybe an apology. I don't know, but I need him, so we take turns touching and tasting each other, our moans and hisses stifled so they won't escape out into the hall.

Tim slides between my legs. We're finally back to where we left off. He's searching my face for permission. I hold up a finger, asking him to wait, and push him off. I want this. Enough to make sure I'd be ready. I stretch, reaching for the floor to hook a belt loop on my jeans. Inside one of the pockets is a small bottle of lube that I bought from a drugstore. I squirt some into my palms. Then I toss the bottle aside so I can stroke Tim with one hand while exploring myself with the other. This stuff works *way* better than lotion. No burning sensation and no flowery scents.

I push the thought from my mind, not wanting a repeat of last time. All is forgotten when he climbs on top of me again. Tim isn't as cautious as he usually is. I'm equally impatient. Even when it hurts I don't push him away or ask him to slow down. My hunger is too great. I ride out the discomfort until pleasure replaces it. I paw at Tim, pulling him down while wrapping my legs around him. He kisses me as his body gyrates against mine. I'm already close. I can tell he is too.

Maybe that's why he finally slows, his hips rocking back and forth in a gentle motion. The pleasure is so intense that it's almost maddening. We continue like that for what feels like an eternity. Longer than we've ever gone before, as if he knows it'll be the last time. The sun can come up for all I care. I don't want him to stop. When we're like this, thoughts are fleeting. The concerns of the real world are distant. It's just us, together in a way that feels inseparable. We've achieved perfection. If only we could resist the temptation to push our luck and go beyond this moment, which will feel good… but ultimately usher in the end. So I tell him again, because of all that I've wanted to say over the past two weeks, they're the only words that truly matter.

"I love you."

Tim pushes himself up to gaze down at me. I still can't read what's behind those eyes. They say ignorance is bliss, and I do feel happy, in this moment. He's everything I ever wanted. My heart swells, filled with so much for him that I fear it's going to come apart at the seams. I always knew he'd break it. One way or another.

I let him push me to the brink. I'm not even touching myself anymore. I don't need to. When I moan, he growls. Together we take the leap, briefly achieving a new height, but that only increases how far we fall. Tim collapses onto me. I clutch him close, but I can already feel him slipping away. I don't want to let go. He doesn't either, judging from how long we lay there holding each other. He stays inside of me. By the time he pulls out, the pain is much worse than when we first started, all of it emotional.

I swallow against more tears. Then I sit up and swing my legs over the mattress. Tim gets out of bed and gestures for me to wait. I watch him go to his desk and switch on a lamp. He returns with an envelope and hands it to me. Then he brings his mouth close to my ear and whispers, "I got in."

I look at him in surprise and hastily pull out the acceptance letter, needing to see it with my own eyes. I open my mouth to say something. He shakes his head and hands me my clothes before grabbing his own. My pulse is racing as we get dressed. Tim got accepted into the same school as me. This could change everything!

I feel a pang of uncertainty. The future is one thing. What about the present?

I'm puzzled when Tim puts on his blue shoes. He smiles at me and tilts his head toward the door. This is new! We leave his room together, part of me desperately hoping that his parents will catch us. I'm even tempted to trip and make a noise so they'll wake up. But I don't, because outing him won't solve the real issue. Tim needs to accept himself. Instead of trying to please everyone else at his own expense.

"What are we doing?" I ask when we're safely at the end of his driveway.

"I'm walking you home." Tim says, leading the way. He pulls the acceptance letter out of his back pocket. "What do you think?"

"That it's our last hope," I say from around a constricting throat.

Tim's smile falters. "Yeah. I figured."

"So you're going? Have you sent your response yet?"

Tim shakes his head. "I'm still working on my parents."

"Oh."

He nudges me. "It's not like all the other stuff. They don't have a religious reason for not wanting me to go."

"Aside from them preferring a Catholic school."

"I guess," he admits. "My mom likes that I'd be closer. And it's cheaper. They aren't against it. But uh... Is there any point?"

"What do you mean?"

He stops and turns toward me. "Do I still have a boyfriend?"

I take a deep breath. I can see our entire future laid out before us, and it's bright and beautiful, except for the silhouette of a person who is standing in the way. "Are you still going to prom with Krista?"

He returns the letter to his back pocket. "Yeah. I have to."

"Then I can't be your boyfriend," I tell him.

A breeze rustles the freshly unfurled leaves above us. Tim's head is bowed, his handsome features lost in shadow, but I want to see them one more time. I place my hand on his cheek, so that he'll look at me. His expression is sullen. If he didn't care about me, he wouldn't feel sad, or fight to go to the same school. Maybe that's enough. For now.

"But after prom is over," I say, "if you're ever single again…" I shrug and leave it at that.

He kisses me, and I allow myself to forget all the reasons I shouldn't kiss him back.

"Wanna keep going?" he asks when letting go of me.

I shake my head with a subtle smile. "I'll find my own way."

I walk backwards a few steps, our eyes locked until the moment I turn away. High school is almost over. Everything must come to an end. I went to him tonight intending to say goodbye. But maybe, when summer finally arrives, it'll be the start of something new.

A melancholy settles over me the day before prom. So many people in school are buzzing with an excited energy. The rest of us put on brave smiles while telling ourselves that such things don't matter. And maybe that's how some people really feel. I wouldn't have cared as much, if Tim didn't want to go to prom at all. If we could have simply been together tomorrow night, that would have been fine with me.

Instead I try to be excited for Allison and Ronnie. Leon asked out a junior, who I got to meet the other day. Half her hair was buzzed short, the rest long and dyed. She spent most of lunch explaining to us why nobody with a heart should eat meat. Leon was grinning the whole time. I'm happy for my friends. As for my enemies, I refuse to look in Krista's direction during my economics class. I hope Tim gets diarrhea tomorrow night. The sudden onset kind. I want it to happen when he's in the middle of a slow dance with her. A petty fantasy, but it does make me chuckle occasionally as I weather the rest of the day.

"Are you going to prom?" Danny asks when we're sitting in our physics class.

"No," I say. "Are you?"

He laughs, like it was a joke. "Who would I go with? Hey, how come you aren't going with your boyfriend? Are you waiting until his school has their prom?"

He's not quiet when asking this. Nor does he glance around as if scared of being overheard.

"No," I answer. "He's going with someone else. A girl, actually."

Danny makes a face. "That's messed up!"

"I think so too."

We sit in silence for a moment. Then I see Danny perk up in my peripheral vision.

"Hey!" he says. "Since neither of us are going, do you want to hang out tomorrow night? You could come over to my place. We'll watch a movie or something fun."

I don't even need to consider the offer. "Sure! Let's do it!"

He writes down his address and we set a time. I'm half-tempted to ask him to prom. We still haven't talked about the gay thing. I'm not sure where he's at with accepting himself, or if I'm reading the situation correctly. I suppose it doesn't matter. The hottest guy in school—besides Tim, of course—could ask me to go with him, and I'm pretty sure I would decline. The last thing I need is a front-row seat to Tim and Krista's magical evening together.

The walls of Danny's room are covered in sci-fi posters, most of them with fold-lines from magazines. Some of the shows and characters are familiar to me. Most are not. He also has action figures and toys, a few of them recent purchases. Which is weird, but I like it. I didn't realize that science fiction was so important to him. Funny how you can sit next to someone for the better part of a year and not really know who they are. I'm eager to get into the personal stuff.

We haven't had much time alone. After he gave me a quick tour of his room, his mother called us to dinner. He lives in a two-bedroom apartment with her. She has frizzy ginger hair and laughs easily. We ate at the table. Pork chops, green beans, and mashed potatoes. She's transparently thrilled that Danny has a friend over, which makes me wish I'd done this sooner, or invited him into my little social circle, which only grew beyond Allison when she started dating Ronnie. It stings knowing I could have had another friend well before then. Someone like me, perhaps.

Danny is explaining what a rock tumbler is and why he enjoys his when he hands me a pale stone speckled with black spots. "That's dalmatian jasper," he says. "I dug it up in the vacant lot across the street. You can keep it if you want."

I suck in through my teeth. "I don't know… A dalmatian sounds like a lot of responsibility. Do I have to take it for a walk? What do I feed it?"

He grins. "Just pet it every once in a while and it'll be fine." Danny peeks into the pouch he's holding. "Or you can choose something different."

"Too late," I say, slipping it into my pocket. "I've already formed an attachment."

He looks pleased.

I glance around his room. "You know, at the baseball game, you said we had a lot in common, but we're actually pretty different."

"Oh," he says. "I know of at least one thing."

"Yeah?"

He nods. "We're both gay."

After nearly a year of trying to get Tim to utter some version of that, I'm almost dumbstruck by how effortless Danny made it seem. "Really?" I ask. "When did you figure it out?"

"This year. I mean, part of me has *always* known, even though I tried not to think about it. When I first heard people talking about you being gay, and that you didn't deny it… It made the way I feel inside okay somehow. I kept trying to work up the nerve to talk to you but…" His face flushes, which is flattering. "I was really happy when we ended up sitting next to each other. That wasn't the first time either. Did you know that?"

I nod. "Math class in the eighth grade."

"That's right! I didn't think you'd remember."

"I do," I tell him. "You were always competing with me."

He looks confused, but only momentarily. "You mean because I was always the first to finish every test?"

"Not *always* the first," I retort. "And for the record, math isn't my best subject or I would have beat you more often."

"Sounds like *you* were the one competing with *me,*" he teases.

That makes me chuckle. "I guess so."

"I do get really good grades," he says with pride that I

previously interpreted as arrogance. "When people pick on me, my mom says it's the best way of getting revenge. Because eventually, being smart will actually be worth something."

I already mourn all the lost years that we could have been friends. "Enough about your big brain," I say. "I've waited my entire life to meet someone else who is gay. Tell me about that!"

He blinks in confusion. "I thought you had a boyfriend?"

"So did I," I murmur. After a sigh, I try to sum it up as best I can. "He's bisexual but can't even admit that much. Which is why he's taking a girl to prom, so everyone will think he's straight. And to make his mom happy."

"She doesn't know?" Danny asks.

"Nope."

"Huh. I already told mine."

"Oh yeah? How'd it go?"

Danny shrugs. "She didn't care. Like at all."

I can't help laughing. "Sorry. He's made it all so complicated. You've just reminded me that it doesn't have to be. What about your dad?"

"I was nervous about telling him," Danny admits. "He's not in my life much. Sometimes I don't see him for years at a time. My mom doesn't like him, since he never pays child support like he's supposed to. So I thought about keeping it a secret from him, in case he stopped coming around entirely. But then I figured I didn't have much to lose."

"How did he react?"

Danny crinkles his nose. "He told me a story about an army buddy who would refuse to go to brothels and strip clubs for religious reasons, even though everyone knew he was gay. But he was one of the toughest guys in their squad, so nobody ever called him on it. I'm not sure what the point was. I think it was supposed to be supportive. My dad isn't good at that sort of thing. He finished by telling me I need to do push-ups."

"Sounds rough. Worse than what my boyfriend is going through."

Danny seems surprised. "You guys didn't break up?"

"I don't know. It's complicated. And hot. But mostly complicated."

"You're lucky," he says breathlessly.

"Even though I'm in a bad relationship?" The words surprise

me after slipping out, because I've never let myself frame it that way before.

Danny nods. "I just want to be with another boy. I've never even kissed someone."

"Be careful what you wish for." I'm tempted to ask which guy at school he finds the most attractive, but I know what his answer will be. And at the moment, I don't want to think about Tim at all. Especially knowing where he is and who he's with. "What should we do next?" I ask, eager for a distraction.

"I have a ton of movies and TV shows."

"I've noticed!"

"Have you ever seen this series?" Danny goes to a poster of a weird-looking guy squatting next to a robotic dog. "It's one of my favorites, since it involves time travel. Hey, where would you go, if given the chance? Into the future or into the past?"

"The future," I reply, not needing to think hard about it. I just want to know if Tim and I end up together. That way I could stop torturing myself by wondering if I should walk away or wait things out.

"Why the future?" Danny asks.

"Because there would be a lot of comfort in knowing what's going to happen."

"That depends on what you see," he replies. "It could be dystopian. Then you'd spend the rest of your life knowing how horrible the future will be. I'd rather go to the past. To change things."

"Like what?"

He licks his lips again. "I would have asked you out at the beginning of the year."

That's so sweet! It's all too easy to imagine an alternate timeline, where the unassuming guy sitting next to me in physics class turned out to be what I'd been looking for the entire time. And maybe he could be still, if I wasn't so wrapped up in Tim.

"I would have said yes," I tell him.

Danny smiles. "Really?"

"Yeah."

He seems a little overwhelmed by this news. His cheeks are burning and he keeps blinking rapidly. He's not stunningly handsome. Nor does he have an impressive physique. But he is taller than me, which I like, and his willingness to be open with his thoughts and feelings is refreshing. I can't though. My heart is too messed up at the moment, so I nod at the poster. "That looks good. Let's watch it."

"Okay!" Danny says. "I'll ask my mom to microwave some popcorn for us. I'll be right back!"

He races from the room, leaving me alone. But thanks to him, I'm not going to spend prom night feeling that way.

I thought prom being over would bring relief, but I'm hounded by questions. Did they kiss? Did Krista say that she loves him? Did he say it back? What if they slept together? I don't want to know. I mean, I totally do, but I'm certain the truth will devastate me. So I avoid Tim by spending the next day with Allison. She tells me all about her evening with Ronnie, and how special everything was. I'm happy for my friend, but being around her means resisting the same temptation to find out more. She would have kept an eye out for Tim. I'm sure Allison saw him, but she doesn't offer any information, and by some miracle I manage not to ask.

I'm lying in bed that night when I hear something pelt my window. The lights are already off, so I remain motionless as Tim keeps trying. Danny comes to mind. I don't have a crush on him, or any feelings that aren't platonic. But I can't help thinking that he would have been a better boyfriend. The attraction between us could have developed slowly and been built on more than just the physical. My parents would love his mom. I'm certain of that. I don't know about his dad, but the parallel doesn't escape me, because it's hard to feel sorry for Tim when Danny has it even worse and still came out swinging. We would have been two nerdy gay guys, defying all the bullies and homophobes by slow dancing together at prom.

The clinking sounds have finally ceased, so while drifting off, I try to imagine what Danny and I could have had. But of course my treacherous imagination soon replaces him with Tim. When I wake up the next morning, the remnants of a dream haunt me, Tim's breath tickling my ear as he whispers *I love you, I love you, I love you,* over and over again. But of course he isn't really there with me, so I get up and welcome the distractions of the day.

Allison comes over around lunchtime. My mom makes us grilled cheese sandwiches and tomato soup. Comfort food.

Afterwards we head over to Leon's house. With the talent show coming up, we've been practicing there almost every day. Leon is still trying to get his ballad ironed out, certain it's our strongest contender. Ronnie thinks we should go with an older song they already perfected, so we've been rehearsing both. I don't really care which we end up choosing. I just like to sing with my best friend.

We're about to play another set when the basement stairs squeak. I look up and see Tim standing there. My heart leaps before recent events catch up with me. Then my stomach sinks.

"Hey," he says sheepishly, his eyes moving from me to Leon. "Your little brother let me in."

"As well he should," Leon replies. "Are you here to jam with us?"

"No," Tim says. "I just need to talk to Benjamin real quick."

Every head swivels in my direction.

My cheeks flush. I don't know why. Maybe because it's awkward. I can picture Danny coming down those stairs, gangly legs and all, his trucker hat whipping back and forth as he excitedly checks out all the instruments and band posters. Instead a hot guy is squirming at the top of the stairs while his expression pleads with me to go somewhere private. I don't like it. I sigh and stand. A minute later, I'm standing outside with him, even though the sky is overcast and drizzling.

"Are you still mad at me?" Tim asks. "I thought we were cool."

"How did it end with Krista?" I ask, unable to resist. "Does she think you're still dating?"

Tim shakes his head. "She never did. Krista is going to study abroad, so prom was always supposed to be a… I don't know."

"Last huzzah?" I suggest.

Tim nods. "Yeah."

"What about you?" I ask. "What college are you going to?"

"I'm working on it. I promise."

He reaches for my hand, but I move it away. Yes, he looks ridiculously good for a guy who is wearing torn-up jean shorts and a simple black T-shirt. His brown skin is alluring as ever, as are the rounded muscles. I want to give into temptation and let his touch chase away my concerns. But not this time. He'll have to use his words.

"Listen," Tim says, taking a step closer before sighing. "I know I fucked up. But now it's over so… Will you let me make it up to you? Friday night. We'll do something really special."

I shrug. "Like what?"

"It's a surprise," he says. "And an apology."

I roll my eyes to hide my weakening willpower.

"Would it help if I let you kick me in the nuts?" Tim says, trying a smile.

I'm instantly disarmed by the shape of those lips as they frame pearly white teeth.

"You know I'm too fond of your nuts to do that."

"I mean, I was hoping," Tim replies.

This time, when he reaches for my hand, I don't resist. He looks relieved. I only wish I felt the same. He must see the uncertainty in my eyes, because his brow furrows up.

"Have you given up on me?" he asks, sounding vulnerable.

I swallow before responding. "No. Not yet."

"Good." He brings my hand to his lips and kisses it. "Friday night. I'll pick you up at home."

"Don't you mean around the block from my house?"

"No," he says. "I'll park in your driveway. Okay?"

I hold my tongue, but only to punish him. I already know my answer.

"Okay."

CHAPTER TWENTY-SEVEN

I want to be happy. And I want to be with him. So during the week, I try to let go of my animosity and return to the feeling I had after we last slept together. The past can't be undone. All we can do is wipe the slate clean and let this be a new beginning for us. I don't know what Tim has planned, only that it's a surprise. By the end of the week, I'm mostly excited by the prospect. Krista puts a damper on this, simply by existing. I can't help but see her during our economics class. She's a living reminder of everything that went wrong.

I don't wait by the door on Friday evening. I make myself look nice, but once I'm ready, I sit in the living room while reading a book. If he wants me that bad, he can knock on the door.

Ding-dong!

Or ring the bell. My misgivings are instantly forgotten. I leap to my feet and throw open the front door. Tim is standing there in a maroon T-shirt and the same torn shorts that I last saw him in.

He looks me over and asks, "What did you get all dressed up for?"

I glower at him and start to shut the door. He puts a hand out to block it and laughs.

"I'm only kidding. It'll all make sense soon, I promise."

"Where are we going? Should I grab a swimsuit or something?"

"Nah." He turns his body to the side and tilts his head toward the driveway. "Everything is all set up. You'll see. Let's go."

As soon as we're in his car, he leans toward me for a kiss.

I pull back and shake my head. "Not on the first date."

"We're *way* past that," he says, trying again.

"No we aren't." I put a hand on his chest and try not to melt. "This is our first date. We're starting over."

"Does that include the other firsts we had? We get to do them all over again?"

"Yeah. *If* we make it that far."

He finally retreats to his side of the car. "Sounds good to me."

He starts the engine and pulls out onto the road.

"So what have you been up to?" he asks when we leave my neighborhood. "Or I guess, if this is our first date, tell me all about yourself."

"It's more of a symbolic fresh start," I say, offering a smile that seems to put him at ease. I explain what the band has been practicing for. And inform him that I have a new friend.

"Danny," Tim repeats. "You mean the kid with the funny hat?"

"Yeah. Turns out he's gay like me. We spent prom night together."

He glances at me with concern. "Should I be worried?"

I think about it and nod. "Yes."

"Okay." Tim takes a deep breath. "Sounds like I've got some competition. Let me see what I can do."

He pushes down on the accelerator. Before long, we end up in a familiar parking lot.

"Your studio?" I ask, already disappointed. Of course we won't be somewhere out in public.

"Yup!" Tim says, not picking up on my discontent.

I figure he wants to paint me again or something. I'm quiet when following him through the dark rows of cubicles. Tim unlocks the door to his studio and turns around instead of opening it.

"I've just got one question for you," he says.

"What's that?"

Tim smiles, his eyes filled with affection. "Will you go to prom with me?"

And with that, he pushes open the door and stands aside so I can see. The first thing I notice are all the sparkling lights, like he spent the past week catching stars with a fishing net to bring them here. Shimmering white curtains cover the far wall, hiding the usual clutter of his work from view. A large crescent moon hangs from the ceiling. Gold, silver, and navy blue balloons are bundled together in clusters. I take a step forward, wanting to see more, but Tim's arm extends to stop me.

"I'm afraid you can't get into this prom without a date," he says. "So who's it going to be? Me or Danny?"

"Hmm," I say, feigning indecision.

"I see." Tim gets down on one knee and takes my hand.

"Please be my prom date, Benjamin. I'm begging you. I know I've been a jerk. I was trying to do the right thing, but I got it all wrong. I'm sorry."

I'm so giddy with excitement that I honestly can't remember what I was upset about. Something involving a girl? Who cares! His eyes are so deliciously vulnerable. I can't wait to kiss away that uncertain expression. "Yes!" I say at last. "I will marry you."

Tim blinks. "Wait, that's not—"

"Too late!" I cry in delight. "You were down on one knee. That makes it official."

Tim laughs while getting to his feet. "I mean, if that's what it takes…"

"You can drive me to Vegas in the morning," I reply. "For now, I'll be your prom date."

"Thank god," Tim breathes.

"The decision wasn't his," I say. "Let's leave him out of this."

"You've got it." Tim bows formally. "Right this way, sir."

He's behind me when I enter but doesn't remain there. Tim dashes around the room to light candles and turn on a boombox. I approach a table covered in a white cloth. More candles surround a champagne bucket full of ice, although it's cooling soda cans instead of a bottle. What really captures my attention are the two chairs that have been pulled out, a black tuxedo draped across each.

"I tried really *really* hard to find a white one for you," Tim says, coming over to join me. "I guess that'll have to wait until the wedding. Here. This one's yours."

He picks up one of the tuxes and holds it out for me to see.

I cover my mouth with my hands, resisting the urge to cry.

"Maybe I should go first," Tim says, setting it down again.

He pulls off the T-shirt he's wearing, and if the situation didn't move me so deeply, I wouldn't mind if he stayed that way. I start unbuttoning my shirt. Soon we're standing there in our underwear, which makes me feel exposed, because glancing around, there are hardly any traces of Tim's studio left. It really does feel like we're in a public ballroom built for two.

"What about the security guard?" I ask.

"Vince is out of town," Tim says with a grin. "Dude is on vacation! I couldn't believe my luck. Otherwise I was thinking of renting a storage unit or something."

The thought makes me laugh. I probably would have liked that too, but this place is special to us. We've made some memories here. Tonight we'll add to them. We keep smiling at each other while putting on the tuxedos. Tim looks absolutely dashing in his, like a suave secret agent. I'm just happy that mine fits. "How'd you know my size?" I ask him.

"I have an artist's eye," he explains. "And an intimate knowledge of your body."

That's certainly true! Tim walks over to straighten my bow tie. Then he leans forward before hesitating, I guess because of my reluctance earlier. Ancient history! I throw my arms around his neck and kiss him. Tim picks me up, swings me around, and sets me back down again.

"Can I offer you something to drink?" he asks.

"Forget that!" I grab his hand and drag him to the middle of the room. "I wanna dance!"

"Yeah, okay," he says. "Uh… Let me put on something slow."

I shake my head. Along with my hips. "This song is great! Show me what you've got!"

"I'm not the best dancer," Tim says self-consciously before starting to swing his arms.

He's not kidding, as it turns out, but that's all right. Tim already has so much going for him, and I *know* he's got all the right moves in the bedroom. I'm happy to outshine him for once. I prance circles around my man, shake my booty, and keep him laughing while he tries his best to keep up.

"I think I'm ready for the punch bowl now," I say after a few songs.

We return to the table, where he cracks open a can of cola for each of us.

"Where did you get all this stuff?" I ask, looking at the paper moon, which doesn't seem to be the type of decoration bought at a store.

"I've got an inside connection," Tim replies. "Stacy is on the prom committee."

"So it's from the actual dance?"

"Mostly." He follows my gaze. "There *was* a moon, but it wouldn't have fit in here so I made my own."

"Can I have it? I wanna hang it in my room."

He laughs. "Yeah! Why not?"

"I might take those lights too," I murmur before something occurs to me. "Wait, what was your excuse for needing everything? Stacy must have wondered."

Tim cringes. "I said it was for a prank."

"Like a bucket of pig's blood?"

"Not *that* kind of prank. I told her how my mom is obsessed with prom and said I wanted to decorate our living room."

I snort. "So you could dance with her?"

"No, so she could go to prom with my dad."

"Aww! How sweet!"

He smiles. "That's the reaction I was hoping to get. From you."

"Well you managed," I tell him. "This is really great."

"You think so?"

"Yeah." I glance around. "What was the actual prom like?"

"Crowded," Tim says immediately. He doesn't offer any more information than that. But I have to know. I wish I didn't, but I do.

"Did you kiss her?"

Tim swallows. "Did you kiss Danny? Because it's okay if you did."

That he's giving me permission, even in retrospect, is more of an answer than he probably intended. I decide to let it go. We were messing around back when Krista really was his girlfriend, so if anything, it's my just desserts. Now that I know how it feels, I promise myself it'll be the last time I do that to anyone.

"Have you responded to your acceptance letter yet?" I ask.

"No. Still working on it." Tim looks stressed, like I'm going to grill him all night, but that's not what either of us want.

"No rush," I say easily. "If worse comes to worst, we can always run away together."

He grins at this. "Yeah?"

I shrug. "Why not? You'll sell your paintings. I'll sing for our supper."

"I'm up for that." Tim leans forward, his expression intense. "When we're together, especially when it's just you and me, I feel like I've got everything I'll ever need."

"Then we'll find a way. No matter what we have to do."

We sit there talking, leaving serious topics behind so we can goof off and make each other laugh. I sing to him when a song comes on that I like, and afterwards, he stands to announce the king and queen of prom, crowning us each with a cocktail napkin that blows off as we walk into an invisible audience to greet our loyal subjects.

"How about that slow dance?" I ask demurely.

"All right." Tim goes to the stereo.

A soulful ballad begins to play. He turns to me and extends a hand. I'm all too happy to be pulled into his arms. I nestle up against his chest. The boy sure can fill out a suit! Tim wraps his arms around me as we pivot in a slow circle. He steps on my foot, murmuring an apology, while I think back to when I first saw those blue shoes of his. We've come so far since that fateful summer night. Throughout all the highs and lows, I've never stopped loving him. I don't think I ever could.

When I look up, he's wearing a subtle smile, like my thoughts are laid bare for him to see. I only wish his were so easy to read. There's something dancing in his silver eyes, especially after he presses his lips to mine and pulls back.

"Hey, Benjamin?"

"Yeah?"

Knock! Knock! Knock!

We both look at the door just in time to see it open. A portly man with a bald dome and ring of gray hair is standing there. He's wearing a uniform. I'm still staring at him when Tim lets go and pushes me away.

"What's going on here?" the security guard asks, eyeing us with unease.

I look at Tim, who puts on a fake smile and walks over to the man with his hand extended, like a car salesman desperate to earn commission.

"Hey!" he says. "I wasn't expecting anyone to be here since Vince is out of town."

"Who?" the security guard asks, ignoring the offered hand.

Tim drops it to his side. "The guy who is usually here at night. He didn't mention me?"

"The agency sent me over," the man replies. "That's all I know. What are you boys up to? What's going on here?"

"Oh nothing," Tim says, moving to the stereo to turn it off. "Our girlfriends were sick on prom night, so we decided to have one here. They'll be around before much longer."

"Looked to me like you were dancing together," the man grumbles.

"We were practicing," Tim says, his voice beginning to sound strained. "Listen, my dad owns the office building. He lets me use this room as my studio." Tim pulls aside one of the curtains on the wall to reveal a stack of canvases. "See?"

The security guard shakes his head. "I know the owner of this building. I met him when I was guarding the construction site. With all due respect, you don't look Chinese to me."

"Okay, maybe my dad isn't the owner, but he is the boss. Look, I've got a key and everything. I even know the alarm code."

"So would a good number of people who work here," the security guard says. "Are you an intern or something?" His eyes dart to me, full of suspicion. "And who are you, exactly?"

I open my mouth to reply.

Tim gets there first. "Nobody. Are you sure Vince didn't leave a note about me? Maybe we could call him so he can explain everything."

"I'd rather talk to the owner," the security guard says. "Or your father, I suppose."

"What for?" Tim demands with an edge of panic in his voice. "We're obviously not sacking the joint." He returns to the wall to yank the curtain, which comes unpinned on one side and flutters open. "Look at all these paintings! I made them. This is my studio! Why else would all this stuff be in here? Sit down and I'll prove it. Ever wanted a painting of yourself?"

The security guard is eyeing Tim like he's lost his mind. But then, so am I.

"This is way above my paygrade," the man says. "I'm going to call it in."

Tim pinches the bridge of his nose. "For fuck's sake, listen to me! You don't need to call anyone!"

"I think I do," the man says warily. "You boys wait right here."

And with that he turns and leaves the room.

Tim covers his face with his hands. Then he drops them and starts looking around. "Oh shit! Oh shit, oh shit, oh shit!"

I watch as he starts yanking down the decorations. He's swearing under his breath. Not all the words are in English. Quite a few involve biblical figures. He needs to calm down.

"Tim!" I shout to get his attention.

He spins around to face me, his eyes wide. "You've gotta get out of here!" he says, marching over.

"Why?" I ask. "It's too late."

"No it's not." He grabs my arm and yanks me toward the door.

"Let go of me," I say, trying to wiggle free. "Let's talk about this."

I'm not sure he hears me. Tim sticks his head out to check for the security guard. We can hear him deeper in the office, talking on the phone.

"I'll say it was Bryce," Tim says to himself as he drags me along with him, "and that we were just goofing around. Wait, that won't work. They *know* we went to prom already."

"Tim," I try again, but it's hopeless. I can either dig in my heels and make it a wrestling match, or I can go along with him until we're somewhere that he feels safe.

He leads me through a break area to an external door with a push bar. Tim kicks it open and puts his hand on my back so that I'll go first. I end up behind the building, on the opposite side of the parking lot, next to a row of dumpsters. I turn around to find him wedged in the doorway, preventing it from closing completely.

"You've gotta get out of here," he repeats.

I shake my head. "Why? We're about to graduate. It doesn't matter anymore! Now that we're adults, we can—"

"Shut up!" Tim hisses. "This isn't the time. Okay? Just get the fuck out of here!"

I cross my arms over my chest. "No."

He looks like he's about to have a stroke. "C'mon man," he pleads. "Just go. Please!"

I grit my teeth before forcing myself to continue. "We can do whatever we want. Even if that means we both get jobs to pay for your tuition. At least we'd be together. Right?"

"I can't deal with this right now," Tim replies. "We'll talk later. Okay?"

He retreats before I have a chance to respond, the door swinging shut behind him. I stare in disbelief as it clicks shut. Then I walk over to one of the dumpsters and kick it, which only makes my toes hurt. I pace back and forth while growling from the pain. I'm tempted to walk around to the entrance and let myself back in, or pound on the door until someone hears me. I don't care who.

The door squeaks open behind me. Tim is standing there with a bundle of decorations in his arms. And my clothes.

"What are you still doing here?" he demands. He drops something so the door can't shut completely. The paper moon, which has been crumpled up. "Fuck it. Here." He walks over to me, tilting my clothes off the top of the pile, like I'm supposed to catch them. I step back so they fall to the ground. "Jesus Christ," he hisses. "Why do you have to make this so damn hard?"

Tim walks to the dumpster, tossing strings of lights and extinguished candles inside. Then he turns around to gather up my clothes.

"You need to make a decision," I tell him. "I know you want to please your parents. And that you're worried about what people will think. It'll be okay, I promise. They'll come around to the idea when they realize how happy you are, and until they do, you'll have me. We'll have each other!"

"I don't need a fucking ultimatum right now," Tim says, shoving my bundled-up clothes into my arms. "I need you to leave!"

"No!" I say, my voice cracking. "You need to choose, because I can't do this anymore, Tim. It hurts!"

He barely seems to hear me, which makes it all the more ironic when he says, "Are you deaf? Fucking go!" Tim grabs my shoulders with shaking hands to spin me around. "Get the hell out of here!" I feel him push from behind. The tip of my shoe catches on something and I trip, but my arms are full of clothes. I barely drop them in time to catch myself. The physical pain is nothing compared to what I feel inside. I'm on my hands and knees, a dumpster inches from my face. I roll over on my butt to stare up at him in shock.

"Oh man," Tim says, reaching for me. "I didn't mean to—"

I slap his hand away. "Don't touch me!"

Tim grabs the sides of his head, like it's about to split in two and he's trying to hold it together. "Benjamin," he says, his voice hoarse when he drops his hands. "I'm sorry. I really am. But you've gotta go."

I stand up and brush myself off. Then I look him square in the eye. "Choose. Last chance."

Tim picks up my fallen clothes. He can't seem to meet my gaze, even when handing them to me. I watch as he turns, kicks the paper moon out of the way, and lets the door close behind him as he goes.

I stand there devoid of thought and feeling until the shock wears off. Then I feel my heart break. I always thought that was merely an expression, but the pain is very real. A mixture of the physical and emotional. I've never felt anything so potent. Not since I fell in love with him.

I don't wait anymore. I turn and walk away from the building, aimless as the darkness envelops me. I'm not sure how long I walk, or in which direction. Only that I end up in a park, the grass wet when I fall to my knees and begin to sob.

The truth will set you free, but that doesn't mean you'll like where you end up. Captivity hurts. This is even worse. I'm sitting in the passenger seat of Allison's car. She came and got me after I exhausted myself by wandering around while blinded by tears. I wept in her arms when she found me and cried again when we parked somewhere so I could tell her what happened. Now I feel drained and exhausted. We've just pulled up to my house.

"Want me to come inside?" she asks.

I glance at the clock. "No. You'll get in trouble."

"I don't think my dad will mind. When I told him that you needed me, he offered to drive. I think you have a new fan."

I manage a half-hearted smile. "Let him know I appreciate it. I'll be okay though. I just want to get into bed."

And cry. I'm not sure that I'll ever stop.

She unbuckles her seatbelt to hug me. "You know I'm just a phone call away. Or just come over. I don't care what time it is."

"Thanks."

"I'll check in with you tomorrow," she says. "I love you, Ben."

"I love you too."

I tromp to the front door, pleading with the universe to give me a break—just this once—because I can't let my mom see me like this. She'll be excited about the tuxedo until she notices my face. Then I'll have to explain what happened all over again. As understanding as she always is, what I need right now is to curl up in a fetal position until the pain goes away.

The house is mercifully silent inside. I make it upstairs to my bedroom door before I hear a voice behind me. My sister.

"What are you wearing?"

I turn around. "My prom dress," I say without a hint of irony.

Karen's face twists up as she looks me over. "Did you get mugged or something?"

"No. Tim and I broke up. Are you happy now?"

"Yes. That guy was an asshole. I could tell from day one."

"You don't know anything about him," I retort, my voice wavering. "Not a goddamn thing."

"Then why do you look like you rolled down a hill and ended up face down in the mud?"

My chin starts to quiver.

"Don't," Karen says. "I mean, if you've gotta get it out of your system, then fine. But once you have, don't waste your time crying over him. I've dated my fair share of assholes. They aren't worth it."

I swallow against my rising tears. "Yeah, but I loved him."

She rolls her eyes. "You're too much like Dad sometimes."

"Meaning?"

"That you've got a bleeding heart."

"I don't remember you ever complaining."

Karen snorts. "Of course not. He lets me get away with murder. Remember the time I ate the rest of your Halloween candy, and when you told on me, Dad lectured you on how important it is to share? I knew I wouldn't get in trouble. That's why I did it. He's a pushover. Just like you."

I glare at her. "Great pep talk. Thanks. Really fucking helpful!"

She seems delighted by my scowl. "Now we're talking! Get angry! I don't know what happened, and sure, I don't know anything about Tim. But I do know my baby brother, and if this guy was dumb enough to hurt you, then it's his loss. The stupid asshole."

My chin quivers again, but only because I feel a surge of affection for her. When I think of Tim… "You're right. He is an asshole!"

"Damn straight," my sister says with a nod.

"Karen?" we hear my mother call from downstairs. "Who are you talking to? Is your brother home yet?"

I cringe.

Karen interprets my reaction correctly. "Yeah. He just went to bed."

"Oh, okay. I'm going to bed too. Sweet dreams, baby girl."

"Sweet dreams," Karen parrots. We listen until the coast is clear.

"It actually was a decent pep talk," I tell her. "Thanks."

"Yeah, no problem. Now stop bothering me."

She hugs me and we say goodnight. Then I shut myself in my bedroom and take off the tuxedo. I lost the clothes I was wearing before. I must have left them somewhere while running on autopilot. I strip down to my underwear and crawl into bed, braced for another bout of tears, and a few do slip free, but they no longer feel cathartic. I keep thinking of what Karen said, and how the evening played out.

Tim said that I was all he ever needed. What happened to us doing whatever it took to be together, even if that meant running away? He promised me the moon, *literally*, the stupid piece of shit. And just like it, Tim threw me out with the garbage. All because of the mere possibility of us getting caught.

My hand clenches into a fist. I get up, grab my backpack, and take out my notebook and a pen. Then I sit cross-legged on my bed. I need somewhere to put everything that I'm feeling. Not so that it can be hidden away. I won't be like him. I want my pain to be immortalized on paper, so I'll never make the same mistake again. And so I begin to write.

CHAPTER TWENTY-EIGHT

"Are you sure you want to do this?"

Allison and I are waiting in the wings of our school's auditorium. The talent show is winding down. We keep taking turns peeking through the curtain while the guys set up their instruments behind us. The rows of seats are filled. Just about everyone who attends our school is out there. At the moment, a brave freshman is doing a stand-up routine, and it's not going well.

"Yeah, I'm sure." I check the audience again. Most people are talking to each other rather than paying attention to the act on stage, although I do see some rolling eyes. It'll be a tough crowd.

"Because if you want," Allsion says, "I can sing the whole thing. You know, instead of just the chorus."

I turn around, an apology on my lips until I see her playful expression. "I just think it's important for a white guy to get the limelight for once, you know?"

"Oh totally," she replies. "The entire history of music has your back on that."

I do feel a *little* bad, but after Tim and I had our meltdown, I stayed up half the night writing. Which resulted in two pages of lyrics that I took over to Leon's house the next day. They fit the ballad he'd been struggling with. Not perfectly. The whole band had to work together and make adjustments, but we ended up with something that sounded fresh, so we decided to make it our entry into the talent show. The lyrics are deeply personal. I don't care what anyone thinks about them except for one person. I'm not sure if Tim is out there in the audience, but I hope he is.

We hear some half-hearted applause, my pulse picking up, because that's our cue. My palms are sweaty when Allison hands me a mic. We check with the guys, who are playing warm-up chords. They nod. A teacher gives us a signal. My stomach churns as the curtain begins to rise. I look to my best friend, who smiles reassuringly.

"We've got this," she says.

"Yeah. Just take over and finish the song if I faint."

She laughs. I wasn't kidding.

We're momentarily blinded by lights. The drum machine starts playing. Ronnie joins it by plucking his bass. Leon coaxes a riff out of his guitar. I step forward and close my eyes, traveling deep inside myself and returning with the words I found there. Then I begin to sing.

"Before you came along, so fine and strong, I'd only known the moon.
Drawn by your fire, and unquenchable desire, I emerged from my
cocoon."

I open my eyes and walk along the front of the stage. I see people making faces at me, or nudging each other, like I'm a joke, but that's nothing new. I've put up with their ridicule for the entirety of high school. Now it's time for them to listen to what I have to say, because this isn't some cloying ballad. The beat is strong, the pace fast. Nobody can talk during this song. Our band is too loud.

"You said I was your butterfly, and to seek the sky, because we were
meant to soar.
Why'd you keep me in the dark, love hidden in a park, where the sun
don't shine no more?"

I hope people pick up on the innuendo, because I'm waving my freak flag with this one. Time for the chorus. I usually don't rap, but it's the only way my part of the chorus felt right.

"I broke the silence, you broke my heart,
Now all that's left is to fall apart."

Allison steps forward to sing the refrain, and unlike me, she draws out the words, filling them with vibrato. Her voice is stunningly beautiful. I search the audience while she sings, seeing the surprise on people's faces turn into rapt admiration. And rightly so.

"He broke the silence, you broke his heart,
Now all that's left is to fall apart."

Some of the audience bursts into applause. Allison and I spin around each other, switching positions so I can sing the next verse.

"Unwilling to be denied, I've got way too much pride, I seduced you with my song.
You took me to your bed, and messed with my head, how could I have been so wrong?"

My voice falters on the last word, because that's when I see him. Those silver eyes are peering at me from the audience. Tim is surrounded by his friends, but my focus narrows along with my eyes. I hate his fucking guts! And I love him. More than ever, because I can't stand the idea of our time together coming to end. My heart aches, right there on stage in front of everyone. I want him so bad. Even now. Which makes me glad that my sister stoked my anger, because these lyrics aren't just a message to Tim. They're a reminder of why we can't be together.

"Your touch burned my wings, baby it still stings, how this mariposa came tumbling down.
Thought I could be your prince, been laughing ever since, you proved I'm just a clown."

Tim's eyes widen. Probably because he's scared I'm going to out him. I dance around on stage, rapping the chorus so Allison can follow it up and wow everyone again. While she's singing, my attention returns to Tim. And his friends. Bryce is leaning over to shout something in Stacy's ear. She makes a face and elbows him in the ribs to shut him up. Krista is clapping along like she's having a grand ol' time. As for the guy next to her... I take a deep breath and force myself to look elsewhere. I notice Danny bobbing his head and wink at him. Then I step forward to sing again.

"You're so full of fear, and make nothing clear, but I was your willing fool.
You said we'd last, that she was in the past, but all those lies weren't cool."

Everything rises up inside me, the pain, anger, love, and hate. I walk to the very front of the stage, so far that my toes are hanging over the edge, my attention on one person alone. Tim is looking at me too. Like a deer caught in headlights, I don't think he has a choice, even as my truck comes roaring down the road. His face is impassive, as if he's trying to hide how he feels. Good luck, buddy, because I'm pushing that gas pedal down to the floor!

> *"Here's the bad news, because it's you who lose, this butterfly has chosen to abstain.*
> *Find someone else to deceive, blind enough to believe, that you're somehow worth the pain."*

The mask slips. Tim's guarded expression becomes wounded. He turns his head away, like he can't handle it. Which sums up our relationship nicely. I don't show any mercy. Not now. I rap the chorus to him, even though he refuses to meet my gaze.

> *"I broke the silence, you broke my heart,*
> *Now all that's left is to fall apart."*

I feel Allison's arm around my shoulder as she joins me to sing the final verse.

> *"He broke the silence, you broke his heart,*
> *Now all that's left is to fall apart."*

The song ends just as suddenly as it began. The moment Allison hits her last note, the instruments fall silent. After a beat, the audience erupts in applause. There's a reason the school put us on last. We brought down the house! I see plenty of derision. People giving a thumbs down or trying to boo, but they're drowned out by everyone else. Allison is leaping around in excitement. She waves at the crowd before hugging me. Then we have to retreat as the curtain drops.

I take one last look at where I last saw Tim. His friends are still there. He is not. I see him heading for the exit, the smile sliding off my face, because singing this song wasn't a magic bullet. I still want him. And I still love him. Even though it's over.

— — —

The final day of school has arrived. I can hardly believe it. I'm sitting in my physics class, occasionally checking the clock like it's New Year's Eve, because we're down to the last minutes.

"When you said you could sing," Danny says breathlessly, "I had no idea! And the way you danced… It was really—" He hesitates before shrugging. "Really hot!"

This makes me chuckle. "Thanks. That's very generous."

"I mean it!" he says. "I bet you'll be famous someday."

"Not if I can help it. I'd rather be happy."

Although it did feel good to take second place. I didn't catch the act that won, but making it close to the top was vindicating. Especially for Leon. We had a nice long talk that evening. He wants to pursue music as a career. I wish him nothing but success, because I don't think many straight guys would be as accommodating. I took a song he wrote about his ex-girlfriend and made it ridiculously gay. And he was nothing but supportive. I'm not going to miss high school, but I do wish I'd become friends with him sooner.

"Can I ask you something personal?" Danny says suddenly.

"Sure," I say with a shrug. "I'm an open book."

"The guy that you broke up with… Did he go to our school? Because it felt like you were singing to him."

My throat constricts. "Yeah. Not only that, but you've met him before."

"Wow!" Danny thinks about it. "Was it Bryce?"

I laugh, mostly out of relief. "No. I can't tell you who it was. He's still in the closet. That's the problem."

"Oh. Well I bet he's sorry now."

"I honestly don't know."

"Five minutes left!" someone shouts behind us.

I check the clock and see that it's true. Then I look at Danny. "This is it."

"Yeah," he says. "I'm glad it's almost over."

"Me too. I feel like we should do something special."

The class gets quieter as we watch the second hand complete another loop.

"Hey," Danny says. "You don't have to. I mean, obviously. But I think I'll always regret it if I don't try so… Umm…"

I turn my full attention on him. He's not wearing the hat, since we're in class, his poofy red hair almost matching the flush of his skin.

Danny licks his lips. Then he flashes a panicked smile. "Would you like to go on a date with me?"

He's not quiet when asking this. I hear someone snort behind us. Me? I'm already smiling.

"Yeah," I say, just before my time in high school officially comes to an end. "I'd like that."

Summer is here again. My bedroom window is open to let in the warm night air. I'm sitting on my bed, staring at a painting of two overlapping hearts, but I'm not alone exactly. Sorrow has become my constant companion. I don't cry anymore. I've tried to accept that it's over and move on. Which is harder than I ever expected.

I slept with Danny.

We went on our date. I had fun, and it was refreshing, because neither one of us felt the need to hide who we are. When he tried to kiss me, I was honest and told him it was too soon for me to get into another relationship. I didn't want to put him through the agony of having feelings for someone who couldn't reciprocate. We're going to different schools anyway. He moves away next month. Allison and I leave not long after that. So even if I'd never met Tim, it wouldn't have been the right time for us to start something serious. Danny listened patiently while I explained all of this. Then he said…

"That's okay. But I'd still like to kiss you."

And so I let him. He's a sweet guy. I have no doubt that he'll make someone happy. And I definitely made him smile later that night. I don't have any feelings for Danny, aside from a genuine fondness. I don't find him very attractive. But I did hope that having sex with him would somehow put distance between me and Tim. Instead it was a reminder of everything that I miss. We had a good time. Sex is sex. But without love, it isn't much better than staying home and jacking off.

I can tell that Danny has a crush on me. I've already explained that we have to go back to being only friends. So no more messing around. He didn't seem too distraught. We've hung out since, and things are cool between us. I can't say the same about me and Tim. Too much has been left unresolved. I guess that's part of breaking up. Our show has been unceremoniously canceled. There will be no season finale. I'll always wonder what happened after we parted ways.

Although I could guess. He's definitely enrolling in that Catholic school. If his father found out about our slow dance,

Tim would have tried to appease him by going there. That was probably inevitable. If not, something else would have tripped us up. I've tried to imagine our future if we hadn't been caught. Living with Tim in another city would have been great until his parents came to town. Like prom at his studio, Tim would've gone around hiding anything personal before each of their visits, erasing us from existence. And of course I'd have to go somewhere else while his parents were there—wait by the dumpsters until he gave the all clear. Our relationship would have ended in disaster eventually. I probably dodged a bullet. It's just a shame that I can't stop thinking about the gun.

Only a glimmer of hope remains. His key still hangs on a chain around my neck. I could let myself in, like I've done before, and get into bed with Tim. That always closed the distance between us, our issues left out in the cold. At least until we returned to the real world. Wouldn't it be worth the pain? I want to be wrapped in his arms again. I want Tim to fuck me and make promises I know he can't keep. As messed up as everything got between us, I could fill the summer with him before circumstances force us apart. If this has to end—and it clearly does—then maybe it wouldn't be the worst way to go.

Or I could return the key. That would finally put the constant temptation to rest.

My eyes move to the stack of clothes folded on top of my dresser. The rented tuxedo. The coat he gave me for Christmas. I stand and gather them up, trapping them beneath an arm. Then I turn to the painting, a lump forming in my throat. I can't part with it. He's in my heart anyway. I'll never be rid of him completely. And it was beautiful. While it lasted.

I breathe in deeply when leaving the house. Bugs serenade me as I walk through my neighborhood, but I don't sing along with them. Not this time. That music is buried inside me, where it will have to remain. For now. The houses I pass are silent sentinels as I proceed along a familiar route. How often had my pace quickened in anticipation of being with him? Now I idle along, knowing that each step is bringing me closer to the end. When I finally reach his house, I stop and stare from across the street, remembering when I saw him mowing the lawn and how intimidating it was to walk past him. I should keep going now. I'm not sure if I can do this. It might simply be another excuse. Part of me wants to be weak, just so I can have him again.

I press my hand over the key, the cool metal warming against my skin, but it won't last. I know that now. I just have to accept it. I cross the street and walk to his front door. The key still turns after I slide it into the lock. I almost wish it didn't. After letting myself in and quietly closing the door behind me, I stand in the entryway, looking up the stairs. I want to linger there and draw this out, but my feet move of their own accord, taking me to him one last time.

The breath is short in my lungs when I let myself in a room awash with moonlight, the shadows blue and hazy around the edges. I freeze when I hear the sheets rustle. Tim is in bed, lying on his side while facing the door. I leave it open so I won't be tempted to stay and walk closer. The blankets are bundled up around his waist, revealing the bare skin of his torso. How am I ever going to find the strength to do this?

I silently pad over to his dresser and leave the stack of clothes there. I'm tempted to open one of the drawers and take a sketchbook so I'll always have a piece of his heart. But then, I guess he gave that to me a long time ago. I'm so glad he managed to rise above his fear on occasion, such as my birthday, even though he always got pulled back down again. Those fleeting moments were glorious. I know he tried. I don't really hate him. It would be so much easier if I did.

I walk to the window with a lump in my throat and look up at the moon. All of this began under its light. How fitting that it will end this way too. I hear the sheets rustle behind me again. I close my eyes, waiting for the sound of his voice to take away my indecision.

Benjamin! What are you doing here? Come get into bed with me.

I would. If he asked. I listen to the sound of his breathing, matching my own to it. Then I open my eyes and turn around. Tim is lying on his back now. I walk around his bed, sitting on the edge of it while angled toward him, like a parent tucking in their child for the night. But my love for him was never so innocent.

I watch his strong chest rise and fall. My gaze moves along the curves of his muscles. I take in every detail, not wanting to forget any of it. The alluring bulge where his legs meet beneath the sheets. The whisps of dark armpit hair. And especially that handsome face. I lean over, wanting to kiss him goodbye. I bring my lips as close to his as I dare without actually touching them. If he wakes up now—if I feel his hand wrap around the back of my neck so his mouth can press against mine—I'll forgive him. For everything. I'll make my peace with being a dirty little secret. We'll spend the rest of our lives together on his terms. I don't care anymore.

But part of me must. Otherwise I wouldn't lean back, my heart breaking all over again. I see a different future. A wife and kids for him. A gaggle of nieces and nephews for me. I bet we'll still smile and laugh. Our friends and family will assume that we're happy and complete. They won't know of the pain deep down inside of us that will never heal. I hope it doesn't, since it'll be the last thing still connecting us. I reach around my neck and undo the chain. The key spins, reflecting the moonlight, as flashes of everything we were together fill my mind.

The first time I saw him jogging at night. Riding in his car. Kissing him on the beach. The sound of his voice on the phone. Singing for him. Being wrapped in his arms. Watching him paint. His hands washing me in the shower. The arguments. The words he never spoke.

Then I stand. I leave the necklace and key on top of the folded clothes. My feet feel heavy when walking to the open door, where I hesitate and turn around, unable to resist. Tim rolls over to face me. His eyes are open, revealing depths of emotion, like he finally decided to stop hiding. I'm surprised by the strength I feel rise up inside of me. And the certainty.

I love him.

But I also love myself.

I take one last look at the handsome boy who stole my heart. He pushes himself up on an elbow and slides his hand across the sheets, as if showing me where I could be. I fight against my tears, but they come anyway when I shake my head. Tim swallows, his face crumpling before he nods, as if he understands. A sad smile tugs at my cheek. His chin trembles before he manages to do the same. I raise my hand in parting. Then I turn and softly close the door behind me as I go.

EPILOGUE

"If you join our Lucky Licks loyalty program, you always get a free topping of your choice. And every ten visits, you'll earn a double-decker cone or cup." I've said these words so often that they haunt my dreams. I found myself singing them in the shower the other day. The jingle I came up with was really catchy too. I might record a demo and send a copy to the rich hippies who founded this frozen yogurt chain.

The customer sighs at my sales pitch. "I simply want a bottle of water," she says. "Can I please just order that?"

"Well sure," I say, not willing to let her off the hook yet. But only because I have an audience. My best friend is standing nearby. "But that would technically count as a visit, meaning I could add a sticker to your new Lucky Licks loyalty card."

"No thank you," the woman says, digging in her purse.

"Would you like the sticker anyway?" I ask. "It's really cute. Just like the one on my shirt."

I breathe in to make my chest swell against the work-issued polo I'm wearing. The woman barely glances at it. "I'm lactose intolerant," she says. "Even breathing the air in here is making my stomach feel funny."

"One bottle of water coming right up."

Slinging frozen yogurt isn't the worst job in the world. Cleaning out the toilets can be, especially in such circumstances.

"Oh my god!" Allison says when we're alone again. "I thought she would never leave! Some people are so rude. We were in the middle of a conversation!"

"Tell me about it," I say. "No really," I add, grabbing a cloth and wiping the counter like a bartender. "You were describing the hot guy who asked you to dance and how he took his shirt off. I'm crushing on him already."

"Well, don't," Allison says, stirring the melted remains of a tiramisu twister. "He started swinging the shirt above his head like a stripper—"

"Still works for me," I interject.

"—and he wouldn't stop. Not until he hit some poor girl in the face."

"Was it you?" I ask.

"No! But only because I have fast reflexes and kept ducking. Then he gets this funny look on his face and says, 'You sure have big lips. I bet they feel good all sorts of places. I've never kissed a black girl before.' So I said, 'There's a reason for that.' before walking the hell away."

"And some people say that romance is dead," I reply. "You got his phone number, right?"

"Oh totally. I'm inviting him to move in with us."

"Perfect! I've gotta see those smooth moves for myself. I've always wanted a ceiling fan."

"There *were* plenty of cute guys at the party," Allison says. "Two of them were dancing together."

"All the good ones are already taken."

"Not all of them," she says pointedly.

I glance behind me, like I don't know who she's referring to. Then I drop the act. "I'm still not ready."

Which is ironic, because I'm spoiled for choice. There are plenty of gay guys around. I'm just one among the herd.

Allison shakes her head. "Nobody is saying you have to leap into another relationship. Get out there and mingle!"

Years have passed since Tim and I broke up, but I still think of him. Every single day. I've dated a few guys and had some flings. None of them recent. I just haven't felt that same spark with anyone. I know from experience that when I do, the choice won't be mine, so I don't see the sense in chasing after what's outside my control. Although, like Allison said, it doesn't hurt to mingle. That would increase the odds in my favor. Not that I'm in a hurry.

"Do you work tomorrow night?" she asks. "There's a secret party at the dorms on campus. We could check it out together. Even if it's lame, they never last long before getting busted."

"Yeah, all right," I reply, since it's not really committing to anything.

Allison checks the clock. Then she swears. "I've gotta get to my study group." She places her cup on the counter. "I'll see you at home. Dinner will be on the stove, if I'm already asleep."

"Okay. I'll try not to wake the children."

She never cooks for me. We don't even have house plants. Living together feels more like a slumber party that never has to end. I've never been this happy in my life. Maybe I can think of a few moments. Although these days, I try not to, preferring to leave the past behind me. High school especially. When I look back on it now—the bullies, the name calling, and the cliques—it all seems so small and insignificant. College is a completely different experience. There are still fraternities and sororities for anyone who wants to continue obsessing over image and status, but most people I've met here are more interested in being themselves while pursuing their passion.

A family of four comes through the door. The first of the evening rush. I keep busy for the rest of my shift, grateful when it quiets down enough that I can start cleaning, so I won't have to stay as late past closing time. I have some studying to do before my classes tomorrow, but it's way more likely that I'll put on some music and soak in a bubble bath. Eager to make this vision a reality, I start mopping the back room until I hear a ding that indicates a customer has entered the shop.

When I return to the front counter, a guy is standing there. He's tall and blond. His green eyes dart from the menu above my head down to me. He flashes a smile, which I return. Then he consults the menu again. I use the opportunity to stare. He has big hands. I bet they're warm. Mine are perpetually frozen when working here. The man looks a little older than me. He's wearing khaki pants and a dress shirt with the sleeves rolled up. He must shop in the big and tall department, but only because of his height. His body is lean enough.

I'm eager to check out that friendly face again. When I do, I realize that he's been watching me. I feel my cheeks flush, which makes him smile. His eyes dart up to the menu but don't remain there long before they return to me. We laugh at the same time. I'm not sure why. All I can think is…

Here we go again!

———

AUTHOR'S NOTE

I write from the heart. Otherwise I never would have created yet another version of Ben and Tim's origin, since I really have no idea how to market this. I imagine the new story might cause some confusion among established readers, but I'll do my best to explain.

When Ben Loved Tim is a partial retelling of *Something Like Summer*, which was so adored by readers (and myself!) that I eagerly wrote eleven sequels. When Ben Loved Tim only covers about the first third of *Something Like Summer*. There's much much more to the story, some of which will be explored in the sequel, *When Ben Loved Jace*. A third installment will follow, completing the trilogy. Much like the book you now hold, the sequels will be written from Ben's perspective.

By contrast, the Something Like... series often switches perspectives. Something Like Winter is Tim's story and is told from his point of view. Something Like Autumn is about Jace—the guy Ben meets in the epilogue. From there, the world continues to expand with a large roster of characters who each have their own story to tell.

I don't intend for one series to replace the other, since each will offer different benefits. The *He Loved Him* series provide san intimate look into Ben's heart. *The Something Like...* series allows you to set off with different characters and experience great swaths of the story that won't make it into the new trilogy.

Whether you're new to my writing or reuniting with old friends, I hope Ben's tale stirred something in you. Love is the greatest gift we can give and receive. Thank you for allowing me to share some of mine with you.

Jay Bell

The story began—

—in the *Something Like…* series, each book written from a different character's perspective, the plots intertwining at key points while also venturing off in new directions. The quest for love takes many different forms, changing like the seasons. Which is your favorite?

Books in the series:

#1: *Something Like Summer*
#2: *Something Like Autumn*
#3: *Something Like Winter*
#4: *Something Like Spring*
#5: *Something Like Lightning*
#6: *Something Like Thunder*
#7: *Something Like Stories – Volume One*
#8: *Something Like Hail*
#9: *Something Like Rain*
#10: *Something Like Stories – Volume Two*
#11 *Something Like Forever*
#12 *Something Like Stories – Volume Three*

I love him. And I'm pretty sure he loves me back… even though he's straight.

When I first met Carter King, I knew he was something special. I imagined us being together, and we are, but only as friends. Best friends! I'm trying to be cool with that, even though I know he has secrets, and there have definitely been mixed signals. I don't want a crush to ruin what we already have. Then again, if there's any chance that we can be together, it's worth the risk, because Carter could be the love of my life. Or he might be the boy who breaks my heart.

Straight Boy is Jay Bell's emotional successor to his critically acclaimed Something Like… series. This full-length novel tells a story of friendship and love while skating the blurry line that often divides the two.

-=Books by Jay Bell=-

The Something Like... series

#1 Something Like Summer
#2 Something Like Autumn
#3 Something Like Winter
#4 Something Like Spring
#5 Something Like Lightning
#6 Something Like Thunder
#7 Something Like Stories - Volume One
#8 Something Like Hail
#9 Something Like Rain
#10 Something Like Stories - Volume Two
#11 Something Like Forever
#12 Something Like Stories - Volume Three

The Pride series

#1 Pride High: Book 1 - Red
#2 Pride High: Book 2 - Orange
#3 Pride High: Book 3 - Yellow

The He Loved Him series

#1 When Ben Loved Tim
#2 When Ben Loved Jace
#3 When Ben Loved Ben

The Loka Legends series

#1 The Cat in the Cradle
#2 From Darkness to Darkness

Other Novels

Kamikaze Boys
Hell's Pawn
Straight Boy
Out of Time, Into You
Switch!

Who the hell is Jay Bell?

Jay Bell is a proud gay man and the award-winning author behind dozens of emotional and yet hopelessly optimistic stories. His best-selling book, Something Like Summer, spawned a series of heart-wrenching novels, a musically driven movie, and a lovingly drawn comic. When not crafting imaginary worlds, he occupies his free time with animals, art, action figures, and—most passionately—his husband Andreas. Jay is always dreaming up new stories about boys in love. If that sounds like your cup of tea, you can get the kettle boiling at my website:

www.jaybellbooks.com